Performance Philosophy

Series Editors
Laura Cull Ó Maoilearca
University of Surrey
Guildford, UK

Alice Lagaay
Hamburg University of Applied Sciences
Hamburg, Germany

Will Daddario
Independent Scholar
Asheville, NC, USA

Performance Philosophy is an interdisciplinary and international field of thought, creative practice and scholarship. The Performance Philosophy book series comprises monographs and essay collections addressing the relationship between performance and philosophy within a broad range of philosophical traditions and performance practices, including drama, theatre, performance arts, dance, art and music. It also includes studies of the performative aspects of life and, indeed, philosophy itself. As such, the series addresses the philosophy of performance as well as performance-as-philosophy and philosophy-as-performance.

Series Advisory Board:
Emmanuel Alloa, Assistant Professor in Philosophy, University of St. Gallen, Switzerland
Lydia Goehr, Professor of Philosophy, Columbia University, USA
James R. Hamilton, Professor of Philosophy, Kansas State University, USA
Bojana Kunst, Professor of Choreography and Performance, Institute for Applied Theatre Studies, Justus-Liebig University Giessen, Germany
Nikolaus Müller-Schöll, Professor of Theatre Studies, Goethe University, Frankfurt am Main, Germany
Martin Puchner, Professor of Drama and of English and Comparative Literature, Harvard University, USA
Alan Read, Professor of Theatre, King's College London, UK
Freddie Rokem, Professor (Emeritus) of Theatre Arts, Tel Aviv University, Israel

http://www.performancephilosophy.org/books/

More information about this series at
http://www.palgrave.com/gp/series/14558

Paula Hildebrandt • Kerstin Evert
Sibylle Peters • Mirjam Schaub
Kathrin Wildner • Gesa Ziemer
Editors

Performing
Citizenship

Bodies, Agencies, Limitations

Editors
Paula Hildebrandt
Berlin, Germany

Sibylle Peters
FUNDUS Theater
Hamburg, Germany

Kathrin Wildner
HafenCity University Hamburg
Hamburg, Germany

Kerstin Evert
Tanzplan Hamburg
K3 - Zentrum für Choreographie
Hamburg, Germany

Mirjam Schaub
University of Art and Design
Burg Giebichenstein
Halle a.d. Saale, Germany

Gesa Ziemer
HafenCity University Hamburg
Hamburg, Germany

Performance Philosophy
ISBN 978-3-319-97501-6   ISBN 978-3-319-97502-3   (eBook)
https://doi.org/10.1007/978-3-319-97502-3

Library of Congress Control Number: 2018963303

PREFACE

New forms of citizenship are developing in the cities of the twenty-first century: self-organized and often independent from the state, they negotiate and shape how we live together.

The graduate programme Performing Citizenship explored new articulations of citizenship, starting from the gap between traditional institutions and a self-confident new citizenry. It combined cultural studies from various disciplinary backgrounds with art-based methodologies and hands-on experimentation in public space.

Performing Citizenship—Bodies, Agencies, Limitations provides insights into our research projects complemented by contributions from an international conference hosted by (the organizers of the programme and) editors of this book in November 2016 in Hamburg. The contributing chapters cover a wide range of academic disciplines, from urban planning, postcolonial studies, philosophy, cultural anthropology, to pedagogy and media studies. Based on a conceptual and methodological framework, they discuss conflicts, tensions and potentialities of doing things with rights. Addressing all kinds of cultural, social and political phenomena—body optimization, corruption, gentrification, global logistics, migration and 'welcome culture'—we claim that a performative take on citizenship offers a fresh and productive look at questions of identity and belonging, rights and responsibilities.

The book as well as the three-year research programme would not have been possible without the generous funding of the Landesforschungsförderung Hamburg, the people working behind the scene, namely the HafenCity University Hamburg, the K3—Centre for

Dance and Choreography, the Hamburg School of Applied Science and the Fundus Theatre Hamburg. Last but not least, we would like to thank Alice Lagaay for her enthusiasm in considering this volume for the Performance Philosophy Series and, most notably, Jules Bradbury for her careful and diligent editorial work.

Berlin, Germany	Paula Hildebrandt
Hamburg, Germany	Kerstin Evert
Hamburg, Germany	Sibylle Peters
Halle a.d. Saale, Germany	Mirjam Schaub
Hamburg, Germany	Kathrin Wildner
Hamburg, Germany	Gesa Ziemer
14.06.2018	

CONTENTS

LIST OF FIGURES

Introduction

Paula Hildebrandt and Sibylle Peters

PERFORMING CITIZENSHIP: TESTING NEW FORMS
OF TOGETHERNESS

Realities and concepts of citizenship have changed radically throughout history and will keep changing. Today, in the beginning of the twenty-first century, new articulations of citizenship emerge in citizen's and non-citizen's practices and struggles, and they often do so in conjunction with artistic practices. In these struggles and practices, citizenship is embodied and changed; new forms of togetherness, new strategies to claim rights and new civic roles are tested and rehearsed. Within this book, the editors want to present insights from a wide range of perspectives into how citizenship is performed and thereby changed; a body of thought across disciplines, based on in-depth-research and artistic experimentation.

Performing citizenship is not only the title of this volume, it is also the title of a research and graduate program, bringing together scholars, artists and citizen researchers in practice-based forms of research. The members of this program investigate the performance of citizenship through

P. Hildebrandt (✉)
Berlin, Germany
e-mail: info@paulahildebrandt.de

S. Peters
FUNDUS Theater, Hamburg, Germany

© The Author(s) 2019
P. Hildebrandt et al. (eds.), *Performing Citizenship*, Performance
Philosophy, https://doi.org/10.1007/978-3-319-97502-3_1

1

artistic experiments which critically highlight long-hidden aspects of citizenship, promote new emerging agencies, create new choreographies and scores of movement in public space or invent and test nascent institutions. Funded by the city of Hamburg, the three-year program is a joint venture of two academic institutions—the HafenCity University Hamburg (HCU) and the Department of Design of the Hamburg University of Applied Science (HAW)—and two cultural institutions—The Theatre of Research/Fundus Theater Hamburg and the K3/Tanzplan Hamburg.

The title of this book and the individual contributions refer back to the international conference, *Performing Citizenship_02*, that took place in Hamburg in November 2016. At this conference, members of the program presented their research, while internationally acclaimed experts from a range of disciplines—such as media studies, urban sociology, philosophy, theater and literary studies, political science, critical gender studies and postcolonial theory—were invited to respond and give insight into the respective artistic and academic research practices. Across the broad span of contributions contained in this volume—from 'Haircuts by Children' in Toronto to 'Claims for the Future' from the Downtown Eastside Women's Centre in Vancouver, 'Citizen Spaces' in Mexico City and back to the 'Department of Paralogistics' and the 'Welcome City Group' in Hamburg—many of the texts offer analytical accounts of artistic and activist research projects that address global transformations of citizenship and their local manifestations. This is complemented by more theoretical contributions and a few key historical examples: the masks that were instrumental in the performance of citizenship in the Golden Age of Venice (Schaub), Friedrich Schiller's concept of aesthetical education (Gunsilius), and mimicry practices of the female jester at the court of King Louis XIII (Jungen).

Citizenship Redefined and Reinvented

Citizenship is back on the agenda of philosophy, together with urban studies, the global governance discourse and international politics (see, e.g., the Oxford Handbook of Citizenship 2017). Some scholars even speculate about a 'renaissance of citizenship' (Faist 2013, p. 4). Multiple publications try to grasp the current transformation of citizenship: citizenship seems to no longer be based primarily on places of origin, and is challenged by new forms of belonging, of representation and sovereignty. A flurry of concepts are celebrating new configurations of citizenship that are not determined by place, origin or nation—variously ascribed as activist

(Isin 2009), flexible (Ong 2006), insurgent (Holston 2007), medieval (Roy and AlSayyad 2006), multicultural (Kymlicka 1995), multilevel (Maas 2013), urban (Lebuhn 2013), transnational (Leggewie 2013), ubiquitous or diasporic (Balibar 2012). These concepts aim to grasp the current dynamics and diversity of border-crossing transfers, intersections and entanglements, with ever more people traversing the physical borders of nation-states and creating new political subjectivities.

Whereas citizenship as a legal and political institution is based on the nation-state as a framework of constitutional rights and obligations enforced by law and related institutions, this foundation of modern citizenship is increasingly and fundamentally challenged by a number of interrelated and indeed accelerated developments. Economic globalization disempowers nation-states and undercuts their sovereignty, while the gap between rich and poor within and across nations is widening, which puts existing social security systems and public health infrastructures under pressure. Changing patterns of mobility and connectivity, migration and transnational cultural interconnections all challenge the legal and political boundaries of sovereign nation-states, their legitimacy and capacity to organize and provide of citizenship (Benhabib 2006; Shachar 2009). At the same time, new alliances, networks and collectives of citizens emerge and assume roles and responsibilities formerly attributed to the state as institutional body and representation of the people.

Given these developments, citizenship today is at the same time associated with old and ineffective protocols, which continue to produce exclusion, and yet is also 'in the making', moving into a position beyond the given. Citizenship is simultaneously in withdrawal and in the process of becoming. At its best, this ambivalent performance of citizenship has the capacity to rearticulate or reinvent citizenship, to link old and new figurations of citizenship—often, if not necessarily, across given thresholds of legal and political institutions, social conventions, disciplinary competencies and discourses, ascriptions and attributions of race, class, culture and gender.

Given these dynamics, the editors of this volume conceive citizenship as 'essentially contested' (Gallie 1956)—a questionable and corrigible concept that has to be claimed, enacted, performed, and therefore is permanently subject to revision and considerable modification.

Accordingly, the editors of this volume suggest a performative take on citizenship in order to think beyond conventional notions of normative or legal definition of a citizen. Moreover, we are convinced that this performative take should not be conceived from the overall viewpoint of an academic master discourse, but has to be informed in multiple ways by the dimension of contestation and struggle itself, in which citizenship is actually performed.

Transforming citizenship in action is a very challenging task. Not only does it require a certain momentum of self-empowerment to start acting in the first place, but it also implies building new and uncertain alliances across given social, cultural and institutional systems which allow for at least a temporary cohesion of collective action. Insights, inventions and new concepts have to be transformed into real and repeatable repertoires of citizen actions, thereby establishing new protocols, rules and conducts of communicating, sharing and 'commoning'. All attempts and each initiative aiming toward a changed reality of citizenship face significant obstacles by challenging powerful counterparties. They confront a set of problems concerning their own 'performance' when claiming, contesting, enacting ... in short, when doing things with rights. A performative theory of citizenship should not only acknowledge these problems but should help to determine and to solve them.

However, in the following, three theoretical concepts will briefly be introduced and connected, which constitute a common ground for the different contributions to this volume. As a result, a first provisional definition of the performativity of citizenship and its different layers will be given.

Doing Things, with Rights: Citizenship as Performance

Firstly, citizenship is understood here as a subject position that allows us to act in the first place. To be a citizen comprises a complex conditional framework that entitles us to certain actions, suggests certain ways of acting and links actors to one another in distinct ways, not only giving meaning to our actions but primarily allowing certain acts and actions to *be* acts and actions, to be real—that is, to constitute reality. How closely such an understanding of citizenship is linked to performativity becomes clear when we look back at the very origins of performative theory and, in particular, at John L. Austin's initial examples for performative speech acts— that is, sentences which are neither true nor false but which constitute the reality of which they speak. As the sentence (as speech act) 'I do' exclaimed in the course of the marriage ceremony (Austin 1962, p. 5) may bring about the reality they speak of, the example also shows that a certain subject position has to be taken in order for them to be carried out successfully. As evident in acts like getting married or the making of a will, which is also among the first examples for speech acts given by Austin, this is the subject position of the citizen, presupposing networks of bodies with institutional power. One has to be a citizen to marry or to make a will. Austin famously argued that, whereas speech acts like these cannot be false in terms of their truth value, they still can fail. Austin termed such speech acts as 'unhappy' (Austin 1962, p. 15). And they potentially do fail and become 'unhappy', if enacted outside of the presupposed network of actors that makes them work in the first place; in many cases, this means outside of citizenship. With this background, 'performing citizenship' first means to act in accordance with the protocols and systems of citizenship, and thereby successfully constitute and produce pieces of civic reality.

Secondly, performing citizenship today also means to claim and enact citizenship in new ways beyond already given subject positions and institutional networks. Though 'acts of citizenship' which shift or reinvent the concept of citizenship in action are by degree 'unhappy' in Austin's sense, and partially failing, individual citizens, citizen initiatives and movements all around the world persist in their trying. To better understand these dynamics, this volume profits from Engin Isin's concept of 'Acts of Citizenship', referring to acts which change and produce citizenship as such. Isin defines these 'Acts of Citizenship' as follows:

> To act, then, is neither arriving at a scene nor fleeing from it, but actually engaging in its creation. With that creative act the actor also creates herself/ himself as the agent responsible for the scene created. (Isin 2009, p. 25)

The proximity of this concept to another layer of performativity is evident in the reference to the creation of a scene. To perform citizenship in this sense means to act *as* citizen in a way that potentially reinterprets the citizen as a role and as a subject position. In other words, to perform citizenship and to act *as* citizen includes a certain dimension of 'fake it 'til you make it' when claiming, enacting or presupposing a right that has yet to gain legal apparatus.

In this context, to focus on how citizenship is performed, also implies a certain take on the crucial question of representation. Evidently, most, if not all, systems of citizenship—in terms of legally enforced rights and duties—rely heavily on structures of representation in which citizenship is performed by speaking in the name of (all) citizens, or in the name of a certain body of citizenship. Conflicts between established formations and new figurations of citizenship are often oversimplified, using a binary opposition of citizenship as a system of representation on the one hand, and citizens claiming to speak and act for themselves and on their own account. Focusing on how citizenship is performed undercuts this binary by suggesting a middle ground, albeit a shaking one. To focus on the performance of citizenship within given systems means to look at the ways these systems are embodied in action; while to focus on the performance of citizenship *outside* of given systems means to be aware that nobody ever just *is* a citizen. Even claiming something like 'direct democracy' necessarily involves processes and constructs of representation in the course of its performance. Purely because performing citizenship outside of given systems also generates forms of representation, it does have a chance to create the scene and the actor in the action itself in an 'Act of Citizenship', as Isin defined it.

A third layer to the performativity of citizenship explicitly regards the body, the embodiment of citizenship to actually take shape. *Habeas corpus*—historically and biographically, the right to control one's own body is what initiates citizenship. The performance of this right, the steady reiteration of corresponding practices, effectively creates the body as 'my body', as something 'I' own, a process that makes 'me' a citizen. It makes 'me' a citizen as 'my ownership' of 'my individual body' is dependent on being a member of other bodies, specific ones, which are dedicated to keeping the space open for individuals to perform their right.

In this third sense, performing citizenship is not so much about individuals and groups who perform citizenship, but about how citizenship *per*forms individuals and groups, as it materializes in the making of our bodies and the bodies with which those form together. Citizenship *per*forms the individual body in a way no less crucial, yet connected to, the process of gendering as it has been famously described by Judith Butler in the 1990s. Of course, control over one's body is necessarily limited and compromised in many ways, through matter and also through discourse. Therefore, citizenship from this perspective might be seen less as a subject position and more as a *per*formance, a constant negotiation between bodies (Butler 2015; Cvejic and Vujanovic 2012).

To summarize, the performativity of citizenship that the contributions to this volume are focusing on comprises three different meanings:

- There is the successful civic performative, allowing citizens to constitute and change civic reality through their actions.
- There is the performance of citizenship outside of given structures that includes a dimension of 'fake it 'til you make it', that enacts and thereby claims citizenship in new ways.
- There is the most basic performance of citizenship, that often resides beneath the radar of our attention, in which citizenship as such is a *per*formance of bodies—institutional and individual—which, through a daily reiteration of practices, contributes to the very constitution of the individual body.

In the light of these three modes of performativity, their cross-references and transitions, it becomes clear that citizenship and performativity are not just two distinct concepts, two theoretical entities simply combined for the sake of this volume. Instead, the three modes constitute an intrinsic relationship between performativity and citizenship, who owe to each other much of their corresponding world-making powers.

This mutual reference, however, might also result in certain circularities. If citizenship has always been performative, then the limitations of citizenship might, to a certain extent, also be the limitations of performativity. Specifically, both citizenship and performativity are western, if not European, concepts. Therefore, this volume also discusses citizenship and 'non-performance', especially with regard to the politics of representation (Hildebrandt), post- and de-colonial questions (Peters), as well as the logistics of citizenships (Frischkorn).

ARTISTIC PRACTICE AND KNOWLEDGE PRODUCTION

To focus on the performativity of citizenship means considering the constant negotiations of bodies, rights and spaces. It also means paying attention to the fact, that these negotiations have always been a major field of artistic practice. Throughout the history of citizenship, there is an abundance of works and practices illustrating the hope that art significantly contributes to the ongoing negotiation of citizenship and empowers citizens to consciously shape and reshape the performance of citizenship. While highlighting a few exemplary historical lines, most contributions to this volume focus on articulations of the relationship between art and citizenship that have developed since the 1990s. The preface to 'The Citizen

Artist', published in 1998, describes this new relationship between art and citizenship poignantly:

> As public space becomes increasingly saturated by corporate culture, a new generation of artists is emerging. Frustrated by the insulated art world, encouraged by the politicization of art in the 80s, and desirous of the rupture between high and low art, artists are looking into the space of everyday life to find a new canvas. (Burnham and Durland 1998, p. 5)

Since then, research has concentrated largely on changes in art practices, on artists and projects that questioned art as a closed discourse and put it to experimental use in, with and for communities of all kinds. Beyond the initial enthusiasm for these new articulations of 'community art', it soon became clear that the question of participation is crucial to this line of practice and thinking (Bishop 2012; Doherty 2009; Hildebrandt 2012). While most corresponding art practices and projects can be called 'participatory' in general, participation can take many forms. In recent years, critical analyses of participation in art have gained in complexity and standing. They have shown, quite simply, that art can hardly ever get participation right. Though participatory projects often seem to question given power relations, they also produce and reproduce them. Citizen artists might counteract missing participation in society, but nevertheless will always mirror it and get caught in the overall structures of participation and non-participation.

The Performing Citizenship research program was partly designed in response to this critical discourse around participation and suggests the turning of tables: though the critique of participation in the arts may be well-founded, the editors of this volume are convinced that the corresponding problems and paradoxes of participation should not be held against participatory art practices in general, but should be interpreted as symptoms for a much wider crisis: the crisis of citizenship as the foundation and form that participation in society takes. Therefore, instead of looking exclusively at how art is changed through its new relation to citizenship, most contributors to this volume use participatory art practice, including and embracing its failures, as an instrument and a vehicle to examine the transformations of citizenship. Art practices—ranging from curating exhibitions to playwriting, urban intervention and performance, video making, and dance—are understood as tools and frameworks for participatory research, within and beyond the academy, that serve to reach new audiences, but also, and more importantly, 'to reformulate these research-relations' (Hawkins 2013, p. 31) toward something that could truly be called citizen research. In this reconfiguration, the exemplary artistic practices discussed in this volume are not solely the subject of critical inquiry; instead, they become experimental methods with which to explore transformations of citizenship as we are experiencing them or envisioning them today. 'What unites them, however, is that they are methods or means by which the social world is not only investigated, but may also be engaged', write Lury and Wakeford in their inventory of inventive methods. 'To describe them as inventive is to seek to realize the potential of this engagement whether it is as intervention, interference or refraction' (2012, p. 6).

In this sense, hundreds of people—citizens and non-citizens—have contributed to the different research projects presented in this volume, not by writing about citizenship, but by performing and articulating it in new and experimental ways. Research into citizenship has to be citizen research. Therefore, while this volume is meant to make these collective research processes accessible to a transdisciplinary—yet academic—discourse, it is by no means the only outcome of the research projects in question, but is part of a multilayered production of knowledge and corresponding realities which take many forms in projects and practices and evolving networks around the world.

ABOUT THIS VOLUME

Writing about performing citizenship constitutes a form of performance in its own right, operating between criticality and creativity and generating new perspectives and practices of artists, researchers and citizens. For which kind of audience do we write and what kind of language do we choose? The challenge of translating artistic practice into text, theory (citizenship) into practice (performance), making connections between abstract and the particular means to navigate the fine line between knowing and not-yet knowing how to perform citizenship, and how to reflect upon our thoughts in the act. When we understand research as an open process that involves, or more precisely builds on, the contribution, the collaboration and co-production of knowledge with other citizen researchers, blurring—if not obliterating—the boundaries of the 'white cube' of art galleries and museums, the 'black box' of the theater or the 'ivory tower' of academic conferences, journals and publications, this relates also to the act of publishing itself. In other words, this volume will be available online and in print; it is peer-reviewed and open access with a creative commons license.

As regards structure, the book is organized into four parts addressing key aspects raised by the intersection of performance and citizenship:

- Part I positions the present and vulnerable body at the center of struggles concerning citizenship. The body itself becomes both a battlefield and a space where values, norms and ideologies are constantly negotiated. With a focus on individual bodily practices as well as social choreographies of citizenship, this section asks how bodily art practices can challenge existing bodies of citizenship. Which individual and collective strategies enable us to intervene in political and social processes? How can these strategies be used in order to discover new forms of agency?
- Part II focuses on the city and urban spaces of citizenship. Diverse (urban) spaces let new figurations of citizenship emerge that bring existing binaries of private and public, art and activism, self-organization and governance, citizen and non-citizen, into question. These spaces arise out of manifold acts, through which diverse protagonists not only claim and challenge the urban as a scene but furthermore implement new relations between the notion of citizens and the city. But what happens on the edge of new-governance practices which always risk co-producing an urban development that counteracts emancipatory aims? Further, inasmuch as the city is constructed by social processes, spatial formations and its historical implications, the city is also shaped by the narratives and cultural representations of diverse communities which enable forms of belonging, identification and participation. What stories does the city tell, what is the 'sound of the city'? And what are the artistic strategies that reveal counter representations or enable a critical reception of hidden narratives in our urban daily life?
- Part III addresses the premises, critiques and speculations of citizenship and (non)performance. While citizenship is often idealized as a means of emancipation, in an exclusive Western discourse, it also serves as a regulatory instrument of domination that relies on things and artifacts to stabilize its rule. The practice of citizenship implicates multiple sutures in the fabric of the common

world, thereby articulating differently empowered realms. A contested matrix of subjectivity and personhood—the position of the fully human—regulates which bodies are allowed to move freely and articulate their interests as citizens. Furthermore, any performance of citizenship seems to be predicated on its other; that is to say, on other delegated performances and the exploitation of the very part(s) it excludes. We ask: How to be aware of the historic violence inherent in the notion of citizenship? Is it possible to shift or weaken the continuing operation of Western hegemonic power that the concept presupposes? And how could performance be the act of renouncing or redistributing agency so that others become present and discernible?

– Part IV, 'Emerging Agencies', essentially deals with new educational practices of knowledge and cultural production. To change citizenship is to change subject positions and forms of representations. In micropractices, new subject positions and ways of addressing a public can emerge. How do they become discernible? How to foster, trace and support these invisible agencies beyond already existing logics of citizenship and performance? How to enable neighborhoods, schools, workplaces and cultural institutions to become hosts for the emergence of new civic agencies? Who invites whom there? Who speaks for whom? Who invents other spaces and where? What role do artists and artistic projects play within these processes of emerging citizenship and its negotiation?

REFERENCES

Austin, J.L. 1962. *How to Do Things with Words, The William James Lectures Delivered at Harvard University in 1955*. London: Oxford University Press.

Balibar, Etienne. 2012. The "Impossible" Community of the Citizen: Past and Present Problems. *Environment and Planning D: Society and Space* 30: 437–449.

Benhabib, Seyla. 2006. *Another Cosmopolitanism*. Oxford: Oxford University Press.

Bishop, Claire. 2012. *Artificial Hells: Participatory Art and the Politics of Spectatorship*. London: Verso.

Burnham, Linda Frye, and Steve Durland. 1998. The Citizen Artist: 20 Years of Art in the Public Arena: An Anthology. In *High Performance Magazine 1978–1998, Thinking Publicly*. New York: Critical Press.

Butler, Judith. 2015. *Notes Toward a Performative Theory of Assembly*. Cambridge, MA: Harvard University Press.

Cvejic, Bojana, and Ana Vujanovic. 2012. *Public Sphere by Performance*. Berlin: b_books.

Doherty, Claire. 2009. *Situation*. Cambridge, MA: MIT Press.

Faist, Thomas. 2013. *Shapeshifting Citizenship in Germany: Expansion, Erosion and Extension*. Bielefeld: COMCAD Working Papers, No. 115.

Gallie, W.B. 1956. Essentially Contested Concepts. *Proceedings of the Aristotelian Society* 56: 167–198.

Hawkins, Harriet. 2013. *For Creative Geographies*. New York: Routledge.

Hildebrandt, Paula. 2012. *Urbane Kunst. Handbuch Stadtsoziologie*, 719–742. Wiesbaden: Springer.

Holston, John. 2007. *Insurgent Citizenship*. Princeton: Princeton University Press.

Isin, Engin. 2009. Citizenship in Flux: The Figure of the Activist Citizen. *Subjectivity* 29: 367–388.

Kymlicka, Will. 1995. *Multicultural Citizenship: A Liberal Theory of Minority Rights*. Oxford: Oxford University Press.

Lebuhn, Henrik. 2013. Local Border Practices and Urban Citizenship in Europe: Exploring Urban Borderlands. *CITY. Analysis of Urban Trends, Culture, Theory, Policy, Action* 17 (1): 37–51.

Leggewie, Claus. 2013. Transnational Citizenship. Ideals and European Realities. *Eurozine*. http://www.eurozone.com. Accessed 2 Nov 2017.

Lury, Celia, and Nina Wakeford. 2012. *Inventive Methods. The Happening of the Social*. New York: Routledge.

Maas, Willem. 2013. *Multilevel Citizenship*. Philadelphia: University of Pennsylvania Press.

Ong, Aihwa. 2006. *Neoliberalism as Exception: Mutations in Citizenship and Sovereignty*. Durham: Duke University Press.

Roy, Ananya, and Nezar AlSayyad. 2006. Medieval Modernity: On Citizenship and Urbanism in a Global Era. *Space and Polity* 10 (1): 1–20.

Shachar, Ayelet. 2009. *The Birthright Lottery. Citizenship and Global Inequality*. Cambridge, MA/London: Harvard University Press.

Shachar, Ayelet, Rainer Bauboeck, Irene Bloemraad, and Maarten Vink. 2017. *The Oxford Handbook of Citizenship*. Oxford: University of Oxford Press.

PART I

Bodies of Citizenship

Yet Another Effort, Citizens, If You Want to Learn How to React!

Kai van Eikels

CITIZENS WHO DO NOT WANT TO REACT

"Move your fucking head!" The choreographer Deborah Hay calls this one of her core mottoes, in dance and in life. What does this instruction imply if taken for a maxim of performing citizenship? What advice can dance, the art of movement, offer to a body that, normally, is a citizen's body by virtue of reflexes, not reactions? A policeman shouts, 'Hey, you!' and you turn around. This movement suffices to define you as a subject, as one subjected to the state's authority, according to Louis Althusser.[1] To the extent that citizenship is a legal status, not an achievement or a competence, the only performative utterance demanded from citizens by the state's representatives consists of such small responsive movements of acknowledgment. The more automated, the more reliably locked into behavioral routines these responses are—the fewer signs of a true performance they show—the better, from a statist point of view. Disobedience, in this scenario, is left with only two alternatives. You either ignore the policeman and walk on; or you turn against him and engage in a confrontation, perhaps put up a fight. The police have been trained to deal with either form of insurrection.

K. van Eikels (✉)
Ruhr-Universität Bochum, Bochum, Germany

P. Hildebrandt et al. (eds.), *Performing Citizenship*, Performance
Philosophy, https://doi.org/10.1007/978-3-319-97502-3_2

They will initiate pursuit or check the attack—calling in reinforcements if necessary. But what if citizens learned how to *continue* the movement of turning their heads around in a way that turns the reflex into a reaction—that changes the situation, slightly but effectively, by using the turnaround as a mode of communication with others, thus referring and relating the policeman's presence to the presence of other citizens—of citizens who understand how to self-organize spontaneously, who are versed in forming a collective, in establishing a *civil constellation* any time and in any place through a sequence of distributed reactions? For this to happen, moving your head in response would indeed have to become a performance, a bodily activity that draws on skills, on practical and theoretical knowledge. It would need to be practiced as a political movement.

In October 2016, I hosted one day of a week-long workshop initiated by the artist Koki Tanaka. I asked the participants to keep moving all the time and to avoid forming a circle during the entire day we were practicing together. How would power have bearing on a host of people who were incessantly turning around, moving their heads, necks, shoulders and torsos in order to circumvent a standstill and to elude the best-established pattern of gathering? And what kind of power would—or could—it be, as they all continued to be citizens of a nation-state throughout the exercises, remaining subjected to its authority that was operative in their bodies? Which qualities of togetherness would evolve from these bodies' interactions when sustained turnarounds challenged the continuity of unquestioned operation by the standard 'citizen' movement repertoire? The workshop's title, *How to Live Together*, echoed that of the lecture given by Roland Barthes at the Collège de France in 1976–77.[2] The schedule mapped out a variety of activities for the eight volunteers, all of whom lived in or near the city of Münster, Westphalia—some of them were born in the area, some had grown up there but came from an immigrant family, some had only recently arrived for study or to find work. The whole workshop was recorded by a professional film team because the artist wanted a multimedia installation composed of edited videos, photos, texts and objects used during the week to become his contribution for the Skulptur Projekte exhibition in 2017. After we had focused on collectively self-organizing through movement for the first half of our workshop day, the exercises in the second half suggested employing language in a way similar to body movement. For one exercise, nicknamed 'G8,' I told the group members to think of themselves as eight sovereign rulers of the world. Whatever they decided would become reality. All of them were equally powerful though. We wrote down a couple of important political topics like 'world peace,' 'solving the hunger problem' and 'tackling sexism,' then selected issues by drawing paper scraps from a pot and addressed them one at a time. Everyone was entitled to make decisions, but one had to react to a decision with another decision. If someone was not satisfied with a decision, they could alter or even annul it with a decision of their own, yet ought to be prepared that the one who had just been overruled might strike back or a third party might come to their aid. For all this wealth of power, the structure called for cooperation among equals; or else, the world management was doomed to fail.

Which it mostly did, for several rounds. While the general atmosphere of mild annoyance never rose to open protest against the rule or against me, the eight participants found it immensely difficult to break away from their conversation habits. They would rather lecture each other: explaining why a decision was wrong or flawed, criticize its ineffectiveness, express ethical indignation, signal sympathy and antipathy (thus creating informal subdivisions of the group), and engage in discussions that promised to be endless. Whereas the task of formulating a decision and deciding on a formulation rendered the citizens-turned-rulers near speechless at times, sophisticated arguments against a decision spouted from their mouths without hesitation. Out of this group of people, some were active with local initiatives helping refugees or had been involved in social activism, and most seemed particularly socially minded. However, the ethos, or even the concept, of help did not cross over to the 'G8' situation; it disappeared as they shared a reality defined by safety, freedom and the power to decide. Emphatic affects to help will likely be triggered in a state of urgency, where others evidently lack something. In *A Paradise Built in Hell*, Rebecca Solnit tells stories about human beings abandoning their distant attitude after a catastrophe has destroyed or temporarily suspended civil life's infrastructures.[3] The extreme situation imposed on all draws many closer together. In less dramatic intensity, such encounters under pressure occur every day. But for the leisurely gathered workshop group, whose members had even become acquainted to being filmed on this third day, what motivation was there to help each other?

The pattern shifted a little when I introduced another rule—namely, that every decision was to be made in the form of a 'Yes, and....' 'Yes-And-ing' is an agreement in improvisation theater and dance: whatever your response will be, you start with an acknowledgement and affirmation of that which you are reacting to, before adding something. And if you are ill-content with what the other one has just said or done, your own reaction needs to *redirect* it. Negation cannot take on the form of rejection; it will have to find a movement that recognizes the other's move's impulse, following it in its original direction for an initial period, then changing the direction and taking it somewhere else than presumably intended, which may ultimately result in a full turnaround. You react like a Judo or Aikido fighter, who never goes against the partner's movement but uses its momentum for accomplishing their own goal. When we played our game with 'Yes-And-ing,' objections interrupted the collective process less often, and the overall tendency was to be more cooperative and concentrate on modifying a measure rather than trying to disable it.

However, despite the occasional show of pleasure when the process of decision-making was proceeding more smoothly, it remained evident until the end that the participants *did not want to react* in this manner. They visibly felt at odds with the position of mighty rulers, and the semi-ironic 'G8' likely added to make the effort unattractive. But a similar resistance against communication with and through decisions would, I assume, have manifested without the fiction of unlimited power, which just served the purpose of barring 'impotence' as a pretext for not deciding on something. The influence might as well have been limited to that of an average citizen and the tasks adjusted accordingly. The deeper problem seemed to consist in a collective dynamic that required you to react without offering anything in terms of a compelling situational force: people were safe and free, yet still they had to react. Since they were free, they might as well *not* react with a decision, instead withdrawing to the position of the critical observer, the member of an audience. Their lives as citizens had trained them for this mode of (non-) participation, therefore it was no surprise that they preferred to remain in this state rather than doing something at which they were inexperienced. In a nation-state with a government of professional politicians, roles are clearly separated between those who make decisions and those who criticize them. Leaving the population with less power to decide puts more emphasis on a kind of criticality that is disconnected from the practical reason of decision-making. The people of a sovereign nation-state may never say 'Yes, and...' to a decision made by the government. The people may not even articulate an *Einverständnis*— an affirmative understanding—which the chorus in Bertolt Brecht's learning play *Der Jasager* claims is 'most important to learn'[4] for living together. They can merely choose between not reacting and critical comments, and both options go hand in hand.

CITIZENS WHO HAD TO REACT ATTACK CITIZENS WHO DID NOT

New protest movements solved some old problems. In 2011 and 2012, the need for quick decisions in the camps, which were beleaguered by the police, prompted useful techniques for facilitating debates. And the agreement to bring only really controversial issues before the general assembly—and otherwise let people pursue their own agendas—in addition to speeding up proceedings, helped build a relaxed, trustful atmosphere.[5] Still, the state of exception defined the occupiers' life in that it provided the problems. Improvised living together consisted of urgent problem-solving, plus free time for sharing knowledge, social activities and discussions about how things would be different in a better world. Whereas external and internal challenges to the protest event created a pressure that called for reactions both effective and efficient, the pastime activities—which expressed the freedom of living together in a gathering that was not only protest but an experiment with 'small-*a* anarchism'[6]—had need to be neither. Organizational improvements, hence, were mostly economic.

This is a well-known phenomenon with improvisation. For the interplay of spontaneous reactions to embrace change—and particularly a change that extends to the collective dynamic's own procedural patterns—an extraordinary urgency is required, ideally, a *sustained* urgency. The much-lauded inventiveness of group improvisation, where 'the new' 'emerges' as a collective surplus, in reality results from a pressure to *reinvent* that which may be taken for granted in ordinary life. Improvisation's originality reflects a death threat, whose more symbolic manifestations, in everyday extempore and in the performing arts' methods of instant creation, still carry the affective tremor of a literal catastrophe.[7] And for political activists, this threat is to be taken at face value: They obtain practical knowledge through improvised self-organization because their fights against the authorities of the nation-state often lead to situations in which their enemy denies them basic citizens' rights. They must learn how to react, as the state's executive forces exercise a power to withdraw the privilege of *not* having to react—the essential privilege of the citizen.

Repeatedly, activism means survival training in a state of suspended citizenship. The acquired reacting skills are therefore often so congenially attuned to situations of duress that they fit in badly with the loose, casual encounters that compose much of citizens' regular social and political undertakings. Once the fighters return to their citizen identities, normality swallows the self-organizational know-how. Sometimes they sink back into attitudes of resentment deeper than those who never cried from tear gas attacks. Reserve—the personal stance corresponding to the citizen's right to not react—has lost its innocence for them. Having endured moments, hours or days of unprotected bare life, their bodies are painfully aware that the freedom to hesitate, to defer, to put off, to neglect, to disregard or to remain indifferent to what others are doing is all but a natural given. Something in these bodies continues to fight, taking revenge for the inflicted wound in a kind of precisely misguided transference, when they attack politically like-minded fellow citizens whose behavior betrays their ignorance as to how the open-ended discussions they enjoy so much are only possible because the nation-state spares them the necessity to react.

Can we, politically like-minded fellow citizens, take a cue from that transferred revenge, learning a lesson from the very unfairness of those attacks? As people born and educated into becoming functional entities within a society that never gives its members much reason to ask a question like 'How to live together?,' can we learn how to deal with the nation-state's effective presence in-between our bodies in a similar way to how dance performers work with the material of movement? Althusser's policeman need not be attendant, as long as the citizens hear the state's voice resonate in other citizen's voices—which all but very few of us usually do. We search in vain for an atmosphere that invites direct democracy in a nation-state, if for the reason that there are no direct encounters between its citizens. In peaceful, quiet times, the weight of sovereign authority feels light to the point of sinking into oblivion. Still, every one of us has a primary relationship with the state; and only in second respect, mediated by the state's institutional structures that pervade the entire social sphere, do we entertain relationships with one another. But what to make of this lightness?

Self-Indulgent Citizens Who React Because They Have Practiced Reacting

Interactions between citizens attest to their indirectness where a certain distance is taken for granted, which the participants experience as their freedom to react because it portends the possibility of not reacting. Citizen behavior expects that the 'together' will be managed. Richard Sennett accused modern individualism of diminishing people's ability to actively create the public sphere through the use of formal, respectfully distant, polite, social performing styles.[8] If such a de-skilling and de-formalization in fact occurred, it has made us even more dependent on a properly separated, buffered co-presence being provided for us by the sovereign authority. What disappeared as people got used to behaving as if in private even when in public—leaving the parade of erect backs for slouched subway-seat ease—is the *identification with that authority*. Gone are the times when you had to *embody* the sovereign in your own comportment for others to recognize you as a dignified citizen.

In the progressively nationalist design of a republic, as it was pursued in Europe from the eighteenth to the early nineteenth centuries, the citizens contributed the distance of public converse to the political life. They employed a rhetorical and behavioral code of 'self-abstraction,'[9] which effectively removed the distinction between strangers and kin by addressing everyone, even family members or close friends, as though talking to a stranger. The civil public sphere thus socialized the sovereign: a 'bottom-up sovereignty' met halfway with the governance from above, reassuring rulers and ruled that *the same* form of control as it had been implemented top-down in the complex of legislative, judicative and executive power could also be established in citizens' self-organization. From the political party running in national elections down to the local pub's savings association, variants of instituted power proliferated on every level. 'We are the people' translated into 'We are the citizens,' which meant 'We are the state.'

As outmoded (and anachronistic in its sporadic reappearances) as that citizens' pride seems today, it still remains to be discovered what a civic sphere abandoned by sovereignty's poses, postures and paternalisms offers to its residents. What does performing citizenship mean, if it no longer means that citizens embody the sovereign? How can performance benefit from a leisurely state of attendance, if the bodies in public are no longer busy negotiating the discrepancy between the role of the obedient subject—whose every move includes a silent nod to the sovereign's watchman hiding behind—and the role of the substitute sovereign on call, who is always ready to take control ('responsibility') and master a situation? What political performativity is there in the slack, laggard, careless, overly confident but then also more versatile, flip-able, soft-necked inhabitation of a public space maintained by a power that *feels exterior* to its citizens—by sovereignty that remains un-internalized because the subjects relate to the *effects* of sovereign power, yet not to its *structures*?

This question might be deemed unworthy of asking. Bad conscience hastens to assert that the liberties I take as a 'spineless,' effete *nth* generation citizen are not expressions of true freedom; that they betray consumer egotism, complacency and *naiveté*. If the users of a social network habitually ignore the provider company (unless the service is down), they deserve to be called sheepish, as their lack of vigilance renders them easy targets for manipulation. Does the same not hold for citizens who let the state be the state? We have been alerted to secret services intruding on our privacies on a scale that exceeds darkest fantasy. Never had citizens less reason to trust in the institutional cluster that makes up the state, we might caution one another. But the object-less watchfulness of those many of us who are not hackers, lawyers or other experts ready to fight the battle for privacy with some promise of success is not politically helpful at all. Rather than fortify statist logic by giving ourselves over to an angry, and yet fascinated, distrust, anarchist reaction training would seek to weaken the state as the potential enemy of its citizens by actually taking advantage of some liberties it provides—by utilizing them for the sake of emancipating reacting.

In the pamphlet *Français, encore un effort si vous voulez être républicains*, embedded in the dialogue *La philosophie dans le boudoir*, the anarchist de Sade suggested principles for a society in which the revolution achieves a continuous reality, not in the permanent and ever-more radical renewal—as attempted by the Jacobin *terreur*—but rather in a series of secondary steps that make comprehensive, unrestricted use of the freedoms gained in revolution's initial victory.[10] In a time when daily news reminds us that democracy might as well not carry on—as one ruler after the other abuses their authority by transforming constitutional democracies into autocratic regimes, and millions of refugees are desperate to reach one of the few remaining states that still seem to respect citizens' rights—we may want to ask ourselves, in de Sade's spirit, what good the protected atmosphere of liberal citizenship affords the political. Especially if we think that the political lies with the people and *their* power to organize living together—and not with the state's administration—we should expose our political intelligence to the following questions: How can we—you, I, any of us—do something that will feel like a free reaction, based on the sovereign's externality? How can the collective self-organization of political action benefit from a mostly carefree, negligent civil life? Where the state assumes an infrastructural, provider-like reality for its people, what point is there in *affirming* that reality—even though it might be (and, in a certain respect, cannot be anything else) but an illusion?

Performing citizenship—in a blunt interpretation of the expression—is to say that we use knowledge acquired in techniques of artistic performance for instructing citizens on how to play games like 'G8,' how to change them in the playing and how to customize them according to different agendas. If learning to entertain collective processes through nuanced and considered, willful reacting were part of everyone's education, equality would quickly cease to be taken for an ideal upon which reality must surely compromise. More technically, it would be recognized as a performative presupposition that informs communication practices. Criticality, then, would mean adding negations instead of withholding approval. Continuation of movement across multiple bodies—casually, even sluggishly, but perpetually 'moving your fucking head,' as several lines of continuing are synchronizing in and through your body, admitting to the presence of others who happen to be around—would become a widely applied understanding of 'public.' So, inclined to keep on moving, people would see the custom of sitting in circles for hours in order to arrive at a single decision as the weird, quasi-religious ritual it is.[11]

Importantly though, the freedom of not having to react should be respected, more than that, celebrated, within these political skills of performing citizenship. The right to hesitate, to defer, to put off, to neglect, to disregard or to remain indifferent to what others are doing, ought to be the very foundation of an educational program for teaching reaction techniques that set the spine swinging from the feet up to the head down. Rather than scold citizens for their alienation from values like empathy, concern and a type of responsibility that creates bottom-up sovereignty, such performing techniques would do well to scan the alienation for what might be politically helpful in its impact on living together. The more constellative artistry the citizens' bodies achieve in navigating the distance, the more thoroughly performing can establish a civil public sphere. No catastrophic urgency needs be imaginatively imported for this. Unless catastrophes happen, let us find out how to play a peaceful arena, playing it loose. And as soon as we break loose from the compensatory fiction of 'getting closer (again),' foreigners may even touch each other, anytime, in any place.

NOTES

1. See, Louis Althusser (1971), 'Ideology and Ideological State Apparatuses', in *Lenin and Philosophy and Other Essays*, trans. Ben Brewster (New York: Monthly Review Press), pp. 121–176.
2. Roland Barthes (2012) *How to Live Together. Novelistic Simulations of Some Everyday Spaces*, trans. Kate Briggs (New York: Columbia University Press).
3. See Rebecca Solnit (2010) *A Paradise Built in Hell: The Extraordinary Communities That Arise in Disaster* (London: Penguin).
4. 'Wichtig zu lernen vor allem ist Einverständnis' Bertolt Brecht, *Der Jasager*, in: Große kommentierte Berliner und Frankfurter Ausgabe, 3 (Frankfurt am Main: Suhrkamp) 1988, pp. 57–65, here p. 57.
5. See David Graeber's account on principles and procedures of decision-making with Occupy, in: *The Democracy Project: A History, a Crisis, a Movement* (Spiegel & Grau), 2013.
6. See, David Graeber (2000), *Direct Action: An Ethnography* (Oakland: AK Press), pp. 211–222.
7. See, Kai van Eikels (2016) 'What Your Spontaneity is Worth to Us. Improvisation Between Art and Economics', in Sabeth Buchmann; Ilse Lafer; Constanze Ruhm (eds) *Putting Rehearsals to the Test. Practices of Rehearsal in Fine Arts, Film, Theater, Theory, and Politics* (Berlin & Vienna: Sternberg Press), pp. 22–30.
8. See, Richard Sennett (1977) *The Fall of Public Man* (New York: Knopf).
9. See, Michael Warner (2002) *Publics and Counterpublics* (Cambridge: MIT Press).
10. See Marquis de Sade, *Philosophy in the Bedroom*, trans. Richard Seaver and Austryn Wainhouse, pp. 91–122, http://www.sin.org/tales/Marquis_de_ Sade%2D%2DPhilosophy_in_the_Bedroom.pdf, date accessed 1 March 2017.
11. On the religious (re-)determination of political gathering, see Kai van Eikels (2016), 'The Togetherness of Those Who Would Not Wait for One Another' in geheimagentur; Martin Jörg Schäfer; Vassilis S. Tsianos (eds) *The Art of Being Many. Towards a New Theory and Practice of Gathering* (Bielefeld: Transcript), pp. 61–68.

An Elephant in the Room / On the Balcony: Performing the 'Welcome City' Hamburg

Paula Hildebrandt

The first rule on the stage of the big city is: Always create the impression to be on the move to a particular place.
Massimo Carlotto, *The Fugitive (Carlotto 2007, p. 46)*

In January 2015, I moved to Hamburg to start a new job at the HafenCity University Hamburg. I was 39 years old. After finishing my PhD, I was working as a freelance cultural producer, lecturer and writer; I also organized a weekly German language class in a reception centre for refugees in Berlin. Since this time, I became curious to discover the way in which my own approach to arriving in a new city corresponds to the situation and strategies of others who have recently arrived; equally, to those who have lived in Hamburg for a longer time but without a feeling of having arrived. My move to Hamburg was in no way comparable to the situation of somebody who left their hometown due to civil war or extreme poverty. I have no experience of war, abuse, torture or traumatizing events. I write this article as a white, gender-conforming woman from a fairly upper-middle-class background, with an international education and a work

P. Hildebrandt (✉)
Berlin, Germany
e-mail: info@paulahildebrandt.de

© The Author(s) 2019
P. Hildebrandt et al. (eds.), *Performing Citizenship*, Performance Philosophy, https://doi.org/10.1007/978-3-319-97502-3_3

contract—albeit part-time and temporary. I am privileged 'as hell'! The research I do is therefore bound to reflect those privileges.

Hamburg, like any other big city in Germany, is characterized by increasing super-diversity and polarization. This often leads to cultural and political conflicts, nevertheless brightened by excitement and expectations for a better life. The recent influx of refugees adds momentum, relevance and urgency to the question of how to live together and explore new modes of exchange and learning, of conviviality, hospitality and solidarity. In 2015 alone, more than 20,000 refugees arrived in Hamburg. These people come in addition to the many people from 'elsewhere', already living here for decades, often doing badly paid and largely invisible work: caring, cleaning, cooking, tailoring, waxing—a fact too often neglected in the discourse about the so-called refugee crisis.

After the initial enthusiasm and subsequent disenchantment with the German *Willkommenskultur* ('welcome culture'), and in opposition to the predominant and restrictive integration paradigm with its essentialist notion of citizenship and naturalization (*Einbürgerung*), I wanted to find out what constitutes a contemporary practice of hospitality. How to create community, make kin and think-with other beings under circumstances where many people, not just refugees, inhabit multiple worlds and questions of identity and belonging are less defined by territory, family or birth? Can a city be welcoming? What does a 'Welcome City' look and feel like? Can you feel at home among strangers? What are the potentials and limits of hospitality as the central concept when thinking about how to live together in a super-diverse society which continues to consider migrants to be strange?

Inspired by a novel by Massimo Carlotto[1]—about his years in exile, in prison and under persecution—I thought to explore the mostly unspoken rules for living and settling in a new city; the rules that you are supposed to know or which you did not even know existed. Which skills and what kind of knowledge are necessary to act and be considered a citizen of Hamburg: to 'show-up' on the city stage of Hamburg? Further, I wanted to better understand how artists/researchers, working with performative methods, can prefigure or suggest new forms of citizenship that have yet to be invented. This means to also investigate my own performance (as citizen).

A performative perspective on citizenship shifts the discussion over *who* is entitled to rights. This involves a change in outlook from a national framework towards emphasis on the actual (physical) centre of people's lives, a closer look at the insurgent practice of people traversing borders and normative frames (Holston 2007; Isin 2009, 2012; Iannelli and Musarò 2017). Engin Isin has advanced the idea of citizenship as 'the right to claim rights' in order to emphasize the activist, process-oriented and self-empowering dimension of citizenship:

> The actors of citizenship are not necessarily those who hold the status of citizenship. If we understand citizenship as an instituted subject-position, it can be performed or enacted by various categories of subjects including aliens, migrants, refugees, states, courts and so on. (Isin 2009, p. 370)

This shift—from the moving to the acting subject, from mobility to the ability of crossing geographical borders and normative frames—draws attention to the fact that prefabricated categories of citizen and non-citizen do not exist as neutral, pre-social, fixed identities, but only in relation to one another. Citizenship is in a permanent state of reconstruction and reinvention—by the state as well as by non-state actors who challenge, disavow, play with, supersede, if not entirely obliterate, supposedly clear-cut roles and responsibilities, social conventions, standard protocols and normal procedure. Citizenship, in the words of Etienne Balibar, is 'ubiquitous' (2012, p. 443) and therefore can be—might be—enacted potentially everywhere.

As for performing citizenship, I do not really know what it is, and I know it less and less. And yet, although I am not sure about how to actually translate a performative theory of citizenship into artistic practice, I would argue that performativity offers a conceptual gateway to escape the trap of 'othering', of getting lost in essentialist notions of culture, considering the complications of class, race and gender. Performativity essentially revolves around matters of citation and contestation, of role and representation. It is precisely this ambivalence and process of transformation that validates a performative investigation of Hamburg as 'Welcome City'. The aim of my three-year research project was not to arrive at some comprehensive definition of a city that is welcoming, or to establish certain criteria, but rather investigate—through practice and process—when and how new forms of hospitality, of rights and responsibilities towards the other—a stranger, our neighbour—emerge, as embodied activity, lived experience, enactment and performance. My general idea was that the methods employed will facilitate the actual happening of the 'Welcome City' Hamburg and also investigate the circumstances and situations, its fragility and relationality, contingency and sensuousness. Some impatience is implied here with the limitations of a linguistic frame of reference towards a more practical—if not pragmatic and materialist—route in dealing with the complexities of citizenship as one of the most urgent matters of our time. In this way, the constraints are apparent: art as research is often a desk job. Despite this, it holds ample capacity to depart from one's comfort zone, transcending the border of the white cube, museums and galleries, the black box of the theatre, not forgetting the ivory tower of the university.

At the outset, I contacted several networks and initiatives which deal in some way with welcoming newcomers. I actively approached others who would be interested to explore Hamburg (as 'Welcome City'). I did this by circulating flyers—in collaboration with Hamburg's organization for refugee accommodation *Fördern & Wohnen*—in the official Hamburg Welcome Center. I chose likely locations for contact, such as launderettes, the New Hamburg Language Café[2] and attending cocktail parties through the expat network InterNations. I invented the so-called welcome city group: a collection of seemingly disparate people who gather to discover what might constitute a contemporary practice of hospitality. Enacting the 'Welcome City' Hamburg was process in action, in the making. The description of the group—its aims and activities—was meant to be broad and inclusive, inviting people with or without a residence permit, on the move or on the run, residents and refugees.

The group quickly grew to more than 40 'members', mostly communicating via a *WhatsApp* group. Meetings took place on Saturday evenings, each prepared by one 'member', dealing with the overall theme of hospitality from a different perspective; for example, in traditional Iranian architecture, Arabic poetry and proverbs, Argentinian milongas or the prostitution/tourism complex. We explored the nightlife in Hamburg's red-light district of St. Pauli (men and women disguised as a bunch of Hen Night party-goers). During the *Hamburg Nacht des Wissens 2015*[3] (Long Night of Sciences) we attended a crash course on 'International Business Etiquette: whether lunch, small-talk or dress code – learn to avoid awkward situations in an international business context' and a game workshop titled 'The next time the Queen comes to visit… be prepared to impress somebody important!'

Meeting by meeting, action by action, we created a kind of performative cartography of Hamburg as 'Welcome City'. My initial ethnographic and topographic approach—of mapping Hamburg through performative

actions in different locations across the city—increasingly turned to sociological questions and group dynamics that do not follow the familiar logic
of community, family or affinity. I became increasingly cautious regarding
matters of hierarchies and privileges, and of authorship and visual representation, especially when working *with* and not *about* so-called refugees,
people with migration background or presumably marginalized groups
(see Castro Varela and Dhawan 2007; Dogramaci 2013; Krause 2017).

What connects the different phases of analysis of this three-year research
project (2015–17) was the method I applied, which I refer to as performative action. Performative actions function on three interdependent levels.
They are as follows:

1. A sensation performed.
2. A formal structure allowing a turning of the sensation into concrete
   experiences and making something happen.
3. A proposition of meaning—an allegory, that is, the art of meaning
   something other than what is actually being said. It is the art of
   decoding meaning, of reading between the lines, the playing and
   contesting of diverse language games.

The purpose of performative action is to capture what is already given—
the city, its citizens—as well as to inspire what may follow, what is not yet
there. They presume that performance, embodied and repeated action, in
the words of the American sociologist Norman Denzin, 'is a way of knowing, a way of understanding, a way of creating critical consciousness'
(2016, p. 12). Based on my own curiosity, questions and sensations, and
through the sending out of invitations and producing minor irritations, I
drafted a series of experimental set-ups. These set-ups each had a conceptual or theatrical frame for dialogue, mutual exchange, encounter and performative action, navigating the fine line between knowing and not
knowing, or rather, the very process of knowledge production. Here,
German philosopher of science Hans-Jörg Rheinberger's theory of epistemic objects helps achieve terms that embrace both: continuity and transformation, citation and contestation, original and cover-version.
Rheinberger's theory examines how new ideas come into existence. He
argues that new ideas in science emerge not simply through a single experiment, but by the repetition of experiments that demonstrate a process of
continual adjusting and contextualizing in order to attain a comprehensive
body of knowledge. In seeing my project in relation to this theory—as a

series of experiments with formal structure—it is clear some parameters changed (location, guests, hosts, subject, time, communication medium). He refers to this not-yet-formulated body of knowledge as its epistemic object: 'A basic unit of experimental activity combining local, technical, instrumental, institutional, social and epistemic aspects' (1997, p. 238). Accordingly, the 'Welcome City Hamburg'—as epistemic object—is to be investigated and, at the same time, produced through an experimental system of performative actions. Rheinberger's theory also shows that experimental systems are, by definition, initially imprecise. Even within the more or less strictly regulated experimental systems that he describes, 'one never knows precisely how the set-up differentiates' (pp. 79–80). An epistemic object has to be precise enough to generate knowledge and carefully imprecise enough to incorporate unexpected results of experiments. Repeated action, resulting in sensitive readjustment and iteration, is key, more than the single—disruptive, heroic, provocative, spectacular or supposedly subversive—action. Indeed, there was a song, *Gym and Tonic* by the band Spacedust (1998), continuously in my mind when working out the experimental set-ups, actually a cover-version of Jane Fonda aerobics instructions—'2 – 3 – 4 – 5 – 6 – 7 – 8 and back. 2 – 3 – 4 – 5 – 6 – 7 – 8 and back. Work it out! Come on, now!'[4]

'What good is sitting alone in your room?', asks Liza Minelli in the film *Cabaret* (1972), 'Come hear the music play. Life is a cabaret, oh chum, come to the cabaret!'[5] In the photo (Fig. 1), it is me that you see sitting alone in a room, and an inflatable elephant on the balcony. This situation appears neither to address the city nor the issue of hospitality. Yet, in spite of—or perhaps because of—its absurdity and idiosyncrasy, these circumstances are well suited to discuss and summarize empirical findings and insights gathered through hitherto performative actions. Critically, this situation provoked a combination of moral dilemma and puzzlement; effectively, a constructed drama of focal significance to an urban society based on notions of hospitality, its inherent tensions, recursiveness and temporality.

When Hamburg's first mayor, Olaf Scholz, presented his new book *Hoffnungsland* ('Country of Hope', 2017), he explained that 'we'—meaning the city and the citizens of Hamburg—were simply not prepared for the huge influx of refugees in 2015. The question of how 'we' might accommodate such dramatic changes and better be prepared for the next, always unprecedented influx of future refugees, however, was left unanswered. Futurologists from the Fraunhofer Institute for Systems and

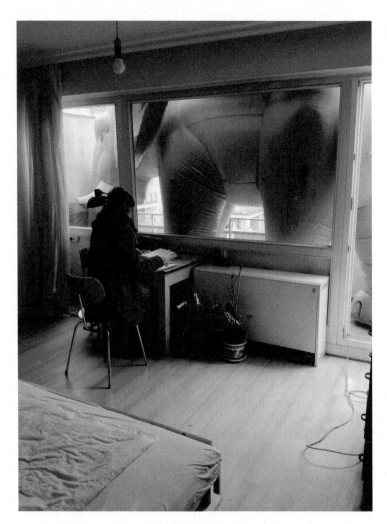

Fig. 1 Elephant on the balcony © Paula Hildebrandt

Innovation Research refer to Japanese foresight methods on science and technology, such as always testing new items and supposed innovations in practice—like, for example, a vacuum cleaner. No sooner said than done. Accordingly, during the 'presentation weeks' of the graduate programme 'Performing Citizenship' in May 2017, I opened a mobile 'BürgerInnenbüro'.

I then invited an inflatable elephant to stay at my place, delivered by AIR promotion, c. 2.5 metres high, powered by a 200watt electric fan that was permanently on. I created a highly artificial and yet real-life experimental situation in order to gain some first-hand experience and insights about how to prepare for those who are yet to come. In other words, this research set-up was conducted in anticipation of future migration due to global warming and possible species extinction. What happens when the prover-bial elephant enters the room? How might we accommodate and com-municate with radically different beings when language cannot reach? Who counts as human? Whose lives count as lives, and what makes for a life worth grievance and protection?

The following gives an account of events and subsequent empirical findings. I include a verbatim transcript of the *WhatsApp* chat with S., a member of the 'welcome city group' from Afghanistan. At that time, he was living with his wife in a temporary container accommodation for asylum-seekers in Hamburg-Billstedt.

03.05.17, 09:37:50: Paula Hildebrandt: I have a guest now. Do you want to meet? Can I bring him/her?
03.05.17, 09:37:50: S.:   Yeah sure my pleasure

Meeting and greeting the elephant caused great excitement and curios-ity, at least in the beginning. Everybody was amused, friendly and helpful when I asked for advice, assistance or a plug to inflate the 'guest'. This initial positive reaction, however, did not last long. It lasted for the exact duration of a selfie.

Finding alternative accommodation, or just getting around the city with this somehow disproportionate guest turned out to be extremely dif-ficult. Due to Road Traffic regulation § 22 StVO, the maximum height for vehicles is 4 m. Therefore, it was not possible to fix the elephant on top of the minivan that I had transformed into a mobile citizen office. To bring my 'guest' to some watering point, the elephant had to be deflated and folded back into the box. Again, upon reaching a sightseeing spot—for example, Elbe beach—the citizens of Hamburg were unanimously very friendly with regard to the inflatable elephant, but only until restaurant owners raised concerned that someone might stumble over the cable for the fan. A joint theatre visit was not possible due to safety precautions, but the elephant was allowed to wait in a rehearsal studio. Hospitality, in other words, is based on the 'priority of affirmation' (Seshadri 2011, p. 127). It requires a first 'yes' or, even better, a first: 'yeah, sure, my pleasure'. Encountering the absolute other—who has no name or a family name—is based on an ethical imperative.

03.05.17, 09:39:58: S.:	I see a white elephant behind the window
03.05.17, 09:40:23: P.:	Yes sir
03.05.17, 09:40:34: S.:	Is that your domestic pet?

Hosting an inflatable elephant is hard work, but also good company. When inflated, the elephant provided a kind of shelter, and conveyed a feeling of calm and security. Furthermore, an inflatable, as a pet, is unconditional in its affection and loyalty. However, the inflatable as temporary guest also severely disrupted well-established routines, familiar comforts, my way of doing things. Simply moving around my tiny flat became cumbersome, and required me having to crawl under or squeeze past the elephant. Which also produced uncomfortable questions: Are you ready to share your bed with a stranger? Is it cruel to accommodate my 'guest', if only for the night, in the bath tub or outside on the balcony? Who has the power to pull the plug and respectively terminate the visit?

I felt trapped in a situation of continuous moral dilemma. Deflating the elephant each time increasingly produced feelings of discomfort and grievance, akin to an act of killing—the sight of the collapsing body, its tail, ears and trunk resuming the form of plastic junk. In other words, yes, it is possible to feel empathy for inflatable material—empathy less in the sense of compassion towards or feeling for, but rather feeling *with* another body (whether human or non-human). And no, a 'guest' is not a pet.

03.05.17, 09:52:07: P.:	Would you host the elephant? For how long?
03.05.17, 09:56:12: S.:	Mmmm as long as I find another place for it
03.05.17, 09:57:14: S.:	Or as long as I can take this burden on my shoulders

The photo (Fig. 1) shows the inflatable elephant on the balcony, and therefore provides evidence that there are limits to taking this burden on my shoulders—what Jacques Derrida described as the impossibility of absolute and unconditional hospitality (Derrida and Dufourmantelle 2000). Not even on the very first day of its stay, was I able to offer unconditional hospitality. Ultimately, it was the sensual experience—the smell of heating plastic, the touch of the rough surface and the noise of the electric fan—that triggered my subsequent action: the eviction of the elephant to the balcony.

03.05.17, 09:57:41: P.:   Nice
03.05.17, 09:57:46: S.:   Or send it back to India or Africa

To be honest, I also googled 'African or Indian elephant', and what difference did that action make? I realized how little I actually know about elephants, their family structures, living conditions, dietary needs and, besides, was it a he or a she? Would a real elephant on my balcony snack away at my Japanese maple tree? Or should I rather feed the elephant with sugar cubes, remembering Benjamin Blümchen? There was no custom of hospitality here; no rule, no tradition, no expert advice or online forum to consult about how to turn an invitation into a conversation, a gesture of hospitality into an act of engaging with a stranger. Put differently, hospitality includes a dimension of not knowing. However, thinking beyond knowing, facing the limits of your own knowledge, might also constitute a positive beginning. According to Mustafa Dikeç, '[t]his is where hospitality poses itself, at the very beginning, at the point where one starts to think about it, placing one at the threshold of knowing, pointing beyond boundaries' (2002, p. 230).

Again, it was the physical presence and concreteness of the elephant in the room that triggered my curiosity about the ecology and psychology of elephants, how to accommodate real elephants in zoos and how to configure citizenship as a conceptual tool to advance animal rights, from an issue in applied ethics to a question of political theory and practice.[6]

03.05.17, 09:58:39: P.:   Oh no
03.05.17, 09:58:48: P.:   Nobody is perfect…

The act of providing hospitality is full of contradictions: the guest as gift or as troublemaker, the tension between expectation and disappointment, the physical demands of another yet unknown, the existence of conventions, rules and regulations as a condition for the possibility to transform these rules. There is always a border—a threshold between guest and host—and a decision to be made about where to draw this line. Each crossing or displacing of this line involves the risk of stumbling or even rejection. There may well be contradictions and misunderstanding, perplexity and stupidity. Hospitality, as a critical responsiveness, is essentially based on the question of who is conceived as part of the family—for whom you care and share certain rights and responsibility. To whom do we owe membership and based on what criteria? What I have in mind here is to understand hospitality not 'simply as a right, but as a sensibility that would encourage the formation of a critical consciousness as to the politico-juridical, as well as ethical and political implications' (Dikeç 2002, p. 235). Hospitality in the sense of sensibility (as distinct from idea) is not a task to accomplish or a certain set of norms and rules to consider; rather it is an ambivalent action (in fact, a series of recursive actions). For that reason, and in order to Enacting the 'Welcome City' requires to be prepared for radical acts of voiding distance, of undoing our privileges and trespassing the border between guest and host, you and me, us and them. This city is built on performative acts of hospitality—action bricks. And life in the 'Welcome City' implies the ability, or at least the willingness, to becoming different, and of continuous transformation. It requires a renewed effort to leave traditional anthropocentric world views and rethink the human, with and in relation to non-human others—such as animals, plants, objects, environments, and so on (Braidotti 2013).

What I hope to illustrate with these explanations is that something performative actions could achieve is the creation of frames for enacting allegories and ambivalent action, temporary spaces and situations where recognition—as well as contestation and conflict—can take place. This means creating situations that are 'performative', insofar as they reject existing frames of reference, they decontextualize, 'break with a prior context', or rather, 'assume new contexts' (Butler 1997, p. 147). Ideally, performative action sets itself apart from other contexts in that it implies no direct function—serving to produce minor irritations, slight shifts in perspective, and small breaks or interruptions that do not hold a specific meaning, but rather expose the very process of making meaning. The aim is less to formulate a certain position, but to put together a proposition and invitation to experiment with new ways of relating and new systems of perception. These actions can be highly allusive and difficult or, by contrast, easily comprehensible and entertaining; perhaps striking to occasional spectators, readers or listeners. At best, they attain a balance between invitation and irritation, pleasure and discomfort, seduction and confrontation, thereby leading others to venture into unexplored territory by jumping into the 'live' picture.

This methodology draws on a growing body of literature that focuses on inventive methods (Lury and Wakeford 2012), live sociology (Back 2012), performance research (Sabatini 2012), creative practice as a form of thinking (Manning and Massumi 2014), sensory ethnography (Pink 2009) and autoethnography (Ellis et al. 2010). Situated in the centre of critical inquiry, of performance research and writing, is the researcher herself: her body, curiosity, sensibility and subjectivity. I am my own case study, the most immediate raw material. In other words, this way of doing research is as radically interpretative as the separation between the research object and the researcher vanishes. The performative body functions as archive, compass, recording device, filter, space of resonance or flow heater; in order to condensate, evaporate, melt, sublimate or translate abstract ideas into concrete action.

In line with Lury and Wakeford, I want to emphasize here,

> [...] the sensory plenitude afforded for knowledge and action by inventive methods. Such methods enable us to acknowledge that we are in medias res, in the middle of things, in "mid-stream", always already embedded in a situation, one both settled and unsettled. (2012, p. 19)

Affirming the presence of the researcher implies critical reflection upon their own privileges and positionality:

> The researcher's presence does not preclude an analysis and interpretation of how social processes are constituted, or what consequences they produce. The researcher stands in the center of the events under consideration. In critical inquiry [...], the researcher is an advocate for change, an activist, a transformative actor, a passionate participant, an agent of self-reflective action, a model of active engagement in the world. [...] the researcher is not a disinterested observer. (Denzin 2016, p. 45)

Contesting the mind/body dualism, I would argue that embodied action constitutes an epistemological category in its own right and is a valid tool for conducting empirical research. It is precisely the force of performative action which allows the reconstructing and reinventing of new forms or new articulations of citizenship by intensifying the present, encouraging a coming to one's senses in ephemeral events that become permanent. Ephemerality and permanence do not exclude but rather presuppose each other. The Farsi word for guest is *mehmān*, meaning 'to stay', and the word for hospitality is *mehmān nawazi*—because a guest stays only for a limited time, but the memory of that stay lingers on.

Every form of representation—in academia, politics, art and cultural production—is deeply afflicted with asymmetries and hierarchies, privileges and complications, in terms of authorship and ownership. Therefore,

I would argue that actions—that is to say, practice- and process-based working methods—run counter to the wish for visible representation. A constant effort is required here to try to escape the trap of what I call 'refugee porn', which I define as socially engaged artists, journalists or researchers using the images and stories of 'the speaking refugee' to increase their own symbolic capital and gain points of distinction. The specific role and responsibility of artists doing—ethnographic, performative, sensual, sociological—research can be described as follows: to communicate and experiment with different languages and keep trying to translate this action into art. Interestingly, Etienne Balibar looks at the power of translation in attempts to overcome the untranslatability of idioms, evident primarily in two extremes of society: 'These are on the one end intellectuals with higher education, uprooted or exiled writers and on the other end anonymous migrants who mostly have a lower position in the current division of labour and employment hierarchy' (2012, p. 289) (author's translation). Whoever possesses the means of academic and artistic representation is not only privileged in representing themselves—due to their ability and knowledge about the prevailing cultural codes and social norms—but also because of their access to certain institutions, speaking and publication opportunities. Performing citizenship as artist/researcher means using these privileges to transform the rules of the game; in the case of research, the procedures and protocols of citing, conferencing, exhibiting, showing, teaching, presenting and publishing, together with those who are not officially authorized or do not feel entitled to speak these languages. And part of the privilege demands the capacity to be open, kind and confused.

EPILOGUE

The 'Welcome City' exists occasionally and is partly fiction, if not fantasy. It is an 'other' city, immanent in the world of human agency, endeavour, perseverance and hypothetical possibility. It can be activated whenever and wherever the seemingly clear roles of the self and the 'other'—us and they, you and me, citizen and non-citizen, resident and refugee, guest and host—start to blur, become unclear and need to be negotiated if not obliterated.

This city is made of actions, just as it is made of houses, cables, concrete and SUVs. It is a moving territory that consists of acts of permanent creation and recreation. Its activity is not reliant on movement, nor pretending to be on the move to a particular place,[7] but rather on personal encounter and unfolding relationships that resist fixed meanings. Building a city on bricks of hospitality—concrete actions that are always contingent and ambivalent—begins with respect for each other and ultimately leads to radically rethinking ourselves, our own approach and relations towards others. It demands being present, that is, being addressable, visible and vulnerable, as our very being as citizens exposes us to the address of others, including injury, insecurity and eventually rejection.

In the 'Welcome City', citizens are able to decide for themselves if they want to stay or move on. It is a paradoxical community of strangers who accept each other as much as they accept their own strangeness. It is performed by individuals who know about their difficulties and paradoxes of showing up as citizens of the stage of the big city. Citizenship—that is, questions of identity and belonging—turns out to be contingent, to be negotiated, and yet founded upon what all human and non-human beings have in common—a body that exists, set apart from the prefabricated, reductive binary categories.

That is the 'Welcome City'. No 'refugee porn', no charity event or zoo visit, not always entertaining, but rather challenging, contradictory, yet something infinitely more interesting.

NOTES

1. Massimo Carlotto (2007) *The Fugitive*.
2. A café located in the Immanuelkirche—a Protestant church located in the city's Veddel quarter.
3. https://www.nachtdeswissens.hamburg.de/index.php?article_id=170
4. Spacedust (1998) *Gym & Tonic*, https://www.youtube.com/watch?v=ANLySahi3fs, date accessed 5 March 2018.
5. Liza Minnelli (1972) *Cabaret*, https://www.youtube.com/watch?v=moOamKxW844, date accessed 5 March 2018.
6. Recommended literature: Bradshaw (2009) *Elephants on the Edge: what animals teach us about humanity*, Meuser (2017) *Architektur im Zoo: Theorie und Geschichte einer Bautypologie*, also Donaldson and Kymlicka (2013).
7. Massimo Carlotto (2007) *The Fugitive*.

REFERENCES

Back, Les. 2012. Live Sociology: Social Research and Its Futures. In *Live Methods*, 18–39. Oxford: Blackwell Publishing.

Balibar, Etienne. 2012. The "Impossible" Community of the Citizen: Past and Present Problems. *Environment and Planning, D: Society and Space* 30: 437–449.

Bradshaw, G.A. 2009. *Elephants on the Edge: What Animals Teach Us About Humanity.* New Haven/London: Yale University Press.

Braidotti, Rosi. 2013. *The Posthuman.* Cambridge: Polity Press.

Butler, Judith. 1997. *Excitable Speech: A Politics of the Performative.* New York/London: Routledge.

Carlotto, Massimo. 2007[1994]. *The Fugitive.* Trans. Anthony Shugaar. New York/London: Europa Editions.

Castro Varela, María do Mar, and Nikita Dhawan. 2007. Migration und die Politik der Reprä-sentation. In *Re-Präsentationen. Dynamiken der Migrationsgesellschaft,* ed. Anne Broden and Paul Mecheril, 19–26. Düsseldorf: IDA-NRW.

Denzin, Norman K. 2016. *The Qualitative Manifesto: A Call to Arms.* New York: Routledge.

Derrida, Jacques, and Anne Dufourmantelle. 2000. *Of Hospitality.* Trans. Rachel Bowlby. Stanford: Stanford University Press.

Dikeç, Mustafa. 2002. Pera Peras Poros. Longings for Spaces of Hospitality. In *Theory, Culture & Society* 19 (1–2): 227–247. London/Thousand Oaks/New Delhi: Sage.

Dogramaci, Burcu. 2013. *Migration und künstlerische Produktion.* Bielefeld: Transcript.

Donaldson, Sue, and Will Kymlicka. 2013. *Zoopolis.* Oxford: Oxford University Press.

Ellis, Carolyn, Adams, Tony E., and Bochner, Arthur P. 2010. Autoethnography: An Overview. *Forum: Qualitative Social Research* 12 (1). Art. 10. http://nbn-resolving.de/urn:nbn:de:0114-fqs1101108. Accessed 7 Mar 2018.

Holston, John. 2007. *Insurgent Citizenship.* Princeton: Princeton University Press.

Iannelli, Laura, and Pierluigi Musarò, eds. 2017. *Performative Citizenship. Public Art, Urban Design, and Political Participation.* New York: Mimesis International.

Isin, Engin. 2009. Citizenship in Flux. *Subjectivity* 29: 367–388.

———. 2012. *Citizens Without Frontiers.* London: Bloomsbury.

Krause, Ulrike. 2017. *Researching Forced Migration: Critical Reflections on Research Ethics During Fieldwork.* RSC Working Paper Series, No. 123.

Lury, Celia, and Nina Wakeford. 2012. *Inventive Methods. The Happening of the Social.* London/New York: Routledge.

Manning, Erin, and Brian Massumi. 2014. *Thought in the Act. Passages in the Ecology of Experience.* Minneapolis/London: University of Minnesota Press.

Meuser, Natascha. 2017. *Architektur im Zoo: Theorie und Geschichte einer Bautypologie.* Berlin: DOM verlag.

Pink, Sarah. 2009. *Doing Sensory Ethnography*. London: Sage.
Rheinberger, Hans-Jörg. 1997. *Toward a History of Epistemic Things. Synthesizing Proteins in the Test Tube*. Palo Alto: Stanford University Press.
Sabatini, Arthur. 2012. Approaching Knowledge, Research, Performance and the Arts. In *Inventive Methods. The Happening of the Social*, ed. Celia Lury and Nina Wakeford, 114–121. London/New York: Routledge.
Seshadri, Kalpana Rahita. 2011. The Time of Hospitality – Again. In *Phenomenologies of the Stranger: Between Hostility and Hospitality*, ed. Richard Kearney and Kascha Semonovitch, 126–141. New York: Fordham University Press.

Doing Rights with Things: The Art of Becoming Citizens

Engin Isin

Performativity, Performance, Enactment

An origin of performativity is often traced back to J. L. Austin (1962) and the controversy that followed with Jacques Derrida's (1988) intervention on its uses by John Searle (1970), and the subsequent uptake of the perspective by Shoshana Felman (2003), Judith Butler (1990, 1997), Eve Sedgwick (2003), and others. This particular trajectory has been well illustrated by James Loxley (2007) (see also Moati 2014). Yet, as I mentioned, performativity has multiple origins and crisscrossing trajectories in philosophy (Mulligan 1987; Reinach 1983), sociology (Goffman 1967, 1961, 1959; Tilly 2008), anthropology (Turner 1966, 1987), and humanities, which led to the emergence of performance studies (Schechner 2002; Davis 2008). As one would expect from a performative perspective, the meaning and uses of performativity and performance were multiple, conflicting, and dynamic (Lloyd 2016). And its uses also involved invoking traditions of thought that may not have used performativity, but its affiliate principles (Youdell 2006).

E. Isin (✉)
Queen Mary University of London, London, UK
e-mail: engin.isin@qmul.ac.uk

© The Author(s) 2019
P. Hildebrandt et al. (eds.), *Performing Citizenship*, Performance Philosophy, https://doi.org/10.1007/978-3-319-97502-3_4

Another origin of performativity is traced to theories of enactment in philosophy (Edie 1971; Ware 1973; Deutscher 1988) and cognitive sciences (Zarrilli 2007; Stewart et al. 2010). The concept of acts has been especially prominent in this trajectory for understanding social and political conduct (Pluth 2007; Perinbanayagam 1985). So 'enactment' has come to acquire a special meaning, to determine the conditions under which social acts occur and the kinds of people or things that such enactments produce (Mol 2003; Law and Urry 2011).

Given these multiple and complex origins and trajectories of the development of a performative perspective in social sciences and humanities, I do not intend to discuss its meanings and uses here. Without giving in to the temptation to singularize, I would still say that in all these origins, trajectories, and developments, performativity is an attempt to understand the ways in which people inhabit and transform specific subjectivities and how these subjectivities follow from acts that are made possible only under certain material and symbolic conditions. Or, as Michel Foucault put it, a concern in social sciences and humanities is to understand 'how should one "govern oneself" by performing actions in which one is oneself the objective of those actions, the domain in which they are brought to bear, the instrument they employ, and the subject that acts?' (Foucault 1997, p. 87). If social sciences and humanities in the nineteenth and twentieth centuries struggled over tensions between agency and structure, or objectivity and subjectivity, it is perhaps not a coincidence that, in the twenty-first century, some scholars are drawn to a performative perspective where understanding people as acting beings in their objective and subjective circumstances involves a dramaturgical language where words such as stages, scenes, acts, performances, actors, and sites that provide a rich repertoire (Rayner 1994) and a performative language where words such citations, iterations, and significations provide a means by which to understand how we inhabit identities, practices, and selves (Nakassis 2013; Holywood 2002).

There are various tensions in using these dramaturgical and performative languages and between performance and performativity. Austin famously excluded speech acts performed on stage from his analysis and thought that these were not ordinary uses of language. He thought that 'a performative utterance will, for example, be in a peculiar way hollow or void if said by an actor on the stage, or if introduced in a poem, or spoken in soliloquy' (Austin 1962, p. 22). This was precisely what Derrida took issue with, questioning a difference between words spoken in literature and ordinary life as though they belonged to separate serious and 'playful' uses of words. He was emphatic:

> for, ultimately, isn't it true that what Austin excludes as anomaly, exception, 'non-serious,' *citation* (on stage, in a poem, or a soliloquy) is the determined modification of a general citationality—or rather, a general iterability—without which there would not even be a 'successful' performative? So that—a paradoxical but unavoidable conclusion—a successful performative is necessarily an 'impure' performative, to adopt the word advanced later on by Austin when he acknowledges that there is no 'pure' performative. (Derrida 1988, p. 17)

Derrida certainly made it difficult to maintain a pure difference between ordinary and literary language, and also between languages of arts, sciences, and politics.

We are now witnessing the increasing use of these dramaturgical and performative languages in understanding how people inhabit citizenship as political subjectivity, and how citizenship is enacted in everyday acts with or without authorization to act under its (legal) prescription (Isin 2017). Both in social sciences and humanities, there are now many contemporary (Ofer and Groves 2016; McThomas 2016) and historical (Farenga 2006; Prauscello 2014) studies that use a performative perspective on citizenship. I want to broadly reflect on how 'performing citizenship' is proving a useful perspective for scholars and how they are making a productive use of it. What I want to discuss below is not various uses of performativity and performance in studying citizenship but to outline a logic of their use: how the need for such a perspective has arisen and how it is challenging our views of citizenship.

WHAT IS CALLED CITIZENSHIP?

Citizenship mediates the relations between the citizen, non-citizens, and polities to which they belong, claim, or inhabit. That simple statement always belies the fact that the citizen of a polity almost never belongs only to that polity but to several nested, if not overlapping and conflicting, series of polities, like the city, region, the state, and the international. Clearly, in the contemporary world, the sovereign polity is the state, but even its sovereignty is now implicated in various international and regional polities evinced by international covenants (such as the European

Convention of Human Rights), multilateral agreements (like the North American Free Trade Agreement), supranational bodies (as in the European Union), and shared sovereignty arrangements (for example, Scotland or Quebec). This is further complicated by the fact that many citizens and non-citizens in the contemporary world do not reside in their birthplace but in—often multiple—adopted countries. All this places citizens and non-citizens as relational subjects within a web of rights and responsibilities, through which they are called upon to performatively negotiate a particular combination that is always a complex relationship.

A Chinese government cannot have a unified and singular relationship with its citizens since their lives are mediated not only through their rights from and responsibilities to the Chinese state but also through human rights, environmental or cultural discourse, and international politics beyond its borders. Similarly, a British government cannot have exclusive relations with British citizens, as their lives are implicated in and interdependent with the European Union as a supranational polity, the European Convention of Human Rights, and myriad other mutual rights and responsibilities toward other polities. Even if the British government decides to end its membership of the European Union, there would still be a web of obligations and commitments that would implicate its citizens and non-citizens. While still dominant, the state therefore cannot be said to have an exclusive sovereignty over a given population within a given territory.

It is then problematic to think about citizenship as a universal, static, and enclosed relationship, as Iris Young (1989) argued in a brilliant and now classic article. We can observe today that the combination between rights and responsibilities is always an outcome of social struggles that find expression in political and legal institutions in different polities. Three conventional rights (civil, political, and social) and three responsibilities (conscription, taxation and participation) define the relationship between the citizen and the state. Civil rights include the right to free speech, to conscience, and to dignity; political rights include franchise and standing for office; social rights include unemployment insurance, universal health care, and welfare. Although conscription is rapidly disappearing as a responsibility of citizenship, taxation remains resolutely in place; jury duty is increasingly challenged under certain circumstances, but still serves a fundamental role. Moreover, new rights have appeared—such as sexual rights, cultural rights, and environmental rights—with varying degrees of success in institutionalization (for example, witness the struggles over same-sex marriage in the United States and Europe). Again, as mentioned, whether conventional (that is, civil, political, social) or expanded (sexual, environmental, cultural), these rights and responsibilities are mediated through other polities that influence the actual combination granted in a given polity at a given time.

Conventional perspectives on citizenship (such as liberalism, republicanism, and communitarianism) make much less sense now, given the contemporary complications just mentioned. Since the combination of rights and responsibilities, and their performance, greatly varies across polities it is probably more accurate to speak about various citizenship regimes that characterize a similar, if not co-dependent, development of certain combinations. We can, for example, talk about an Anglo-American regime (for example, Britain, USA), a North European regime (such as Denmark, Norway), a continental regime (such as France, Germany), a South American regime (such as Brazil, Chile), a South Asian regime (such as India, Malaysia), and so forth. We can also talk about postcolonial citizenship regimes (for example, India, Brazil, Ghana), post-communist citizenship regimes (such as Poland, Hungary, and even China), neoliberal citizenship regimes (such as Britain, USA), and post-settler citizenship regimes (such as Canada, Australia). Arguably, each of these regimes sets out a different combination of rights and responsibilities of citizenship, but each displays a recognizable culture with regard to how citizenship is performed.

Yet, in each of these polities, citizenship does not exist in a singular and unified form either. There are struggles over its meaning in courts, education, services, taxation, and many other spheres of life. How we approach citizenship in our contemporary world is then a complex question because, as James Tully (2014) argued, we inherit not single but multiple, overlapping, and conflicting uses of institutions, laws, and traditions that use the word 'citizenship'. He warns against defining a meaning that is ostensibly universal while attempting to apply it to different circumstances. He identifies an attitude within this desire, for example, in the attribution of a universal meaning such as 'modern' and an attitude that desires to see it as 'diverse' as 'critical'. A modern attitude is marked by its will to develop citizenship as a civil code and a critical attitude is marked by seeing citizenship as a negotiated and dynamic relationship (Tully 2014, pp. 5–8). For Tully, the challenge to be found in citizenship is in identifying its diverse forms in different places, yet maintaining a productive language about the ways in which we speak and write about it. Tully draws on Wittgenstein, who was also a source of inspiration for Austin. Although Tully does not use the language of performativity, his use of words—such as games, enactment, and play—to understand citizenship as negotiated practices, strongly resonates with performativity; or at least it shows a logic as to why scholars are increasingly drawn into a dramaturgical language in the face of its practical complexities.

DOING RIGHTS WITH THINGS

This increasing use of dramaturgical and performative languages—such as 'performing citizenship', 'enacting citizenship', or 'acts of citizenship'—by scholars recognizes two key aspects of citizenship. First, that there is a recognition that citizenship that exists on paper is an expression of inert or passive rights, yet citizenship rights (and responsibilities) are brought into being only when performed. It is not only that rights that have been won through long and hard social struggles (such as freedom of speech or social insurance) would disappear if not performed, but also that such struggles require performing rights that may not exist (for example, sexual rights, animal rights, or ecological rights). Second, since citizenship is brought into being by performing it, non-citizens can also perform citizenship. The political subjects—individual or collective—of citizenship are not given in advance, they too are brought into being performatively. Those who do not have the status of citizenship, but obtain it by making claims to it, often negotiate many rights and responsibilities. These two performative aspects of citizenship have often been recognized by studies that examine tensions or gaps between different articulations of citizenship in public discourse.

These two aspects of performing citizenship permeate social and political life more than meets the eye. When people mobilize for legalizing same-sex marriage, rally for social housing, protest against welfare cuts, debate employment insurance, sign petitions, occupy squares, advocate the decriminalization of marijuana, apply for citizenship, renounce their citizenship, wear attire such as turbans or headscarves in public spaces, seek affirmative action programs, demand better health care access and services, or practice their graffiti art across borders, they may not express themselves as struggling for the maintenance or expansion of social, cultural, or sexual citizenship rights. Governments may not recognize them as such either. Instead, people invest in whatever issues seem most related and closest to their social and political lives—and dedicate their time and energy accordingly—and governments respond, or fail to respond, to these demands. There are two points to make about such struggles. First, they are irreducibly political struggles that arise from social, economic or cultural conditions in which people are situated. To classify such struggles either as redistribution (economism) or recognition (culturalism) misses their complexity. Second, in the absence of clear articulation, it is important to acknowledge that when people enact themselves through such performances or acts—whatever differences may separate them in values, principles, and priorities—they are performing citizenship, even those who are not passport-carrying members of the state (non-citizens). This means that they are being playful, creative, and innovative in drawing upon various repertories of becoming or unbecoming citizens.

I would like to propose formalizing these points by naming different senses in which citizenship exists. I think citizenship is performed or played in the gaps or tensions between and among these different senses of citizenship. There is, for example, citizenship (in) theory. This is where contestations over the meanings, functions, and uses of citizenship take place. There may be statements about ideas of universal, egalitarian, fairness concerns around citizenship. There may be normative or positive claims to represent citizenship. These senses of citizenship (in) theory often struggle and contest with each other over these meanings and functions of citizenship. There is then citizenship (in) practice, where people uptake or inhabit citizenship through rituals, habits, manners, and gestures. People vote, protest, petition, and pay (or avoid or evade) their taxes. We can then also speak about citizenship (in) law where it is codified, enforced, and revised. There is then citizenship (in) acts where it is resisted, revoked, deprived, claimed, demanded, and so forth. These different senses in which citizenship exists are not mutually exclusive, but interrelated senses that come into conflict with each other. A citizenship that is advocated (in) theory may well fall short of what transpires in law and how citizenship (in) practice comes to function may confront citizenship (in) law. Citizenship (in) acts may disrupt what we do with citizenship (in) practice.

I think citizenship (in) theory, citizenship (in) practice, and citizenship (in) law signify different senses of citizenship in the following ways: the dramas played out in courts and legislatures for citizenship (in) law find their counterparts on streets, squares, assemblies, and cyberspaces of citizenship (in) practice. These dramas are played out no less intensely in articles, books, and conferences; developing citizenship (in) theory rather than in elections, referendums, and plebiscites of citizenship (in) acts. Although these plays mediate between citizens and polities, performing citizenship does not always take the form of demands on government. To put it differently, performing citizenship always involves a citizenship-as-yet-to-come. If Austin characterized performativity as doing things with words, it is tempting to describe performativity of citizenship as 'doing rights with things' to emphasize not only the actual social and political struggles that mobilize it, but also practical, material, artistic, expressive, and articulate ways in which people enact citizenship on a stage that may or may not be of their choosing.

These may provide us with some reasons why scholars are drawn to a performative perspective on citizenship. As Mary McThomas argues, for example, to make sense of the struggles of undocumented migrants requires an understanding of the tensions between citizenship (in) law and citizenship (in) practice. This is because, she asserts, 'a performance-based conception of citizenship, which focuses on the carrying out of civic duties instead of nation-state authorization, more accurately reflects our current situation and recognizes obligations we have to those living among us' (2016, p. 2). She illustrates that, in the USA, there is a disconnection between 'paper citizenship and performing citizenship, [which] expose[s] the gap between the reality of our neighborhoods and conventional theories of citizenship and political obligation' (2016, p. 37). She argues that instead of understanding obligation to be what citizens owe to the state, we should flip it and ask 'what the state owes to those who perform the role of citizen, regardless of their documented status' (2016, p. 38). This resonates with many scholars with regard to undocumented migrants who have studied it as performing citizenship (Jeffers 2011; Aradau et al. 2010; McNevin 2011; Nyers 2008, 2011; Erel 2009; Squire 2016).

As Inbal Ofer and Tamar Groves (2016) and their colleagues illustrated, citizenship is being performed in social movements across the world, traversing many state borders. They argue that we are witnessing 'multiscalar dynamics: global logics and institutions reinforce local structures and channels of interventions, which generate new understandings of citizenship as a form of being and of interacting with other social groups' (Ofer and Groves 2016, p. 8). As I mentioned earlier, there are differences in the ways in which acts, enactment, performance, and performativity are used by these scholars, and yet their perspective—on how active (and activist) ways in which citizens and non-citizens become citizens on a stage of not necessarily their choosing—is common.

The Art of Becoming Citizens

If indeed citizenship mediates the relations between citizens, non-citizens, and polities to which we belong, claim, or inhabit, then it also involves the art of being with others, negotiating different situations and identities, and articulating ourselves as distinct yet similar to others in our everyday lives. Through these social struggles, we develop a sense of our rights as others' obligations and others' rights as our obligations. As Christopher Kutz (2002) reasoned, this a collective work of citizenship. This is especially true for democratic citizenship, as it approaches the combination of rights and responsibilities as a dynamic (and thus contested, but changing and flexible) outcome and its creative performance as a key aspect within a democratic polity (Zivi 2012).

Citizenship, especially democratic citizenship, depends on the creative and organizing capacities of citizens whose performance of citizenship is not only the driving force for change but also the guarantee of the vitality and resilience of the polity. Governments may see domains of citizen performativity and enactment as separate from each other in the everyday governing of the polity and in the social lives of its citizens, but occasionally, an event reminds everyone that people (citizens and non-citizens) are performing or enacting themselves as citizens. The gaps—traversed between citizenship (in) theory, citizenship (in) practice, citizenship (in) law, and citizenship (in) acts—are increasingly where articulate, effective languages of everyday politics emerge and are where literary and artistic performances are playing out serious roles. For all these reasons, a dramaturgical language, combined with a language of performativity, is proving both productive and suggestive in order to give accounts of ourselves both individually and collectively struggling as citizens and non-citizens.

References

Aradau, Claudia, Jef Huysmans, and Vicky Squire. 2010. Acts of European Citizenship: A Political Sociology of Mobility. *Journal of Common Market Studies* 48 (4): 945–965.

Austin, J.L. 1962. *How to Do Things with Words*. Oxford: Oxford University Press.

Butler, Judith. 1990. *Gender Trouble: Feminism and the Subversion of Identity*. London: Routledge.

———. 1997. *Excitable Speech: A Politics of the Performative*. London: Routledge.

Davis, Tracy C. 2008. Introduction: The Pirouette, Detour, Revolution, Deflection, Deviation, Tack, and Yaw of the Performative Turn. In *The Cambridge Companion to Performance Studies*, ed. Tracy C. Davis, 1–8. Cambridge, University of Cambridge Press.

Derrida, Jacques. 1988. *Limited Inc*. Trans. G. Graff. Evanston: Northwestern University Press.

Deutscher, Max. 1988. Simulacra, Enactment and Feeling. *Philosophy* 63 (246): 515–528.

Edie, James M. 1971. The Problem of Enactment. *The Journal of Aesthetics and Art Criticism* 29 (3): 303–318.

Erel, Umut. 2009. *Migrant Women Transforming Citizenship*. London: Ashgate.

Farenga, Vincent. 2006. *Citizen and Self in Ancient Greece: Individuals Performing Justice and the Law*. Cambridge/New York: Cambridge University Press.

Felman, Shoshana. 2003. *The Scandal of the Speaking Body: Don Juan with J.L. Austin, or Seduction in Two Languages*. Stanford: Stanford University Press.

Foucault, Michel. 1997. Ethics: Subjectivity and Truth. In *Essential Works of Foucault, 1954–1984*, ed. P. Rabinow, vol. 3. New York: The New Press.

Goffman, Erving. 1959. *The Presentation of Self in Everyday Life*. Garden City: Doubleday.

———. 1961. *Encounters: Two Studies in the Sociology of Interaction*. Indianapolis: Bobbs-Merrill.

———. 1967. *Interaction Ritual: Essays on Face-to-Face Behavior*. Garden City: Doubleday.

Holywood, Amy. 2002. Performativity, Citationality, Ritualization. *History of Religions* 42: 93–115.

Isin, Engin F. 2017. Performative Citizenship. In *The Oxford Handbook of Citizenship*, ed. Ayelet Shachar, Rainer Bauböck, Irene Bloemraad, and Maarten Vink, 500–523. Oxford: Oxford University Press.

Jeffers, Alison. 2011. *Refugees, Theatre and Crisis: Performing Global Identities*. New York: Palgrave Macmillan.

Kutz, Christopher. 2002. The Collective Work of Citizenship. *Legal Theory* 8: 471–494.

Law, John, and John Urry. 2011. Enacting the Social. *Economy and Society* 33 (3): 390–410.

Lloyd, Moya. 2016. Performativity and Performance. In *The Oxford Handbook of Feminist Theory*, ed. Lisa Jane Disch and M.E. Hawkesworth, 572–592. Oxford: Oxford University Press.

Loxley, James. 2007. *Performativity*. London: Routledge.

McNevin, Anne. 2011. *Contesting Citizenship: Irregular Migrants and New Frontiers of the Political*. New York: Columbia University Press.

McThomas, Mary. 2016. *Performing Citizenship: Undocumented Migrants in the United States*. London: Routledge.

Moati, Raoul. 2014. *Derrida/Searle: Deconstruction and Ordinary Language.* Trans. Timothy Attanucci, and Maureen Chun. New York: Columbia University Press.

Mol, Annemarie. 2003. *The Body Multiple: Ontology in Medical Practice.* Durham: Duke University Press.

Mulligan, Kevin, ed. 1987. *Speech Act and Sachverhalt: Reinach and the Foundations of Realist Phenomenology.* Dordrecht: Kluwer Academic Publishers.

Nakassis, Constantine V. 2013. Citation and Citationality. *Signs and Society* 1 (1): 51–77.

Nyers, Peter. 2008. In Solitary, in Solidarity: Detainees, Hostages and Contesting the Anti-Policy of Detention. *European Journal of Cultural Studies* 11: 333–349.

———. 2011. No One Is Illegal Between City and Nation. *Studies in Social Justice* 4: 127–143.

Ofer, Inbal, and Tamar Groves, eds. 2016. *Performing Citizenship: Social Movements Across the Globe.* London: Routledge.

Perinbanayagam, R.S. 1985. *Signifying Acts: Structure and Meaning in Everyday Life.* Carbondale: Southern Illinois University Press.

Pluth, Ed. 2007. *Signifiers and Acts: Freedom in Lacan's Theory of the Subject.* Albany: State University of New York Press.

Prauscello, Lucia. 2014. *Performing Citizenship in Plato's Laws.* Cambridge: Cambridge University Press.

Rayner, Alice. 1994. *To Act, to Do, to Perform: Drama and the Phenomenology of Action.* Ann Arbor: University of Michigan Press.

Reinach, Adolf. 1983. The Apriori Foundations of the Civil Law. Trans. John Crosby in a special issue of *Aletheia* 3: 1–142 (original edn. 1913).

Schechner, Richard. 2002. *Performance Studies: An Introduction.* London: Routledge.

Searle, John R. 1970. *Speech Acts: An Essay in the Philosophy of Language.* Cambridge: Cambridge University Press.

Sedgwick, Eve Kosofsky. 2003. *Touching Feeling: Affect, Pedagogy, Performativity.* Durham: Duke University Press.

Squire, Vicki. 2016. Unauthorised Migration Beyond Structure/Agency Acts, Interventions, Effects. *Politics*: 1–19.

Stewart, John Robert, Olivier Gapenne, and Ezequiel A. Di Paolo, eds. 2010. *Enaction: Toward a New Paradigm for Cognitive Science.* Cambridge, MA: MIT Press.

Tilly, Charles. 2008. *Contentious Performances.* Cambridge: Cambridge University Press.

Tully, James. 2014. *On Global Citizenship: James Tully in Dialogue.* London: Bloomsbury.

Turner, Victor Witter. 1966. *The Ritual Process: Structure and Anti-Structure*. New York: Aldine de Gruyter.

———. 1987. *The Anthropology of Performance*. New York: PAJ Publications.

Ware, Robert. 1973. Acts and Action. *The Journal of Philosophy* 70: 403–418.

Youdell, Deborah. 2006. Subjectivation and Performative Politics: Butler Thinking Althusser and Foucault: Intelligibility, Agency and the Raced-Nationed-Religioned Subjects of Education. *British Journal of Sociology of Education* 27 (4): 511–528.

Young, Iris Marion. 1989. Polity and Group Difference: A Critique of the Ideal of Universal Citizenship. *Ethics* 99 (2): 250–274.

Zarrilli, Phillip B. 2007. An Enactive Approach to Understanding Acting. *Theatre Journal* 59 (4): 635–647.

Zivi, Karen. 2012. *Making Rights Claims: A Practice of Democratic Citizenship*. Oxford: Oxford University Press.

Performing Citizenship: Gathering (in the) Movement

The Choreographic Format of Circle Dancing and the Round Dance as a Matrix of Collective Action in the Context of Political Assemblies, Protests and Occupations

Liz Rech

Introduction

If one speaks in the activist context of 'the movement', the concept of movement with regard to the 'moving body' is always threefold: the political movement; the actual physical, choreographic movement; and the associated inner movement and its personal affections.

The experience of collective and coordinated movement in public space plays an important role on the political field. This applies not only to the

Translated by Daniel Caleb Thompson

L. Rech (✉)
Graduate Program Performing Citizenship, HafenCity University Hamburg, Hamburg, Germany

57

P. Hildebrandt et al. (eds.), *Performing Citizenship*, Performance Philosophy, https://doi.org/10.1007/978-3-319-97502-3_5

kinaesthetic and somatic potency of body experience—which has a direct effect on the social movement itself—but also to the efficacy of its reach to potential viewers because, through its movement in public space, the body's 'indexical force'[1] (Butler 2015, p. 9) becomes visible in a very special way and demands recognition. Butler points out that assemblies, irrespective of specific demands, have meaning: 'The gathering signifies in excess of what is said, and that mode of signification is a concerted bodily enactment, a plural form of performativity' (Butler 2015, p. 8). The resulting questions are:

What forms do these corporeal productions assume?
Which choreographic formats are applied in contexts of political assembly?
Why are such applications extant?

This article deals specifically with the choreographic format of Circle Dancing, which regularly arises in the context of political meetings and occupations. What defines this practice of collective movement? What is its political dimension? And lastly, which roles are played by the body and its 'response/ability' in the context of the ethics of political responsibility and mindful practice of movement?

GATHERING IN THE MOVEMENT

The German word *Versammlung* (a gathering) is related etymologically to the verb *sammeln* (to gather) and the noun *Sammlung* (a collection). In the context of this article, *Versammlung* can be translated to English as either 'gathering' or 'assembly'. Whereas a 'gathering' describes the 'collection' of clearly defined members, an 'assembly' refers to a meeting that takes place for a specific purpose and is open to the addition and departure of (temporary) participants to the meeting. This presumably explains why the term of 'assembly' has become widespread in the context of contemporary activism; it not only describes the temporary, the fleeting and the incomplete, but also addresses a greater heterogeneity within contemporary political collectivity as witnessed in political protests, such as the Gezi Park protests in Istanbul, 2013: '93.6 per cent stated that they had come to Gezi Park as a "simple citizen", whereas only 6.4 per cent of the participants said they were part of an organization or political party'[2] (Uluğ and Acar 2015, p. 122).

The term 'assembly' also refers to a new understanding of the collective: the collective is no longer considered a homogeneous, closed collective but as an open collective with fraying edges.[3] This leaves more room for heterogeneity and is reflected in formulations for the description of political performance, such as 'acting plurality', 'body alliances' and 'assemblage' (all three from Butler), 'group subject' (Guattari), 'multitude' (Virno) or 'arrangement' (from the French: *agencement*, Deleuze).

Accordingly, contemporary political formats of assembly must facilitate space for the integration of diverse positions and heterogeneous bodies. It is not surprising that, in this context, the concept of choreography appears because choreographic formats can assemble heterogeneous bodies in a very specific way through dance-like movement. Kunst highlights the ability of choreographic formats to create temporary communities:

> Instead of staging the communities, choreography creates communities through the process of becoming a multifaceted and conflicting mobilization of the body and aesthetic experiences, thus challenging our democratic and political practice. (Kunst 2014, p. 18, translation by author)

In addition to the assembly of heterogeneous bodies, there is another aspect which is significant in the relationship between politics and choreography: (public) space.

In a fundamental way, the relationship between politics and choreography is often determined by the distribution of bodies in space: 'Thinking politics (…) is therefore by definition linked to the idea of choreography in the truest sense of the word: The art of choreography consists of distributing bodies and their relations in space' (Hölscher and Siegmund 2013, p. 12). Kunst and Hölscher/Siegmund present a line of reasoning used herein—one that presumes a political dimension is to be found in the choreographic *arrangement* of bodies. The body is seen as an actor that participates in the production of social reality.

The concept of *social choreography* describes this expanded concept of choreography and transfers it to social and societal spaces. The term *social choreography* describes a practice that constructively creates a performative order of the social field (as an order of spatial conditions, architecture, body, movement, subjects, collective bodies, objects, materials etc.). *Social choreography*, as a performative concept, aims at establishing a link between the social and the aesthetic; the aesthetic is assigned a central role in the description of the political, as well as the social (Hewitt 2005, p. 3). It is therefore a question of the constitution of social orders which are always determined (through situational) social practices.

The utopian moment of newly materializing 'social figurations' (Elias 1978) in public space is relevant to the way in which citizenship is 'performed' because, in this case, it is about the presence and movement of resisting bodies within the context of social movements. This expanded understanding of choreography has been conceptually extended by many authors writing about resistive choreographic practices, such as Milohnic (2013),[4] and also Klein (2013).[5]

This concept will be useful for the analysis of Circle Dancing, since it enables its choreographic structure to be interpreted as a social order and uncovers the degrees to which sociability is inherently present.

The question now is how to evaluate (temporarily generated) communities when they are not merely constituted by origin, group membership and association with a political party or other organization. It is a community that is primarily instantiated by the presence of the individual bodies. In Nancy's book *Being Singular Plural*, he writes of *co-existence* as a simultaneity of the differences and 'co-presences' of those present and that the quantity is not characterized by cohesion but by dispersion (Nancy 2000, p. 40). If one reads Nancy's concept from the perspective of social choreography (as with Hewitt), there arises the challenge of perceiving the choreographic movement as an open system rather than a closed one. The assembly is no longer a closed system, as it necessarily has porous boundaries that allow for 'just turning up' as well as 'departure' from the fabric of the collective. Choreographic formats that emerge in the context of protest should accordingly enable precisely this staging of collectivity; my thesis posits that the choreographic format of Circle Dancing does exactly this.

Circle Dancing in the Political Context

Circle Dancing as happenings within political movements in the context of assemblies were most evident during the occupation of public spaces— such as Occupy Wall Street (2011), the protests in Syntagma Square, Athens (2011), the aforementioned Gezi Park protests at Taksim Square in Istanbul (2013), and during the Arab Spring (2011). Jamshidi describes how in 'the face of brutality and repression from security forces, the festive atmosphere created by outbursts of dance and music has helped keep people on the streets' (Jamshidi 2014, p. 90f). The 'festive atmosphere' joyfully supports the efforts to maintain a presence in the square, a purposeful act used as a strategy to counter violent and extremely physically challenging situations, such as when tear gas is being used. Tsomou describes—with regard to the protests in Syntagma Square 2011, Athens— how dancing 'has become a sustainable strategy on the square' (Tsomou 2014, p. 133) (translation by author). Tsomou, as with Uluğ Acar, understands that:

> The community of the 'we', the '99%' or the 'indignant' is not constituted by origin, group association or membership – its operative idiosyncrasy is to be found in the presence of the individual as well as in the practices in the squares. (Tsomou 2014, p. 116f, translation by author)

Walton confirms this finding in his investigation of the carnivalesque nature of the Gezi Park protests[6] at Taksim Square, Istanbul 2013:

> Gezi was defined by the conglomeration of multiple political identities. What linked the protestors was not an identity, but a novel, emphatic practice of citizenship, a public performativity. (Walton 2015, p. 51)

Among other aspects, Walton goes into detail about the YouTube video *Everyday I'm Çapulling*.[7] In this video, which consists of a series of short moments and situations in Taksim Square, one can see groups of protesters Circle Dancing *(halay çekmek)*. The festive character of the protest can clearly be witnessed. Walton quotes Bakhtin in his study, who describes the carnival as an exceptional social situation along with its potential for change (Bakhtin 1984, cited in Walton 2015, p. 51).

Accordingly, it is possible to speak—in the context of protest—of an *atmospheric territory* that is permanently defended by aesthetic strategies such as dancing, singing, choric speaking, music making and so on. Böhme describes the way in which atmosphere is generated as a type of power (Böhme 1993, p.125). Tsomou points out—on the occasion of the Circle Dancing at Syntagma Square in Athens, 2011—that dancing works as a strategy for preventing a place from being evacuated quickly:

> The circle dancing at Syntagma Square had a double quality: On the one hand they emerged as a tactical response to conflicts with the police; and on the other hand they were not a planned strategy of confrontation, but rather were an end in and of themselves in the sense of experiencing shared happiness [...] [and] self-care, a self-oriented ritual of perseverance in order not to

let the place be so easily cleared [...]. (Tsomou 2014, p. 134f, translation by author)

The citation suggests that by 'experiencing shared happiness', the creation of a certain atmosphere is inseparable from the question of power (or *who is allowed to stay where?*). Circle Dancing serves, above all, to define an *atmospheric territory*. The carnivalesque functions as an integrative element, which is able to gather different social and political identities. It incorporates a wide range of social and cultural practices.

'IF I CAN'T DANCE, I DON'T WANT TO BE PART OF YOUR REVOLUTION': CHANGE AND NEW TEMPORALITIES

The practices that can be observed in different places are usually amassed from the experience of different types of protest. These can be seen in measures such as the installation of camps or tent sites; strong self-organization to meet existential needs, based on the development of a corresponding infrastructure; direct democratic meeting structures; the renunciation of hierarchical structures and the rejection of political representation; work with media and social networks; creative interaction with oppression; physical practices (such as yoga courses); and, among other things, performative formats such as collective dancing. Teune speaks about 'prefigurational politics [...]that anticipate the needs of the desired society by taking concrete action' (Teune 2012, p. 34, translation by author).

This 'experimental conduct' within the framework of prefigurational politics is a form of open and future-oriented action that enables the testing of new cultures and configurations of movement. The mobilization of bodies and 'communities in the making' (Kunst 2014, p. 18, translation by author) imbues a processual and transformative character that makes the movement open for change, conveying 'utopian moments'. This is also reflected in German formulations such as *etwas bewegen* ('to make change') or *die Verhältnisse zum Tanzen bringen* ('to make the circumstances dance'). According to Gormly, dancing seems particularly predestined to actually make change possible: 'Dance is a state of excitement in a system where change becomes possible, desirable, fluid and pleasurable' (Gormly 2012, p. 1).

The theme of transition and change ('Time for change')[8] is closely tied to a shifting temporality; it is not only about the experiences that the participants gain by investing time in the various protest practices mentioned above, but also about the construction of new temporalities via collective practices, and 'pertains to the dynamics that are ultimately decisive in determining the timbre of the present moment in time' (van Eikels 2013, p. 176, translation by author). Della Porta, who has dealt with events that characterize protests within social movements, speaks of 'eventful protests' in this context that enable processes through which collective experiences can be made. 'Eventful temporality' is characteristic of these 'protest events' (della Porta 2008, p. 3). 'Eventful temporality recognizes the power of events in history [...]' (Sewell 1992, p. 262, quoted in: della Porta 2008, p. 3).

Hardt and Negri, together with Aristotle, emphasize the importance of the movement between a *before* and *after* for phases of social transition and upheaval, by describing the transformation of the time horizon as an active process: 'In particular, the multitude takes hold of time and constructs new temporalities [...]' (Hardt and Negri 2000, p. 401). They further develop this idea into the following definition of time: 'Time might thus be defined as the immeasurability of the movement between a *before* and an *after*, an immanent process of constitution' (Hardt and Negri 2000, p. 402, author's emphasis).

Thus, the physical movement is that which is constitutive for the moment of the transition and, in the case of collective movement, becomes a 'performance of a reciprocal measurement and admeasurement of time' (van Eikels 2012, p. 170, translation by author). This admeasurement of time is executed in dance via synchronization through the duration of movement, which is organized chronologically by rhythm. Dance can thereby enable a new provisional 'timeline' to be practised and lived. 'Dance in its most potent form manages to momentarily "live" new orders' (O'Ros, quoted in: Gormly 2012, p. 1). Thus, the choreographic movement becomes an aspect of the aesthetic of change (Klien 2008, p. 2).

In the next chapter, I will show why the choreographic format of Circle Dancing is particularly suitable for staging a new social order.

CIRCLE DANCING AND THE ROUND DANCE
AS CHOREOGRAPHIC FORMATS

Circle Dancing is generally understood as a dance with a circular line-up of dancers, in which the dancers stand next to each other, hold hands or shoulders and face the middle of the circle.

As the penultimate geometric symbol, the circle stands for the universe, the globe, unity, harmony and the perfection of the world. Circle Dancing is one of the oldest anthropologically symbolic expressions of humanity, making possible a dialogue between interior and exterior worlds. Traditionally, dances have accompanied important rituals of transition, rituals in which the theme of change is present. Such transitional rituals are celebrated by the whole community as transformational ceremonies. The location for the ritual is the ceremonial 'village square', where a fire burns in the centre; there is singing, drumming and dancing. In dance rituals, psychic energies materialize. With their bodies, dancers express communicative concerns that go beyond themselves.

In the present day, Circle Dancing is often practised in the context of folk dance. The folk dance, as a concept in Germany, is saddled with negative connotations due to its 'cultural-political instrumentalization in National Socialism and the GDR' (Evert 2014, p. 45, translation by author), as it served as a space for compositional, ideological and functional attribution. For, of course, in the context of 'folk dance' the question always arises, 'Who are "the folk"?'[9] The pleasure of dancing, in particular, served as a 'gateway for assimilation by political ideologies from left and right' (Evert 2014, p. 40) (translation by author). Hanna Walsdorf proposes the following ahistorical definition for the concept of folk dancing:

> Folk dancing is arranged and socially produced, experienced and mediated. It is a sociable dance that can be learned by everyone, which constitutes, confirms and represents a community; however, the moment it is placed on a stage it is transformed from a social event to the demonstration of expository spectacle. (Walsdorf 2010, p. 2, translation by author)

Dance as 'exposition' joins the political fray when it is performed on the stage of public space. In the activist context, it is important that this formation of community does not take place via an idea, but rather through physical practice. This makes it an interesting method within the scope of the recent occupations of public space, as these gatherings are composed of extremely heterogeneous groups. The dances contribute,

> [...] to the formation of community. [...] When people from different walks of life dance together, they put the differences between them into the background. Their dance movements only succeed when they relate to each other and cooperate. [...] In the scope of this deferment of differences they create a feeling of togetherness in rhythmic movement. (Wulf 2010, p. 38f, translation by author)

Circle Dancing and the Round Dance are easily accessible to ordinary people as a choreographic format. One does not need previous knowledge, special dance skills or a professional dance education; the dance steps are easy to learn through clear instruction—often musically supported—and are repeated in cycles, which encourages people to join in. It succeeds through participation. One does not need a dance partner; partners are interchangeable, allowing a fluid stream of dancers to join in. The movements are an open system, an assembly with porous membranes allowing for both a 'showing up to' and a 'departing from' the movement (see section "Gathering in the Movement"). In the case of a closed circle, the newcomer simply picks a spot to break the circle, takes the hands of the dancers on either side and fills the space between with their body. When a dancer leaves the circle, the circle is simply closed once more with the joining of hands.

Unclosed circles can often be observed, in which case there are openings and a round formation is extant. These openings make it even easier to get started. 'The round open structure seems particularly suitable as an entrance and a foundation for dancing together [...]' (Evert 2014, p. 47, translation by author) In the case of Kurdish Round Dances, usually an experienced dancer initially 'leads' the dance and is visually marked by a swath of fabric held in the free hand. The cloth is exchanged when a new leader takes over. Despite these small differences, Circle Dancing is, by its nature, non-hierarchical—there is no 'starting-point'—every dancer is equally important.

The differences within the movements that result from the varying levels of experience of the dancers, and contrasting body shapes and personal movement characteristics are decisive aspects of the choreographic format of Circle Dancing.

Another important aspect is that the circle formation offers the greatest possible visibility of the dancers, both as members of the circle dynamic and from the perspective of the audience. Whereas each of the dancers can see all of the other dancers of the group at any time, those outside of the circle can see the dance as a whole and watch the individuals pass by as the circle rotates.

There is no central perspective from which one could best see the dance. There are only multiple, ever-changing views to the situation. This corresponds to a multiperspectivity of content which, in the context of protest, generally (and by definition) stands in opposition to the prevailing state ideology.

Another aspect of the non-hierarchical character of Circle Dancing is that each dancer leads and is led by their neighbours at the same time. Lepecki calls this 'a-personal leadingfollowing' (Lepecki 2013, p. 37). This leading/following in Circle Dancing corresponds to self-organizing structures of social movements. In the context of larger assembly, the individual assumes personal responsibility, while also transferring a great deal of responsibility to the collective. This requires that the individual trusts the group and shows flexibility regarding their dynamic position within it. 'Feeling valued' and 'being seen' are important factors of emotional well-being in large groups, which is why the maintenance of visibility for each Circle Dancing member is of positive psychosocial merit and not merely a side effect.

Another very important effect of Circle Dancing is that it facilitates the synchronization of a large group. Synchronization is essential for a functioning collective, and the choreographic format of Circle Dancing can serve to establish a very specific form of collectivity, namely that of the collective movement that is needed by the body's response/ability. This is a description of the practice of 'attuning', which Prades describes as a way 'to harmonise'.[10] It points to the importance of finding a common rhythm for a movement or action. Decisive here is that the process of synchronization[11] never leads to perfect uniformity—it is always in the making; it is transient, volatile and reversible, even if it appears to be stable for a certain time. That means that one has to 'attune' again and again.

A precondition for synchronization is a great attention ('body awareness') for both one's own body and those of the other(s). The dance creates a state of alertness and can thus also be seen as a form of body meditation. The physical disposition is described by Prades as a state of fluid attention, in which all the senses are adjusted to the reception of the environment: 'Our senses must be receptive and our body absolutely present' (Prades 2013, p. 214). This state of physical attention emerged as early as 1965, in one of the classics of activist practice. In the handbook, *Manual for Direct Action: Strategy and Tactics for Civil Rights and All Other Nonviolent Protest Movements,* Oppenheimer and Lakey recommend 'ideal body awareness when engaging in protest' (Oppenheimer and Lakey 1965, quoted in Harrington 2016, p. 7). These physically challenging situations require mindfulness, which is about the active discovery of possibilities of movement.

Another important effect of the circle is the phenomenon of rhythm, which helps overcome exhaustion. Within the group, the common body experience and the 'vibe' are experienced as self-empowerment. McNeill describes the mechanism of rhythm structures and how the visceral phenomenon of 'muscular bonding' leads to 'emotional bonding' between the jointly moving people (McNeill 1997, p. 2f). This type of community formation by 'the euphoric fellow feeling' (joyful proximity to a neighbour) is of great importance for social movements, as it builds trust. The physical aptitude of the dancers thereby leads to an intuitive, affective, empathic pre-linguistic understanding of moving jointly in rhythm.

Circle Dancing as Staged Social Order

And so, in the most ideal instances, an alliance begins to enact the social order it seeks to bring about by establishing its own modes of sociability. (Butler 2015, p. 84)

Based on the considerations from the previous chapters, the following can be said:

Circle Dancing orchestrates equality, visibility, multivarious positions in space and continuous changes of perspective. The person is understood as a relational and social being, moving in a collective context to which one can 'show up' and from which one can 'depart'. Thus, the community is staged as an open structure. Furthermore, dancing in public space is a very fundamental way of staging of freedom. 'I will dance despite everything'[12] was the title of a flashmob performance in Tunis, initiated in December 2012 by Art Solution working with a Tunisian group, Service de l'Underground, who promoted dancing by 'citizen dancers' in public spaces as resistance against extremists trying to limit the freedom of the body in public. Butler describes how the human body at assemblies 'is on the line, exhibiting its value and its freedom' (Butler 2015, p. 17). This is especially true for the dancing body. It stands for freedom; a body in motion is difficult to control. In the case of the aforementioned flashmob, the body is liberated, at least temporarily free.

The strength of a group in Circle Dancing or Round Dance is performed offensively and concentrated inwards. This demonstration of strength is also underlined by the fact that, even in violent demonstration situations, the dancers can 'afford' to turn their back on the oppressive forces. Thus, the body is exhibited in its vulnerability from which it gains its immanent strength, as Butler convincingly shows. Circle Dancing marks a specific place in the public realm as its own space ('our place') and thereby temporarily claims atmospheric territory. Circle Dancing instantiates an alliance that is based on equality in a situation that is usually characterized by extreme imbalance of power: 'They are asserting equality in the midst of inequality' (Butler 2013). This equality is founded upon closeness and connectedness, which is made clear by the touch of the dancers on each other's arms and/or shoulders. The German formulation *Schulterschluss demonstrieren* (demonstrate shoulder to shoulder) displays implicit knowledge about the real and symbolic power of this bodily gesture. People sit 'shoulder to shoulder' for a common cause at a difficult time; the term *Schulterschluss* (closing of the ranks) describes the merger of several people into an alliance. The image of people gripping each other's shoulders stands for solidarity and fraternity. In addition to strong symbolic content, this kind of touch holds great importance in the field of affection.

AFFECTION AND TURMOIL: CONTACT IN CIRCLE DANCING

Touching others physically and being touched is essential for people to maintain connection with the world. As Böhler notes, there is a direct connection between touch and reality: '(...) this is the very meaning of touching: it gives us a sense of reality (...) it actually gives a feeling of something that in fact exists outside oneself' (Böhler 2011, pp. 39–40). He emphasizes that this is an act of extroversion in relation to the activity of touching (Böhler 2011, p. 41).

The moment of leaving one's personal universe—a factor in the active contact—also has an unmistakable influence on the degree of the individual body's ability to experience affection. Thus, Mittmannsgruber and Schäfer define the contact as follows: 'The touch is the body's "moving beyond". Its stretching, the spreading and widening of its aptitude' (Mittmannsgruber and Schäfer 2013, p. 197, translation by author).

If, in this sense, the dancing body is imagined in a protest situation, the importance of physical contact for this temporary community becomes clear; the bodies recall their power of affecting others through the touch inherent in the dance. The success or failure of social movements depends on the way these powers of the protesters are realized and used in order to affect their environment. Mittmannsgruber and Schäfer describe the intrinsic power in the body as resulting from a mobile field of forces in this situation: 'Bodies are fields of force [...] they are relationship braids [...]. And every single body is to be regarded as power, namely, to affect and be affected by power. To touch and be touched' (Mittmannsgruber and Schäfer 2013, p. 196, translation by author).

The experience of being a member within the dancing group, part of the force field and realizing its energy, is felt in the group as a moment of self-empowerment. It is both a sense of self-efficacy and a very concrete assessment of possibilities for action. Slaby, who is concerned with the connection between affective states and the awareness of possibilities for action and agency, emphasizes the importance of affective states as an 'interface' for the capacity of acting of a group (Slaby 2012, p. 152). The mutual awareness of possibilities for action—'we can' or 'we cannot'—is important as an ongoing process of self-assurance and positioning for groups that want to remain active in the political space. Flam describes the form of emotional work undertaken by social movements and how they re-socialize their members by working on emotions: '[...] social movements re-define dominant feeling rules' (Flam 2005, p. 19). She continues by describing ways in which cultural elements, such as various forms of rhythm and loud sounds, serve as fear-management devices (Flam 2005, p. 29). The choreographic formats of Circle Dancing and the Round Dance can be regarded as *affective work* in this context—on the one hand, to collectively manage negative emotions such as anxiety and, on the other hand, to maintain agency and a capacity to act. The mindsets of the dancers are changed by experiencing themselves as human beings in contact and connection with other people (Slaby 2012, p. 154).

To be active in the political arena, it is important to feel agency and the world as a space of specific (action) opportunities. This is the reason why a classical form of protest, such as the demonstration, still makes sense in today's media-democracy; shared movement in public space is being 'in motion' in a double sense. The state of being 'in motion' is experienced in a very special way when dancing in public space: The affective state—arising through touch and dancing together—can lead to a euphoric, prerevolutionary state. In his essay *Rühren, Berühren, Aufruhr* ('Stirring, Stirring Up, Uprising'), Nancy describes the connection between touch and political uproar from an analysis of the word *ruhr*—a common wordstem in the German language:

> *Rühren, Berühren, Aufruhr.* German makes it possible to gather three notions in the semantic family of *ruhr*, which we can match in French with *le bouger, l'agiter, le toucher* and *le soulèvement* [and in English: 'moving', 'agitating', 'touching' and 'uproar']; and each of these terms can be understood with its own array of possible values. 'Moving' and 'agitating' convey some physical as well as moral senses, as do 'touching' and 'uprising'. The latter term, for its part, gives its moral value a socio-political orientation. (Nancy 2011, p. 8)

The word 'family' refers to the field of movement, a movement which is directly connected with the range of affections, the *e-motions*. Nancy points out that one must move in order to touch: 'Now, one can only understand the identity of touching and touched as the identity of a movement, a motion and an emotion' (Nancy 2011, p. 12).

Touch—and being touched—are the point of convergence of the political movement; the real physical, choreographic movement, and the associated inner movement and affectation.

Circle Dancing and the Round Dance are aspects of a physical practice within which the gathering bodies, in their performance and vulnerability, open up a field of meaning in the public where the political takes place in the relational 'in-between-ness' of the moving bodies. Nancy described the socio-political turmoil in which the dancing body is located, essentially dealing with overcoming body boundaries: 'The body rises up, as the German word *Aufruhr* suggests, designating, as I pointed out, a socio-political uprising. [...] A body rises up against its own enclosure' (Nancy 2011, p. 15). Thus the isolation of the individual is also broken in Circle Dancing and the Round Dance.

In summary, it can be said that the interpersonal contact and affection extant in the choreographic formats of Circle Dancing and the Round Dance (within the framework of the social convention of dancing) demarcate an atmospheric territory. Through this, the world can be concretely experienced as a space of specific (action) possibilities. This realm is a space of multiple movements: the political, the choreographic and the emotional. These overlapping experiences of movement and 'emotional bonding' that it triggers lead to the formation of a resilient community, which is the prerequisite for any kind of political action. Moreover, in the choreographic format of Circle Dancing and the Round Dance, a form of future-oriented sociability is temporarily established, staged and practised as a matrix of collective action. When these choreographic formats appear in the context of political meetings, protests and occupations, they become part of a prefigurative policy. The body's abilities to touch and be touched, along with its 'response/ability', are at the centre of this practice of collective movement that simultaneously exercises and celebrates sharing itself in a gathering in (the) movement.

NOTES

1. 'After all, there is an indexical force of the body (...): it is *this* body, and *these* bodies, that require employment, shelter, health care, and food, as well as a sense of a future (...)' (Butler 2015, p. 9).
2. See the socio-psychological investigation about the protests in 2013 in Istanbul by Özden M. Uluğ and Yasemin G. Acar (2015) 'We are more than Alliances between Groups' in *Everywhere Taksim. Sowing the Seeds for a New Turkey.*
3. See the collective concept of Kai van Eikel's in Kai van Eikels (2013) *Die Kunst des Kollktiven: Performance zwischen Theater, Politik und Sozio-Ökonomie.*
4. Milohnic (2013) *Choreographies of Resistance/Partisan Choreography, Walking Theory,* 21 Social Choreography, 15–20.
5. Klein, G. (2013) 'Collective Bodies of Protest: Social Choreographies in Urban Performance Art and Social Movements', Walking Theory, 21 Social Choreography, 29–33, http://www.tkh-generator.net/portfolio/tkh-21-social-choreography/, date accessed 23 February 2018.
6. See Walton, Jeremy F. (2015) '"Everyday I'm Çapulling!" Global Flows and Local Frictions of Gezi' in *Everywhere Taksim. Sowing the Seeds for a New Turkey.*
7. The video is available at https://www.youtube.com/watch?v=QV0NT UY0Zls, date accessed 19 September 2017.
8. Halliday identifies the following four meanings that are important to the theory of revolution: (1) Commitment of the population, (2) Progress, (3) Beginning of a new age, (4) Total change. See, Fred Halliday (1999) *Revolution and World Politics.*

9. For in-depth discussion of this problem, please refer to Hanna Walsdorf (2010) *Bewegte Propaganda. Politische Instrumentalisierung von Volkstanz in den deutschen Diktaturen.*

10. Prades, Pepón (2013) 'Ideas that are born from the body. Brainstorming and improvisation' in A. Böhler; Ch. Herzog; A. Pechriggl, (eds) *Korporale Performanz. Zur bedeutungsgenerierenden Dimension des Leibes.*

11. On the topic of synchronization, see Kai van Eikels (2012) 'From "Archein" to "Prattein" – Suggestions for an Un-creative Collectivity' in E. Besteri; E. Guidi; E. Ricci (eds) *Rehearsing Collectivity. Choreography Beyond Dance.*

12. Video documentation of 'I will dance despite everything', http://www.freearabs.com/index.php/art/79-video-gallery/304-jb-span-tunisia-jb-span-dancing-in-the-street, date accessed 19 September 2017.

References

Berger, C., and S. Schmidt. 2009. Körperwissen und Bewegunsglogik. In *Ordnung in Bewegung. Choreografien des Sozialen. Körper in Sport, Tanz, Arbeit und Bildung*, ed. K. Brümmer, R. Kodalle, and T. Pille. Bielefeld: transcript.

Böhler, A. 2011. On Touching. In *Tanzquartier Wien*, Scores N°1 touché. http://www.tqw.at/sites/default/files/Scores_1_Kern_Web_FINAL.pdf. Accessed 9 Oct 2017.

———. 2014. 'Do We Know What a Body Can Do?' #1 Interview with Arno Böhler and Erin Manning. In *Wissen wir, was ein Körper vermag? Rhizomatische Körper in Religion, Kunst, Philosophie*, ed. A. Böhler, K. Kruschkova, and V. Susanne. Bielefeld: transcript.

Böhme, G. 1993. Atmosphere as the Fundamental Concept of a New Aesthetics. *Thesis Eleven* 36: 113–26. Sage. http://journals.sagepub.com/doi/pdf/10.1177/072551369303600107. Accessed 9 Oct 2017.

Butler, J. 2011. *Bodies in Alliance and the Politics of the Street* (2017a). http://www.eipcp.net/transversal/1011/butler/en. Accessed 18 Jan 2017.

———. 2013. *Freedom of Assembly or Who Are the People.* Given as a Lecture at Boğaziçi University, Istanbul (2017a). https://www.youtube.com/watch?v=Yd-7iT2JtXk. Accessed 9 Oct 2017.

———. 2015. *Notes Toward a Performative Theory of Assembly.* London: Harvard University Press; eBook.

della Porta, D. 2008. *Eventful Protest, Global Conflicts* (2017a). https://www.bc.edu/content/dam/files/schools/cas_sites/sociology/pdf/EventfulProtest.pdf. Accessed 9 Oct 2017.

Elden, S. 2011. *Die Entstehung des Territoriums* (2017a). http://www.geographie.nat.uni-erlangen.de/wp-content/uploads/EBK_1.pdf. Accessed 18 Jan 2017.

Elias, N. 1978. *What Is Sociology?* Trans. Stephen Mennell, and Grace Morrissey. London/New York: Hutchinson and Columbia University Press.

Evert, K. 2014. Gemeinsam Tanzen. In *Versammlung und Teilhabe*, ed. R.V. Burri, K. Evert, S. Peters, E. Pilkington, and G. Ziemer. Bielefeld: transcript.

Flam, H. 2005. Emotions' Map. A Research Agenda. In *Emotions and Social Movements*, ed. H. Flam and D. King. Oxon/New York: Routledge.

Gormly, J. 2012. *What Is Social Choreography?* http://www.choreograph.net. Accessed 24 Nov 2014.

Halliday, F. 1999. *Revolution and World Politics: The Rise and Fall of the Sixth Great Power.* Durham: Duke University Press.

Hardt, M., and A. Negri. 2000. *Empire.* Cambridge/London: Harvard University Press.

Harrington, H. 2016. *Site-Specific Protest Dance: Women in the Middle East.* http://dancercitizen.org/issue-2/heather-harrington/. Accessed 9 Oct 2017.

Hewitt, A. 2005. *Social Choreography: Ideology as Performance in Dance and Everyday Movement.* Durham/London: Duke University Press.

Hölscher, S., and G. Siegmund, eds. 2013. *Dance, Politics & Co-immunity.* Vol. 1. Zurich/Berlin: diaphanes.

Jamshidi, M. 2014. *The Future of the Arab Spring: Civic Entrepreneurship in Politics, Art and Technology Start Ups.* Oxford: Butterworth-Heinemann.

Kaltenbrunner, T. 2004. *Contact Improvisation. Moving – Dancing – Interaction.* Trans. Nick Procyk. Oxford: Meyer & Meyer Sport.

Klein, G. 2013. Collective Bodies of Protest: Social Choreographies in Urban Performance Art and Social Movements. *Walking Theory* 21 Social Choreography: 29–33. http://www.tkh-generator.net/portfolio/tkh-21-social-choreography/. Accessed 23 Feb 2018.

Klien, M. 2008. *Choreography as an Aesthetics of Change* (Dissertation – Edinburgh College of Art, Scotland) (2017a). https://www.academia.edu/3809926/CHOREOGRAPHY_AS_AN_AESTHETICS_OF_CHANGE. Accessed 9 Oct 2017.

Kunst, B. 2014. Die partizipative Politik *des* Tanzes. In *Kampnagel; Internationales Theaterinstitut Katalog Tanzplattform Deutschland.* Berlin: Kampnagel Internationale Kulturfabrik GmbH und Internationales Theaterinstitut - Zentrum Deutschland.

Lepecki, A. 2013. 'From Partaking to Initiating: Leadfollowing as Dance's (a-Personal) Political Singularity. In *Dance, Politics & Co-Immunity*, ed. S. Hölscher and G. Siegmund, vol. 1. Zurich/Berlin: diaphanes.

Lorey, S. 2014. Performative Sammlungen. Sammeln und Ordnen als künstlerische Verfahrensweise – eine Begriffsbestimmung. In *Versammlung und Teilhabe*, ed. R.V. Burri, K. Evert, S. Peters, E. Pilkington, and G. Ziemer. Bielefeld: transcript.

McNeill, W.H. 1997. *Keeping Together in Time: Dance and Drill in Human History.* Cambridge, MA: Harvard University Press.

Milohnic, A. 2013. Choreographies of Resistance. *Walking Theory* 21 Social Choreography: 15–20.

Mittmansgruber, M., and E. Schäfer. 2013. Immer wieder – die Körper! In *Korporale Performanz. Zur bedeutungsgenerierenden Dimension des Leibes*, ed. A. Böhler, C. Herzog, and A. Pechriggl. Bielefeld: transcript.

Nancy, J.-L. 2000. *Being Singular Plural.* Trans. Robert D. Richardson, and Anne E. O'Byrne. Stanford: Stanford University Press.

———. 2011. Rühren, Berühren, Aufruhr (Stirring, Stirring up, Uprising). Trans. Christine Irizarry. In *Tanzquartier Wien,* Scores N°1 touché. http://www.tqw. at/sites/default/files/Scores_1_Kern_Web_FINAL.pdf. Accessed 9 Oct 2017.

Oppenheimer, M., and G. Lakey. 1965. *Manual for Direct Action: Strategy and Tactics for Civil Rights and All Other Nonviolent Protest Movements.* New York: Quadrangle Books.

Prades, P. 2013. Ideas that Are Born from the Body. Brainstorming and Improvisation in A. Böhler; Ch. Herzog; A. Pechriggl, *Korporale Performanz. Zur bedeutungsgenerierenden Dimension des Leibes* (Bielefeld: transcript).

Slaby, J. 2012. Affective Self-Construal and the Sense of Ability. In *Emotion Review* 4/2. http://janslaby.com/downloads/slaby2012_affectiveselfconstrual_ emorev.pdf. Accessed 9 Oct 2017.

Teune, S. 2012. Das produktive Moment der Krise. Platzbesetzungen als Laboratorien der Demokratie. *WZB Mitteilungen Heft* 137: 32–34.

Tsomou, M. 2014. Der besetzte Syntagma-Platz 2011: Körper und Performativität im politischen Alphabet der ›Empörten‹. In *Versammlung und Teilhabe,* ed. R.V. Burri, K. Evert, S. Peters, E. Pilkington, and G. Ziemer. Bielefeld: transcript.

Uluğ, Ö.M., and Y.G. Acar. 2015. "We Are More Than Alliances Between Groups". A Social Psychological Perspective on the Gezi Park Protesters and Negotiating Levels of Identity. In *Everywhere Taksim. Sewing the Seeds for a New Turkey,* ed. I. David and K.F. Toktamis. Amsterdam: Amsterdam University Press.

van Eikels, K. 2012. From "Archein" to "Prattein" – Suggestions for an Un-creative Collectivity. In *Rehearsing Collectivity. Choreography Beyond Dance,* ed. E. Besteri, E. Guidi, and E. Ricci. Berlin: Argobooks.

———. 2013. *Die Kunst des Kollektiven: Performance zwischen Theater, Politik und Sozio-Ökonomie.* Munich/Paderborn: Wilhelm Fink Verlag.

Walsdorf, H. 2010. *Bewegte Propaganda. Politische Instrumentalisierung von Volkstanz in den deutschen Diktaturen.* Würzburg: Königshausen & Neumann.

Walton, J.F. 2015. "Everyday I'm Çapulling!" Global Flows and Local Frictions of Gezi. In *Everywhere Taksim. Sewing the Seeds for a New Turkey,* ed. I. David and K.F. Toktamis. Amsterdam: Amsterdam University Press.

Wulf, C. 2010. Anthropologische Dimensionen des Tanzes. In *Konzepte der Tanzkultur. Wissen und Wege der Tanzforschung,* ed. M. Bischof and C. Rosiny. Bielefeld: transcript.

On Bodies and the Need to Appropriate Them

Antje Velsinger

In this essay, I would like to deal with the following questions:

Are citizens in western societies, early in the twenty-first century, actually
the owners of their bodies?
If so, how do these citizens use this ownership?
Could ownership of one's body lead to a subversive, or even utopian, potential for escaping today's cultural requirement of body-optimization?

Throughout the ages, people have retained a fascination with designing
and actively shaping bodies. Cultures have always provided a huge variety
of tools to implement such modification. In Ancient Egypt, for example,
people already used various techniques such as masquerading, tattooing
and mummifying as ways to fashion bodies and to preserve them from
inevitable decay.[1] But although bodies have always been possible to modify, the question of *who* designs them—or which social group has the *right*
to manipulate and rule over them—has always been answered differently,
depending on the society of any given time or place.

A. Velsinger (✉)
Graduate Program Performing Citizenship, HafenCity University Hamburg,
Hamburg, Germany
e-mail: mail@antjevelsinger.com

© The Author(s) 2019
P. Hildebrandt et al. (eds.), *Performing Citizenship*, Performance
Philosophy, https://doi.org/10.1007/978-3-319-97502-3_6

When the Parliament of England passed the Habeas Corpus Act in 1679, for the first time in European history, a citizen suddenly owned the right to his or her body, at least to a minimal degree. Due to this law, which can be translated from Latin as 'you may have the body', a first form of ownership of one's body—an ownership in the subjunctive—was granted to citizens, in order to prevent their unlawful or arbitrary imprisonment. This redefined similar ideas from the Magna Carta of 1215. Before the actual imposition of the Habeas Corpus Act, the king was the one who owned, and therefore ruled over, the bodies of all the subjects living in his kingdom.

Ever since that Act, bodily self-determination has been a key issue of citizen rights. According to the sociologist Jürgen Mackert, citizenship is considered to be a contract between governmental agents and the citizens of a state. This automatically implies a set of mutual rights and obligations. These rights and obligations are sufficiently defined that either party is likely to express indignation and take corrective action if the other fails to meet expectations.[2] Through the enactment of the Habeas Corpus Act, ownership of the body became an integral part of this contract between the representatives of the state and the individual citizens: owning one's own body became a right of the individual citizen and thus formed the basis of all later additions to the concept of citizenship.

As a consequence of the Habeas Corpus Act, the king's former right to arbitrarily own his subjects' bodies suddenly disappeared in European constitutional monarchies and democracies. Since then, in most western societies, ruling over another person's body—which is the case during punishment or rehabilitation in detention—has been regarded as a violation. This new concept has led to the citizens' insistence on rightful and justifiable binding laws and an executive that adheres to legal procedures. Consequently, in all cases where bodily self-determination is ignored, such as in torture, wrongful imprisonment or other forms of physical violation, citizen rights are automatically ignored at the same time. Being a citizen in western societies implies being entitled to particular rights, and these rights include ownership of one's own body. Although, of course, being a citizen implies much more than the right to own one's body,[3] one can say that the least being a citizen means is that it is only the individuals themselves who can own their own body.

When I speak about the body, I refer to a phenomenological concept of the body. According to the phenomenological philosopher Merleau-Ponty, the human body simultaneously lives out its existence in two ways;

as an *object* and as a *subject*.[4] As an *object*, the body is what *we have*, it is physical and expanding material. As a *subject*, the body is what *we are*, as our body, because we can only perceive the world through our physical senses. Consequently, we can state that it also becomes characterized as an agent that perceives and transmits the outside world. This perception of the world in turn depends on how we physically use our bodies. According to phenomenology, the body is our medium to have a world[5] and—as our perception of the world depends on the actions we perform with our bodies—it is also our medium to actively create a world with the help of, and as a consequence of, bodily actions and practices. I will come back to this potential of the body to create the world through particular bodily use later on.

What consequences have the citizens of today's western society developed from their ownership? In the seventeenth century, ownership of one's body was still an endangered concept and rather referred to a passive form of property, without any need for particular activities. Yet today, in our contemporary western culture, we not only own, but rather *possess*, our bodies, which implies a very active use that is based on physical practices.

Since the Act of Habeas Corpus, a cultural shift has taken place from passively owning a body to actively possessing it. Today the body is something that is treated and thought about as something that can be designed and possessed by every individual. According to Michela Marzano, at the beginning of the twenty-first century, the body seems only acceptable if it is mastered and controlled by the individual.[6] Exhibiting a controlled body has become an individual form of proof that one is in control of one's self. This is why the well-shaped and controlled body is the quintessence of social success, happiness and the degree of perfection the individual has reached.

What physical practices do the citizens of the beginning of the twenty-first century utilize to actively possess and control their bodies? In the following, I will outline some examples of practices applied with the aim of controlling and possessing a body.

THE FITNESS INDUSTRY

In contrast to normal sports that aim at conditioning the body through physical activity, the fitness industry in the last ten years has developed new methods, such as EMS[7] or HYPOXI,[8] that require only modest physical activity to shape the body. By using electrical muscle stimulation (EMS) or low-pressure machines (HYPOXI) on very particular body parts, the body can be 'designed' in a very planned and specific way.

PLASTIC SURGERY

While in past decades plastic surgery was an exclusive and expensive service that only very few people were able to use, today, it has become part of pop culture and can be considered a common method used to modify body shapes and manipulate ageing processes.[9]

THE PHARMACEUTICAL INDUSTRY

In today's society, bodily malfunction can be controlled extensively with the help of the pharmaceutical industry. The use of drugs is a widespread method that aims at alleviating physical suffering, such as pain, and also controlling psychosomatic disorders—for example, through heightening powers of concentration to decrease depression.

THE USE OF APPS

Digitalization has brought about an increasing number of apps that allow full body monitoring.[10] These apps allow the user to control and work on individual bodily functions—such as heart rate, muscular movement, sleep patterns, and so on. What is different from the other methods described so far is that this method for full bodily monitoring affects issues of ownership of personal body information. As apps produce data that is stored online, the information provided by an individual becomes part of big data and can then also be used by external institutions and users.

The methods described above show that the 'design-ability' of a body in the beginning of the twenty-first century meets with both economic interests and a culture of self-optimization. The cultural urge to transform, develop and optimize the body in western culture changes also the notion of habeas corpus. The subjunctive of habeas corpus has shifted to an imperative; it is no longer 'you may have the body', but rather, 'possess your body and get the best out of it!' One might conclude that the citizens of today use the ownership of their bodies mainly for enhancement and self-optimization, which are the cornerstones of the current neoliberal ideology.

At the same time, the concept of *ownership* of one's body becomes blurred. Today's citizens readily share the rights to their bodies with other players—such as app providers or the pharmaceutical industry, all of whom have an enormous economic interest in the control and possession of the body of every citizen. It is salient that these economic enterprises not only *possess* but even *appropriate* the body of every citizen, and at a speed that compromises the ability of individuals to realize or to be able to cope with this new outcome. So, are we experiencing a new cultural shift today, towards possessing, appropriating and controlling bodies? Are today's citizens therefore voluntarily running the risk of losing their rights to their own bodies again and, consequently, falling into a newly developed passivity and alienation from their own bodies?

When debating these issues around these questions, Merleau-Ponty's notion of the body as an agent[11] contributes a helpful view. He considers the body to be an agent that creates a reality as it receives it. If the body is our medium to perceive the world, and this perception depends on actions we perform, then the body is a potential medium to actively create a world by applying or rejecting particular bodily actions and practices. Instead of just accepting—or perhaps not seeing—the unpleasant economic reality of being appropriated, or instead of confirming a neoliberal ideology of self-optimization, today's citizens would have the choice to critically rethink their particular form of ownership of their bodies.

The sociologist Robert Gugutzer regards the body as a societal phenomenon in two ways: as a product of society on the one hand, and as a producer of society on the other.[12] The human body is a *product* of society in the sense that our handling, our knowledge, our feeling and our notions of the body are defined by societal structures, values, norms, technologies and systems of ideas. On the other hand, the human body is a *producer* of society because our living together, our social organization, is essentially affected by the physicality of socially acting individuals. Social reality results from social actions and outcomes, and social action always involves bodily action. Therefore, bodily (inter-)actions play a crucial part in the construction of social reality.

This interdependence of social reality, social action and bodily action allocates a very powerful role to everyone who is designing, possessing or appropriating bodies—in other words, a political role.

As an artist, I consider the appropriation of bodies as a potentially critical tool with which to create other forms of reality—realities that escape the ideology of self-optimization and control. Consequently, in the research I do within the frame of the graduate school 'Performing Citizenship', I investigate a contemporary approach to utopian bodies. In this context, I understand utopian bodies as bodies that experiment with a different approach to the neoliberal logic of self-optimization and control.

In the following, I will discuss three examples of body appropriation in the artistic field to show how the appropriation of a different body can be used as a tool to produce a different social reality.

Paul Beatrix Preciado: Testo Junkie

The first example is the pharmaceutical and physical experiment of Paul Beatriz Preciado, as documented in his book *Testo Junkie*.[13] Paul Beatriz Preciado is a contemporary writer, philosopher and curator who focusses on topics relating to identity, gender, pornography and sexuality. Preciado was originally known as a female writer and identified as a lesbian. In 2014, he announced that he was 'transitioning' and, in 2015, he changed his name from Beatriz to Paul.

Ten years before that, in 2005, Preciado started an eight-month experiment with self-administered testosterone. Interestingly, Preciado did not consider himself a 'transgender', so the reason why he took testosterone was not that he felt the desire to become male. However, Preciado identifies with a group who declare themselves 'gender pirates' or 'gender hackers'. Gender hackers call themselves *copyleft* users, who consider sex hormones to be free and to open bio-codes whose use they believe shouldn't be regulated by the state or dictated by pharmaceutical companies.[14]

Consequently, without seeking medical monitoring, Preciado bought testogel from illegal sources and started his body experiment. While he was taking the drug, it was not only his physical bodily appearance that changed, but also his whole way of thinking, writing, feeling, moving, imagining and acting. His body became the place where all these changes were negotiated. By using testogel as a tool, Preciado appropriated a different body. With his experimental practice, documented in the book *Testo Junkie*, Preciado 'hacks into gender', simultaneously rejecting any regulation either by the state or by pharmaceutical companies who normally control gender changes.

In an interview Preciado said, 'I also thought about the project as a kind of collective adventure, in a sense, because I'm thinking about the body, not even just my own, as this kind of a living political fiction.[…] We must manage to actually create some political alliance of minority bodies, to create a revolution together'.[15] With the aid of testogel as a technique to appropriate a different body, the body of the artist becomes a container for physiological and political micro-mutations. The body qualifies as a container in which alternative drafts of a transitioning gender model come into being and into action. Coming back to habeas corpus, in Preciado's case, 'you may have the body' implies the right to decide on your gender by self-determined use of a drug. In Preciado's bodily self-determination, gender becomes something that can be freely appropriated by every citizen.

Leonardo Selvaggio URME

The second example of an artistic strategy to appropriate bodies is the project *URME*, created by the Chicago-based artist Leonardo Selvaggio,[16] based on the appropriation of only one body part—namely, the face. Selvaggio is an interdisciplinary artist whose work examines the influence of technology on identity. In his recent work, he is engaged in the idea of considering identity as data that can be manipulated or even corrupted.

In his project, *URME*, Selvaggio develops alternative ways to use the human face in order to subvert new technological developments in the field of facial recognition. With the help of the new facial recognition app 'FindFace', any stranger needs only a photo of our face in order to get access to any information we have ever communicated via our social media profiles.[17]

In order to protect people from this new form of surveillance, Selvaggio is developing his own defence technologies. In his art project, *URME SURVEILLANCE*, he allows anyone to appropriate his face by wearing a photo-realistic, 3D-printed mask. When a person takes on the face of the artist—in the form of a mask—camera systems equipped with facial recognition software identify that person as Selvaggio, thus attributing all of their actions to the identity of the artist. With this strategy of appropriating someone else's face, people can hide and protect their own identity in surveyed areas. Further, they also actively contribute to designing a new persona, as their physical actions are linked to another person, in this case the artist.

In the project *URME*, the appropriation of someone else's face produces an interesting malleability of identities. The shared face is subverting facial recognition systems because information cannot be read correctly; as a consequence, the data is connected to the wrong social media account.

Coming back to habeas corpus, the project *URME* Surveillance produces an interesting new form of malleable utopian body. In this case, 'you may have the body' implies the *right* to hide, confuse and rebuild the identity of a body. A group of people can share multiples of one reproduced individual body part, in order to create a new identity mapped out by their physical actions, so that economic and governmental surveillance loses overall power and is thus ridiculed.

ANTJE VELSINGER *THE BODIES WE ARE*

The third example is my own research project *The Bodies We Are*, which is located in the choreographic field.[18] In the project *The Bodies We Are*, I work with the appropriation of movement and perception patterns of foreign bodies; in other words, bodies outside the realm of the performer's experience. Based on the assumption that the body is our medium through which we have a world, the appropriation of a foreign body offers a tool for the perception of the world from a different perspective.

In the first part of the research project,[19] I asked three performers/choreographers[20] to select and bring images of bodies with which they do not identify. Interestingly, the majority of these images were images of marginalized or non-mainstream bodies: obese bodies, extremely muscular bodies, bodies involved in BDSM practice,[21] anorexic bodies, extremely flexible yoga bodies, bodies using different kinds of prothesis, and so on. Starting from the thesis that a body is not a stable entity but consists of movement patterns, bodily perception and imagination, I was interested in the following questions:

What happens if the performers try to appropriate these bodies by speculating on and taking over their movement logics?

What happens to the performers themselves if they try to step out of their own bodily reality and jump into an unknown territory of a body totally different from their own? What happens in the process of appropriation?

Let's assume the body is not a stable entity, but rather, a complex system in which particular movement and perception patterns, particular desires and imaginations interact with each other.

Let's assume everyone has a choice of plenty of potential bodies. Can anyone enter, or 'hack into', any bodily system, if he or she appropriates its movement patterns?

Let's do one experiment. Please go online and open the following homepage: http://www.yossiloloi.com/portfolio/fullbeauty-project. Now, please go to image 6/16. Let's assume this is one of our potential bodies that we want to appropriate. What kind of choreographic or performative strategies can be used to appropriate it?

If one considers this body to be a system, the performer first has to speculate and decide, what the characteristics are and which of them are significant. These decisions depend on the individual person who is doing the appropriating. Accordingly, the appropriation of a foreign body always implies a transfer process which then provokes a deviation from our particular individual experience.

A possible performative strategy to appropriate this body:

Movement: Concentrate on weight and volume while you move. Use every movement to perceive as much gravity, heaviness and volume of your body, as possible. Try to intensify this by using your imagination.
Flesh: Focus on the masses of flesh and how these masses are rubbing against each other while you move. Frequent actions are draping your flesh around you and therefore having to grab and pull at your flesh to rearrange it.
Pace: Move slowly.
Breath: Breath goes slowly and against the resistance of the flesh—you have to produce this physically.
Movement orientation: Movement is rather initiated from the centre, not the periphery. **Movement motivation**: You expose as much volume to the space around you as possible. **Use of object:** Use an object to drape your volume on it. The object will help you to expand even better in space.

If a person wants to enter into the system of this body—these 7 points might be helpful as one possible strategy of appropriation. Plenty of others, of course, are also tenable. The combination and interaction of these different characteristics will produce a system that will change how he or she perceives and constructs the body. Interestingly, entering into this foreign physicality will also change the imagination and desires of the person who is appropriating. Consequently, appropriating a foreign body means not only appropriating its physicality and movement patterns but, through its physicality, also appropriating its imagination, its visions and desires. The person, who is appropriating this body will experience that there exists a direct interrelation between bodies and what is imagined and desired.

Relating all this to the habeas corpus theme, it can be said that the project *The Bodies We Are* expands its scope from a singular law to its utopian plural. It does not merely say 'you may have the body', it goes far beyond that; it claims that it is possible to appropriate a variety of—even plenty of—bodies depending on your own interests and needs. Therefore, my thesis is this: If a concrete interrelation exists between the physical actions of a body, its individual desires and its particular environment, then the appropriation of foreign bodies also implies a utopian potential. Appropriating a body can be used as a tool to encounter and experience the not yet known. It can be used as a tool to allow change in the way we perceive our bodily and social reality. Consequently, the appropriation of a foreign body can be used as a vehicle to jump into different systems—to hijack, seize or capture foreign spaces and realms of actions, thoughts and visions.

My final look at the implications of habeas corpus—'you may have the body'—can be summarized as follows: As I have discussed above 'having a body' in the beginning of the twenty-first century meets with a culture of self-optimization, and the right to own one's body has shifted into an imperative of enhancement and control. However, when accepting the body as an agent that has the capacity to produce concrete realities, ownership of one's body could also lead to a subversive, or even utopian, potential for escaping today's cultural requirement of body-optimization. If we use the artistic field to shift from passively being appropriated to actively appropriating a body, we gain space for redefining bodily self-determination. If we consider the body a space for action that produces concrete realities, not only artists, but every citizen can use his or her body to produce concrete bodily realities—realities that not only aim at enhancement and control, but that are also open to include the foreign, the unknown, the scary, or the challenging to imagine.

NOTES

1. Cf. Pommerening (2007) 'Mumien, Mumifizierungstechnik und Totenkult im Alten Ägypten: eine chronologische Übersicht' In: Wieczorek, Alfried (Hrsg). *Mumien. Der Traum vom ewigen Leben*, pp. 71–88.
2. Mackert, Jürgen (2006) *Staatsbürgerschaft. Eine Einführung*, p. 18.
3. As Engin Isin puts it: 'critical studies of citizenship over the last two decades have taught us that what is important is not only that citizenship is a legal status but that it also involves practices of making citizens – social, political, cultural and symbolic'. But following this thesis, it has to be stated that the medium for taking part in all these social, political, cultural and practices is the body. Cf. Isin, Engin F. & Nielsen, Greg M. (eds) (2008) *Acts of Citizenship*, p. 17f.
4. Cf. Merleau-Ponty, Maurice (2012) *Phenomenology of Perception*, trans. Donald Landes, p. 94.
5. Cf. Merleau-Ponty (2012, p. 147f).
6. Marzano, Michela (2013) *Philosophie des Körpers*, p. 24.
7. http://www.stern.de/gesundheit/fitness/sportarten/ems%2D%2D-elek-trische-muskelstimulation-schwitzen-unter-strom-3524208.html, date accessed 28 August 2017.
8. http://www.designyourbody.com, date accessed 28 August 2017.
9. See, MTV series 'I Want a Famous Face', which documents how normal citizens are getting a 'famous face and body' through the use of plastic surgery, https://www.youtube.com/watch?v=H3TeYTTNdSs, date accessed 17 March 2018.
10. One example is Apple's 'Health' app that gathers information in four distinct categories: Activity, Sleep, Mindfulness and Nutrition. The app consolidates health data from an iPhone, Apple Watch and third-party apps that the individual uses, allowing the user—and the provider—to view all the information in one place. http://www.apple.com/uk/ios/health/, date accessed 28 August 2017.
11. Cf. Merleau-Ponty (2012, p. 74).
12. Gugutzer, Robert (2015) *Soziologie des Körpers*, p. 8f.
13. Preciado Beatriz (2013) *Testo Junkie*.
14. Preciado (2013, p. 55f).
15. http://www.theparisreview.org/blog/2013/12/04/pharmacopornog-raphy-an-interview-with-beatriz-preciado/, date accessed 28 August 2017.
16. For a full documentation of the project see, http://www.urmesurveil-lance.com, date accessed 28 August 2017.
17. https://www.theguardian.com/technology/2016/may/17/findface-face-recognition-app-end-public-anonymity-vkontaktedate accessed 28 August 2017.

18. For full documentation of the project, see: http://antjevelsinger.com/
    arbeiten/thebodiesweare/, date accessed 28 August 2017.
19. The first part of the research project took place between 9 and 29 February
    2017 at the choreographic centre of PACT Zollverein, in Essen, Germany.
20. The performers/choreographers involved in the collaboration were Juli
    Reinartz, Johanna Roggan & Vania Rovisco. The fine artist Sophie Aigner
    was also part of the research team.
21. BDSM is a variety of often erotic practices or role-involving bondage, dis-
    cipline, dominance and submission, sadomasochism, and other related
    interpersonal dynamics.

References

Gugutzer, Robert. 2015. *Soziologie des Körpers*. Bielefeld: transcript.

http://antjevelsinger.com/arbeiten/thebodiesweare/. Accessed 28 Aug 2017.

http://www.designyourbody.com. Accessed 28 Aug 2017.

http://www.stern.de/gesundheit/fitness/sportarten/ems%2D%2D-elektrische-muskelstimulation-schwitzen-unter-strom-3524208.html. Accessed 28 Aug 2017.

http://www.theparisreview.org/blog/2013/12/04/pharmacopornography-an-interview-with-beatriz-preciado/. Accessed 28 Aug 2017.

http://www.urmesurveillance.com. Accessed 28 Aug 2017.

Isin, Engin F., and Greg M. Nielsen, eds. 2008. *Acts of Citizenship*. London: Zed Books.

Mackert, Jürgen. 2006. *Staatsbürgerschaft. Eine Einführung*. Wiesbaden: Verlag für Sozialwissenschaft.

Marzano, Michela. 2013. *Philosophie des Körpers*. Munich: Diederichs Verlag.

Merleau-Ponty, Maurice. 2012. *Phenomenology of Perception*. Trans. Donald Landes. London: Routledge.

Pommerening, Tanja. 2007. Mumien, Mumifizierungstechnik und Totenkult im Alten Ägypten: eine chronologische Übersicht. In *Mumien – der Traum vom ewigen Leben: Begleitband zur Sonderausstellun*, ed. Alfried Wieczorek. Mainz am Rhein: Zabern.

Preciado, Beatriz. 2013. *Testo Junkie. Sex, Drugs, and Biopolitics in the Pharmacopornographic Era*. New York: Feminist Press.

PART II

Citizenship and (Urban) Space

Silence, Motifs and Echoes: Acts of Listening in Postcolonial Hamburg

Katharina Kellermann

There is a strong movement in Hamburg 'Recht auf Stadt' ['Right to the City']
*which, of course, also implies the understanding that the city is for the many. Who
defines the city? Who defines the culture of remembrance in the city? Is this culture of remembrance always top-down-politics or are there other forms, too?*[1]

Political communities, such as cities, emerge in part through their
approach to their own history. The question of citizenship is therefore
always connected to a culture of remembrance. This question is particularly pertinent in the case of Hamburg, a city which, 'as a gateway to the
world for the German Empire played a key role in the colonization of
Africa' (Möhle et al. 2006, p. 7). Which perspectives on this colonial legacy are represented in the public discourse is always a matter of political
contestation.

Presently, the urban space of Hamburg shows traces of colonialism,
most of which are hard to clearly identify as such. They can be found
within city planning in the form of architecture, street names and monuments, within cultural institutions, where knowledge is made apparent, as
well as in the political discourses that shape the public discussions.

K. Kellermann (✉)
Graduate Program Performing Citizenship, HafenCity University Hamburg,
Hamburg, Germany

© The Author(s) 2019   93
P. Hildebrandt et al. (eds.), *Performing Citizenship*, Performance
Philosophy, https://doi.org/10.1007/978-3-319-97502-3_7

Following Pierre Nora, such historic traces can serve as sites of memory (Nora 2010, p. x), since they contribute to the formation of identities and are therefore constitutive of the urban community. In this sense, the debate on colonial history—as it is being held in Hamburg and many other major European cities—can serve as an example for the constitutive nexus of citizenship and culture of remembrance. The political and cultural manner by which these sites of remembrance are being handled, especially in a postcolonial and post-fascist Germany, is crucial for debates and modes on participation and exclusion. For example, in 2014 in Hamburg the Senate, in its paper 'Coming to Terms with the Colonial Legacy – a New Start for the Culture of Remembrance' (https://hhpost-kolonial.files.wordpress.com/2014/07/senatsbericht-koloniales-erbe2014.pdf), proposed a variety of ideas for dealing with the city's colonial vestiges. Grassroots organizations and communities from former colonized countries subsequently criticized the paper in an open letter because it completely failed to take their own knowledge production, their experiences, expertise and points of view into consideration (http://www.hamburg-postkolonial.de/PDF/PM_NOTWITHOUTUS.pdf).

This question of which perspectives on historic events are being represented and whose narrative is being heard in this debate[2] is not solely of symbolic meaning. The matter of the social positioning of the relevant agents—in terms of who is able to speak for themselves and who is privileged to speak for and about others—is rather just as much part of the city's memoryscape as the material traces remaining in the urban space and the colonial continuities in the public discourse. Urban space with its historic dimensions is constituted by a specific 'distribution of the sensible' (Ranciere 2004), in which acoustic materializations—such as 'acts of speech' and voices, but also sounds, music and atmospheres—mark social actions and influence individual and collective imaginations of the city. Accordingly, a critical social and artistic analysis of postcolonial cultures of remembrance should also take into account that urban memoryscapes are not solely materialized, for example, in the form of architecture, street names or monuments; they also have specific acoustic materiality.

In the following, the classic concept of the term *soundscape* is explored. Using examples from the artistic research project *How to Hear the Invisible* (How to Hear the Invisible—an acoustic map of the postcolonial memoryscape of Hamburg—is the artistic part of my research project 'Citizenship and Politics of Remembrance. Sound as a commemorative cultural medium in postcolonial Hamburg' in the framework of the graduate school Performing Citizenship. http://performingcitizenship.de/data/ katharina-kellermann-forschungsprojekt/), the project deals with the city as an acoustic space that displays itself as a sonic realm of urban, social and political experience and maps its soundscape as a space of remembrance. Referring to three soundtracks of the project—individually named: 'Silence', 'Motif' and 'Echo'—I show, through artistic work with sound, how the realm of the acoustic can function, beyond its perceptive intent, as an epistemological tool within the context of postcolonial culture of remembrance. Finally, I will outline the concept of 'acts of listening' and the implications for acoustic forms of remembrance, as well as the potential for sound as a medium of performative historiography.

THE ARTISTIC RESEARCH PROJECT WWW.HOW-TO-HEAR-THE-INVISIBLE.ORG

According to Henri Lefebvre, the city is constituted by a variety of representations, imaginations and practices (Lefebvre 1991). These representations frequently have an acoustic dimension that I will take into account by analysing the city as a soundscape. My artistic research is based specifically on the classic notion of the soundscape—as developed by the Canadian composer and author R. Murray Schafer—following the work of Brandon LaBelle and paying attention to 'auditory figures' (La Belle 2010, p. 25). Schafer's concept of the soundscape analyses the variety of sounds that arise from an environment as well as the listeners' perception of them. In his work, he focusses on the so-called *Lofi Soundscapes* (Schafer 1977, p. 97)—that consist of the congestion of industrial and electronical noise. In focusing on these soundscapes, there is an emphasis on the experience of 'sound pollution' (Schafer 1977, p. 97). However, the project of *How to Hear the Invisible* artistically encounters the soundscape with an acoustic approach, based on the ways in which sound and voices operate in everyday life, and also in terms of narrative. In addition, there is focus on the cultural, political and social significance of auditory figures:

Which motifs repeat?
Where is silence?
What echoes?

By answering these questions, the project endeavours to enable an acoustic experience that locates and dislocates remembering through sound. In various sound tracks,[3] Hamburg's daily urban soundscape is augmented through new sounds and voices. 'Motif', 'Silence' and 'Echo' serve as formal structures for the production of sound material (interviews, samples, compositions, field recordings), as well as featuring in the editing and montage. They mark places, like the Rothesoodstrasse and Hafencity and draw—in form and content—a connection from colonialism to post- and neo-colonialism within Hamburg's urban space. Likewise, these tracks are used as metaphors to describe postcolonial debates around the general lack of representation of anti-colonial resistance in the urban space and public discourse. For example, the famous pan-Africanist George Padmore organized the first conference of the *International Trade Union Committee for Black Workers in Hamburg* in 1930, and was head of the organization's office in Rothesood Strasse in Hamburg, till it was closed by the Nazis in 1933 (Möhle et al. 2006). The missing reference to his legislating at the place of his former office can be described as silence. Similarly, the tendencies of romanticizing colonialism by using its context (through references on colonial emperors and so-called colonial goods) in contemporary issues like urban planning in the Hafencity can be described as a neo-colonial echo. In this way, 'Motif', 'Silence' and 'Echo'—the titles of the tracks—also function as auditory figures, depicting how colonial history affects the contemporary daily life of the city and its people today.

The project thus explores which acoustic dimensions the (unmarked, and therefore seemingly mute) colonial traces of Hamburg's urban spaces may have. The montage searches for a possibility to make them audible—historical connections, continuities and contemporary references being rearranged through sound. By layering and mixing a variety of sounds, voices, vibes and atmospheres, the project tries to map the postcolonial city as an acoustic space, focusing on political functions and perceptive modes of operation of sounds and voices within that space. The function of the auditory figures—the respectively acoustic materials and montage that are developed in order to enhance a possibly, different imagination of the postcolonial city through a shifting, editing and alienating of the material—is now discussed for the tracks 'Motif', 'Silence' and 'Echo'.

Motifs

Acoustic motifs structure our sonic memory. Their repetition and variation are the basis for processes of remembrance, as well as for spatial imagination. In Hamburg, such motifs also serve as signature sounds for the city's self-promotion as a cosmopolitan metropolis and 'gateway to the world'. Horns, ship engines and screeching seagulls are typically representative of the city's soundscape, and thereby trigger strong associations. However, they do not only sound on-site, but are also being used to aestheticize and brand other spaces, for example, the subway station at Hafencity University. These selected and edited sounds serve to fabricate the image of the new district of Hafencity, but also draw on sonic continuities. The city's acoustic representation, as well the specific spatial imagination of the city through these motifs, range from colonial activities—such as mission and trade in the late 1900s—all the way to the daily life of the modern city. By connecting these sounds to keywords from a respective discourse, the soundtrack 'Motif'—from *How to Hear the Invisible*—attempts to depict these sonic continuities and highlight the harbour's significance for German colonialism. The montage of those sounds and site-specific field recordings with spoken information serves to re-signify the denotation of the signature sounds.[4] 'Motif' attempts to trigger 'acts of listening' that realize this process of resignification in one's own cognition. By adding a postcolonial sense to the everyday sonic motives, the daily perception of urban soundscape is being shifted through listening.

Silence

The harbour itself is not the only example of a location of the intertwining of German colonialism and Hamburg's traders. Other sites of significance, such as the landmark building Afrikahaus, built by the company C. Woermann, or the naming of two streets after the slave-trader Schimmelmann, can be found throughout the city. In this way, perpetrators and beneficiaries of German colonialism have ingrained themselves into the urban image, as well as into the collective memory of the city as local protagonists, while knowledge of anti-colonial resistance or decolonial practices are less visible. An example of such a lack of visibility can be found at the Rothesoodstrasse, near Hamburg's city centre, where the office of George Padmore—an internationally renowned pan-African thinker and activist—had been located up until its destruction by the Nazis in 1933. From his Hamburg office, Padmore organized the international conference of black Workers of the League against Imperialism and published the magazine *The Negro Worker*.

Today, this (historical) place is not marked with any information provided to indicate significance. The soundtrack 'Silence' attempts to make Padmore's story audible, as well as to raise awareness for the acoustic phenomenon of silence, by using signal-generated sound materials and working with strong variation of volume. The lack of representation in public spaces and within the collective urban consciousness is a form of silence and can be perceived by listening carefully—and can thus be opened up to discursive interpretation. 'Acts of listening' perceive silence within this context as a certain inaudibility of narrative, and thus recognize the non-sounding of Padmore's story—within the symbolic canon of the city—as a form of not knowing, an omission and exclusion from Hamburg's soundscape and culture of remembrance.

Echo

The manner in which historic events and the hegemonic perspectives towards them are present in the urban space can be seen clearly in Hafencity.[5] The acoustics of the district are not only shaped by the materiality of newly constructed building complexes but also by echoes of colonial history. Historic references are present all over the district. While imperialist sailors and conquerors—like Vasco da Gama and Ferdinand Magellan—had already been honoured during German colonialism with their own monument in Hamburg's Speicherstadt, once more we see streets in Hafencity named after them (Informationszentrum 3. Welt, https://www.iz3w.org/zeitschrift/ausgaben/318_grenzen_und_migration/fab). Buildings that have been named after former plantations and colonial commodities—such as Java, Arabica and Silk—might well have been conceptualized with the goal of generating a cosmopolitan 'feel' for the white majority population; however, the city planners failed to recognize and integrate diverse perspectives on global processes, such as migration or a postmigrant urban change, into the shaping of the new district. Due to particular echoes such as these, the Hafencity becomes a space of culture of remembrance in which certain perspectives are being amplified and reinforced while others barely linger. The following quote, taken from an interview with Tania Mancheno,[6] which forms part of the track *Echo*, describes this dynamic:

> [...] if you look at all these buildings, really, they are all named after plantations. And with these plantations, especially in the awful Überseequartier

(literally 'overseas district'– a part of the new Hafencity area), you once again encounter an echo. To me, by definition, Übersee divides the world into north and south, rich and poor, black and white, woman and man; all these blatant segregations that once gave justification to allow a large number of people on this planet to be treated as not human. So, the core of racism lie 'overseas' concepts... and we're placing this right in the centre of this city; however because it is also a new centre, a new centre or heart of Hamburg [...] it's, like, again, this longing for exoticism, again another echo and, as already mentioned, all these buildings that have been named after plantations, that were of worldwide significance to Hamburg. Therefore, here is an echo that is based on colonial power, and that does not remotely consider the racism that was justified by its adoption. So ultimately, it is an echo of the civilizatory wound of colonialism.[7]

The soundtrack 'Echo' tries to create an audible playing-out based on the acoustic research about the architectural materiality of the Hafencity, as well as of echo as a sound phenomenon (by using analogous sound effects). Thus, colonial echoes can be experienced in an acoustic, as well as discursive, manner. Through 'acts of listening', it becomes perceivable which perspectives actually resonate in the urban daily life of a postcolonial city.

City and Commemoration as Acoustic Territories

These examples from *How to Hear the Invisible* are given in order to show the approach of the project to the memoryscape of Hamburg as an acoustic territory,

[...] specific while being multiple, cut with flows and rhythms, vibrations and echoes, all of which form a sonic discourse that is equally feverish, energetic, and participatory. Sound is shared property onto which many claims are made over time, and which demand associative and relational understanding. (La Belle 2010, p. 24)

With this in mind, listening to the sound tracks reveals the fact that social processes, like the field of remembrance culture, constantly interact with an auditory world, which thus contributes to the experience of the city and its inhabitants. As Stefan Militzer puts it, the act of listening involves the act of 'investigating the origins of a sound and thus becomes an attempt at finding and positioning oneself' (Militzer 2015, p. 68).

In this sense, the use of the auditory figures in the artistic research aims to understand the city as a realm of contemporary (Motif) and historic (Silence) narratives, and draw attention to the discourse on their representation (Echo). Motif, Silence and Echo function as auditory figures by assigning specific characteristics to spaces and their perception and by giving shape to their specific significance and effects. Thereby, they not only serve to identify a specific acoustic quality, but their effectiveness also allows for identity formation, permits participation and produces exclusions. In this sense, sound phenomena are used to perceive and understand the urban space as a memoryscape, auditory figures add a performative dimension to such sound phenomena beyond their mere semantic meaning. Through their use, *How to Hear the Invisible* examines the city as a space in which its postcolonial legacy—its consequences and the manner in which it is being dealt with—are manifested acoustically.

The soundtracks transform the significance of spaces and enable possibilities of remembering within the city. In this way, they propose to perceive and discuss the city as a space of remembrance through different ways of listening. The project tries to make the urban space legible as an acoustic one, in which 'sonic materiality operates as "micro-epistemologies", [....] opening up to specific ways of knowing the world' (La Belle 2010, p. 25).

Since they produce and represent cultural modes of signification, the auditory figures of Motif, Silence and Echo serve to analyse Hamburg's memoryscape through sound and by listening. This focus on listening and exploration through acoustic concepts undergoes, in the sense of an acoustic turn, a 'shift away from the privilege of the visible towards an overlooked acoustic dimension' (Meyer 2007, p. 18). According to Petra Meyer, this acoustic turn challenges the paradigm of the visual which, since Plato's *Allegory of the Cave* (Lee 2003, p. 365) and the subsequent formation of a philosophy that mainly operates with metaphors of light and sight, has dominated European culture. Instead of deeming 'visual coordinates to be the main points of orientation for experience' (Militzer 2015, p. 70), the realm of the acoustic and the act of listening as categories of analysis and experience can be fruitfully applied in artistic research; with this awareness, I adopted the use of sound to reveal obscured dimensions. As I will outline in the following, an acoustic turn can also open up a new perspective with regard to the issue of remembrance culture that, especially in the German context, is usually still conceptualized in mostly visual terms.

LISTENING TO THE URBAN SPACE AS A POLITICAL PRACTICE

As I have pointed out through examples from *How to Hear the Invisible*, listening can alert us to the condition of Hamburg's memoryscape and also enable a political practice of positioning within the city's social structure. By perceiving the tracks, listening becomes a way of decoding and also a way to 'achieve an awareness for the underlying sense (something that is experienced, postulated or aimed at as hidden)' (Barthes 1985, p. 253). By applying this experience to urban space and the local politics of remembrance, listening gains a performative dimension, which I will explain in greater detail by referring to the 'acts of listening' model later on, but first, I want to shed some light on the acoustic sphere of the urban space. It is crucial to acknowledge particular modes of operation, which I want to call the 'surround effect' of the city. While Lefebvre, in his 'rhythmanalysis' (Lefebvre 2004) of the city, presupposes that the listener has to remain outside of the acoustic happening in order to recognize its rhythms, my artistic research identifies the listeners themselves as an essential part of the soundscape of the city. Listeners cannot place themselves outside of—or opposite—the city's soundscape, such as happens when watching a film or looking at a painting. While the act of seeing produces an outside horizon, the act of listening knows no such horizon at all, rendering it impossible for listeners to distance themselves from what is happening; acoustically, we cannot separate ourselves. The city's 'surround effect' therefore always already situates the inhabitants of the city as listeners. The acoustic experience creates positioning in the sense of proximity and distance, as well as political positionality within the city's social context, by paying attention to these questions:

Which sounds are familiar to whom and who can identify with them?
How can we articulate and express ourselves?
How are we being perceived in the soundscape of the city?
To whom do we listen and whom do we try to understand?
Who has a voice and what makes a sound?
Which sounds and voices can be perceived and what spaces do they create?

Returning to the opening question regarding forms and possibilities of commemoration as an articulation of citizenship, 'acts of listening' reveal the possibility to politically position one's own sounding in the city and to take responsibility for a diverse approach to the city's history through listening. In their essay on postcolonial feminism, Nikita Dhawan and Maria Do Mar Castro Varela introduce the concept of 'subversive listening'. According to the authors, subversive listening is a specific mode of listening in which the listener gains an awareness of her privileges, as well as of the possibility of losing them. Subversive listening thus enables the self-aware subject to refrain from speaking and let others do the talking (Castro Varela and Dhawan 2003, p. 279). In this sense, the soundscape of the postcolonial city, as the basis of the artistic research project *How to Hear the Invisible*, calls for us to listen in a bi-directional way, which is to say to pay attention to the surrounding space with its atmospheres, noises and linguistic significations, along with its continuities, breaks and silences. Accordingly, this soundscape cannot be deciphered through conventional forms of listening that are still modelled on the linearity of writing, thereby eliminating everything that seems to be insignificant. 'Acts of listening'—as a concept explicated in the next section—create a relationship between the subject and the city that is neither selective nor distanced. The listener is always already part of that urban and social space in which commemoration takes place. It is listening that enables the subject to position itself in the debate about adequate forms of postcolonial commemoration.

ACTS OF LISTENING AND POLITICS OF SOUND

Based on the soundtracks I have discussed, the auditory figures of Motif, Silence and Echo carry political significance because their specific resonance creates a memoryscape of Hamburg. The project *How to Hear the Invisible* tries to offer an acoustic experience in which this political significance reveals itself only through 'acts of listening'. In this respect, listening is to interpret the sounding out of particular voices and the silencing of certain narratives as a sign of exclusion (silence). Further, listening is to recognize sonic continuities and their significance for the self-conception of the city (motifs). And finally, by acknowledging the political impacts of city planning, listening is to realize neo-colonial echoes within our daily life in Hamburg.

Thus, the examples help to distinguish the difference between hearing and listening. While hearing is predominantly a (passive) perception of sound, listening also implies a form of participating and interpreting. The importance of George Padmore, for example, is not present in the city's narrative, therefore, his story is not audible, but through listening it is possible to become aware of its absence, and thus, to comprehend it as silence. In the context of debates about a postcolonial culture of remembrance, listening is one possible approach to the mute urban land-scape sketched at the outset, which enables us to experience the gap between the historic past and its aftermath in our daily urban life. Critically, by asking which voices and stories enter common narratives of the city's history and which ones remain mute, the focus on the unheard and the non-sounding can be extended beyond the phenomena of sound to the nonetheless acoustic realm of discourses, standpoints and positionalities.

This dialogue between speaking and listening is based on structures of participation and exclusion that are expressed through vocal phenomena, as I tried to demonstrate with the help of the example of neo-colonial imaginaries echoing in the area of Hafencity. The technique of the mon-tage of both verbal and non-verbal elements used in the project *How to Hear the Invisible* takes into account that the matter of the research—the dealing with traces of colonial politics in the urban space—is initially inau-dible. The 'acoustic dimension of the experience of a certain place cannot be reduced to a simple materiality or a nonbiased hearing' (Fiebig 2015, p. 75). The perception of the sounds and field recordings is itself influ-enced by the voices of postcolonial protagonists, framing all tracks. Their voices offer the contextualization of the sounds and were also chosen for reasons of representation politics.[8] Voices and sounds as different acoustic signs are being related to each other when listening. By listening, both the vocal body of the speaker and the listening subject enter into an affective relationship with each other that goes beyond the discursive impact of the interview.

Voice as acoustic material, as well as philosophic phenomena, forms an important part of the research project. As it maintains a productive con-nection to my original question of the nexus of citizenship and commem-oration because, in addition to its appellative attributes, ethical aspects characterize voice. Voice interaction is necessarily marked by a reference to the other; it always establishes a relationship and is fundamentally directed towards somebody else. The conversation is dependent on the other's response, besides different modes of addressing the other. Voices address us in the form of sound—even if we don't understand them. According to Roland Barthes, voice gives us 'instruction' to listen (Barthes 1985, p. 255). This form of address leads to a situation of perception in which silence is just as active and meaningful as speaking: 'listening speaks'.

I want to apply and broaden this mode of address—in which, according to Barthes, voice is being responded to with 'words or deeds' (Barthes 1985, p. 255)—to a critical discussion of a postcolonial culture of remembrance in Hamburg and outline some theoretical thoughts that evolved through the course of artistic research. I propose a way of listening in which one feels genuinely addressed by non-linguistic acoustic expressions—like continuous motifs, neo-colonial echoes and discursive silence—as much as by voice-based signals. The idea of 'acts of listening' is an attempt to acknowledge these different acoustic forms of address. In this way, listening constitutes an acoustic space in which different sounds, with their respective levels of meaning, work in a performative way. Through 'acts of listening', those levels of meaning are channelled, and an acoustic space is created in which Motif, Silence and Echo—as auditory figures—call for us to listen as a way of reworking history and a form of commemoration. If listening 'speaks' to us, as Barthes put it, then the experience of this acoustic space requires translation: translation of sound and voices into a social experience of the postcolonial Hamburg, as well as translation of an acoustic relationship into knowledge about the city. This translation relates to a process of interpretive participation. 'Acts of listening' increase the sensitivity to the postcolonial in the city. Thus, to listen also means to feel addressed and to transfer this address into conceptual and aesthetic categories. In this sense, it is not only the speech act that constitutes a performative, but also the act of listening.

Acoustic Remembrance and Performative History Writing

As illustrated, listening is not a given phenomenon that works in non-political or trans-historical ways. Sound is associative and ephemeral in nature, but it is also an essential component of the world it participates in and constructs. For Brandon LaBelle, sound 'comes to reconfigure the spatial distinctions of inside and outside, to foster confrontations between one and another, and to infuse language with degrees of immediacy' (LaBelle 2010, p. xxi). Therefore, listening produces spaces and social materialities, and it thus intervenes in the field of the visible. Precisely the associative character of sound makes it inherently political—which sounds we hear, and how we hear them is open for interpretation, and therefore, a political issue. The knowledge and the experience that we associatively generate through sound lead to modes of awareness other than seeing.

Thus, one aim of the artistic research, *How to Hear the Invisible,* is to facilitate a knowledge production beyond the familiar ways of perception. Dealing with sound is in this way a matter of dealing with the processes of decoding and identifying. While listening is connected with normative notions and criteria, at the same time, it is able to inspire our imagination in different ways. 'Acts of listening' enable a critical engagement with the 'subconscious ideological structures (of the language, thinking and experience) which guide our knowledge and our actions (Hall 2004, p. 145).' Stuart Hall describes representation as the power 'to label, give meaning to or classify someone or something'. It is precisely this form of power that can potentially be undermined by non-visual practices such as listening. 'Acts of listening' thus encompass a critical mode towards normative discourse that impacts our visual perception. If we understand such politics of representation as a set of notions, realizations and political stand-ins, then 'acts of listening' can fragment their structure and quality, and unfold it through different forms of perception and imagination in a productive way.

Returning to the project, the idea of *How to Hear the Invisible* is to make various fragments of space and its history *audible*; the soundtracks reinforce different forms of listening and enable a change of perspective in the current perception of the city and its history. In this case,

> [...] the temporality of the location is no longer a mere continuity – it becomes an experience of constellations, disruptions, asynchronicities and consequentially demands the listener to question their own role as contemporary and as witness. Listening may have always been an associative act, an associative happening, but only specific media-based or artistic approaches activate the different aesthetic, political and social potentials of association. (Albrecht and Wehren 2015, p. 13)

Thus, the access to history remains fragmentary and develops only in the listener's specific and subjective imagination. Imagination in this context means the ability to conjure up something which is absent. This imagination is always specifically situated and applicable to one's own reality. Imagination in the context of a postcolonial culture of remembrance means approaching events from the colonial history with a certain kind of awareness. From today's perspective, one can only begin to fathom the violent nature, rather than fully comprehending it. The attempt to understand this history also always depends one's own social positioning. In this sense, *How to Hear the Invisible* tries to enable 'acts of listening' that can play a part in decolonial politics within the urban space: by critically examining representation, by promoting awareness for motif, silence and echoes and by encouraging one to deal with the consequences and aftermath of colonial politics. The project proposes a practice of remembering where 'acts of listening' use our sonic memory, and today's city, as the starting point of a performative historiography through sound. In the context of a postcolonial culture of remembrance, it is a productive challenge for a critical historiography to examine its own concept of culture. The soundtracks produced and the concept of 'acts of listening', developed within the frame of the artistic research, form an attempt to broaden the range of the culture of remembrance—traditionally dominated by written and monumental concepts. *How to Hear the Invisible* demands a practice of remembering and a historiography that repeatedly questions, contests and challenges their ways of transferring knowledge.

The project comprehends listening as a practice of cultural remembrance (*erinnerungskulturell*) and a performance of citizenship. Using sound as a medium, and triggering 'acts of listening', makes possible specific orders of relationship between the city's inhabitants as senders and receivers. Here, an intersubjective space emerges that allows for a specific form of commemoration. Performing citizenship means experimenting with the political potential of sound in the sense of experimenting with modes of listening, which create a new sociality in, and new perspectives on, the city. Speaking with Gerald Fiebig, new sociality here means to overcome 'the formation of identity in the metropolis according to predefined actions, functions and occupations'. 'Acts of listening' do not only lead to the sounds and voices themselves but, as Fiebig puts it, they enable an encounter with 'categories of experience and identity; with questions of the naturalness of normality of a class of activities; and with other selves engaged in their own categories, experiences, questions and activities' (Fiebig 2015, p. 80).

Therefore, listening—as one mode of working through and commemorating historical events, and thus, a critical way of performing citizenship—has the potential to mark the city as postcolonial, following the traces of the unheard within the heard, of the unknown within the known; becoming aware of one's own position within it. 'Acts of listening' triggered by artistic work with sound are 'a form of listening that allows for switching between different frames of reference: a mode of listening of many modes of reading' (Ungeheuer 2002, p. 205). They can help us to understand the urban community in a different way and to reconfigure it—as location and de-location of sounds and voices that offer alternative historical and political perspectives with formerly unacknowledged dimensions, and also act as an undermining of orders of representation. Acoustic forms of commemoration thus allow for different forms of listening, of speaking and of sounding, as social practices within the postcolonial city. It might even be used to create a new imagination of the city, as an urban and social practice of perception, and so, reformulating commemoration as a performance of citizenship.

NOTES

1. Artist and curator Hannimari Jokinen, interviewed by Katharina Kellermann, April 2016 (translated by author).
2. In this context, the author of this article acknowledges that she is white, and thus benefits from a host of social privileges. Her privileged position affects both the artistic and scientific, as well as the activist perspective on the subject.
3. These audio tracks are available on the website: www.how-to-hear-the-invisible.org
4. Artistic Research Project *How to Hear the Invisible* (2017). The following is an excerpt transcribed from the track 'Motif':

   > *Hamburg – the city. It's harbour – Bismarck memoria – 'Colonial capital of the German Empire'. Berlin Conference. Africa Conference 1884 – Colonialization of Africa – Cameroon, Toga, today's Namibia – as the German South West Africa – as well as today's Tanzania, Rwanda and Burundi – as German East Africa. – Also German New Guinea, Samoa, Kiautschou – Resistance – Rudolf Duala Manga Bell – Mpondo Akwa – Resistance. – In Duala 1884 – At the 'Waterberg' 1904 – the Maji Maji from 1905 on. – Violent counter-insurgency by German soldiers.*

5. Hafencity is Hamburg's newest district, in development since 2008.
6. Tania Mancheno is a historian and a cultural worker living in Hamburg. She developed critical city tours through Hafencity and Speicherstadt, dealing with the colonial history of Hamburg. The term 'echo' I borrowed from the tour: 'Hafencity Inbetween Cosmopolitan Flairs and Colonial Echoes' (conducted by Tania Mancheno and the city planer Andreas Schneider). Their valuable contribution to this research is acknowledged with thanks.
7. Tania Mancheno, interviewed by Katharina Kellermann, February 2016 (translated by author).

8. All interviewees—Millicent Adjei, HMJokinen, Israel Kaunatjike, Tania Mancheno and Andreas Schneider—are members of the groups that signed the open letter: 'Not about us without us'. Under this slogan, various civil societal groups and communities have commented on their exclusion from the proposals of the Hamburg Senate for the reworking of the colonial heritage of the city, and called for participation. See also their open letter: http://www.hamburg-postkolonial.de/PDF/PM_NOTWITHOUTUS.pdf, date accessed 4 January 2017.

References

Albrecht, M., and M. Wehren. 2015. Verortungen/Entortungen. Urbane Klangräume und die Frage nach einer Politik des Sounds. In *Verortungen – Entortungen: urbane Klangräume*, ed. M. Albrecht and M. Wehren. Berlin: Neofelis.

Barthes, R. 1985. *The Responsibility of Forms*. New York: Hill and Wang.

Castro Varela, M., and N. Dhawan. 2003. Postkolonialer Feminismus und die Kunst der Selbstkritik. In *Spricht die Subalterne deutsch? Migration und postkoloniale Kritik*, ed. E. Rodriguez and H. Steyerl. Münster: Unrast.

Fiebig, G. 2015. Soundscape und Aura. Zur Verortung und Entortung von Soundscapes in der zeitgenössischen Audiokunst. In *Verortungen – Entortungen: urbane Klangräume*, ed. M. Albrecht and M. Wehren. Berlin: Neofelis.

Hall, S. 2004. Das Spektakel des ›Anderen‹. In *Ideologie, Identität, Repräsentation* Ausgewählte Schriften 4, ed. S. Hall. Hamburg: Argument.

LaBelle, B. 2010. *Acoustic Territories: Sound Culture and Everyday Life*. New York: Continuum Books.

Lee, Desmond, ed. 2003. *Plato. The Republic*. London: Penguin.

Lefebvre, H. 1991. *The Production of Space*. Oxford: Blackwell.

———. 2004. *Rhythmanalysis: Space, Time and Everyday Life*. London: Continuum.

Meyer, P. 2007. *Acoustic Turn*. Paderborn: Fink.

Militzer, S. 2015. Der Klang der Stadt. Ansätze zu einer Phänomenologie des urbanen Hörens. In *Verortungen – Entortungen: urbane Klangräume*, ed. M. Albrecht and M. Wehren. Berlin: Neofelis.

Möhle, H., S. Heyn, and S. Lewerenz, eds. 2006. *Zwischen Völkerschau und Kolonialinstitut. AfrikanerInnen im kolonialen Hamburg*. Hamburg: Eine Welt Netzwerk Hamburg e.v. und St.Pauli Archiv.

Nora, P. 2010. *Les Lieux De Mémoire, Volume 4: Histories and Memories*. Chicago: The University of Chicago Press.

Ranciere, J. 2004. *The Politics of Aesthetics: The Distribution of the Sensible*. London and New York: Continuum.

Schafer, R. 1977. *The Tuning of the World*. New York: Alfred A. Knopf.

Ungeheuer, E., ed. 2002. *Elektroakustische Musik*. Laaber: Laaber.

WEBLINKS

Arbeitskreis Hamburg Postkolonial. 2017a. http://www.hamburg-postkolonial.de/PDF/PM_NOTWITHOUTUS.pdf. Accessed 18 Jan 2017.
———. 2017b. https://hhpostkolonial.files.wordpress.com/2014/07/senatsbericht-koloniales-erbe2014.pdf. Accessed 12 Feb. 2017.
———. 2017c. http://www.hamburg-postkolonial.de/PDF/Stadtrundgaenge HafenrundfahrtenHamburg2016.pdf. Accessed 12 Feb 2017.
Artistic Research Project *How to hear the invisible.* 2017. http://how-to-hear-the-invisible.org. Accessed 18 Jan 2017.
Graudiertenkolleg Performing Citizenship. 2017. http://performingcitizenship.de/data/katharina-kellermann-forschungsprojekt/. 18 Jan 2017.
Informationszentrum 3. Welt. 2017. https://www.iz3w.org/zeitschrift/ausgaben/318_grenzen_und_migration/fab. Accessed 18 Jan 2017.

Claims for the Future: Indigenous Rights, Housing Rights, Land Rights, Women's Rights

Elke Krasny

In 2011, a year-long programme of cultural events and exhibitions celebrated Vancouver's 125th anniversary. On the occasion of this anniversary, the Audain Gallery, the Downtown Eastside Women's Centre (DEWC), and myself, as the gallery's visiting artist, entered into a collaboration that resulted in the research and exhibition project *Mapping the Everyday. Neighbourhood Claims for the Future*, with its articulations of situated indigenous and immigrant perspectives as they are contingent to the specific local histories and globalized neoliberal conditions. The purpose of this essay is to provide critical contextualization to the project and its making public of the claims put forward by women from the DEWC. Claims-making is understood here as a political act that constitutes subjects of rights. The politics of collectively formulating demands and making a public claim to them is at the heart of this project, as it tests what it means to perform citizenship under Vancouver's specific conditions as they are defined by coloniality and neoliberalism. My triple commitment to feminist political thought,

E. Krasny (✉)
Academy of Fine Arts Vienna, Wien, Austria

© The Author(s) 2019   111
P. Hildebrandt et al. (eds.), *Performing Citizenship*, Performance
Philosophy, https://doi.org/10.1007/978-3-319-97502-3_8

involved curatorial practice, and critical urban research provides the basis for the following feminist materialist and locationally specific close description and analysis of the *Mapping the Everyday. Neighbourhood Claims for the Future* project.

Vancouver's 125th Anniversary

Founded in 1886, Vancouver's beginnings were, in fact, owed to the expansion of the Canadian Pacific Railway. This huge infrastructural investment effort was central to Canada's nation building, with the Canadian Pacific Railway's express purpose to 'physically unite Canada and Canadians from coast to coast.'[1] Even though most of the province of British Columbia (BC) remained unceded land, colonial legislation sought to ensure control of and power over the territory. 'In BC, aside from a small number of treaties on Vancouver Island (the 1850s Douglas Treaties), and Treaty No. 8 in the northeast portion of the province, all of BC remains unceded Indigenous territories.'[2] Today's Vancouver is located on the traditional unceded territory of the Sḵwx̱wú7mesh (Squamish), xwm θkw ẏ m (Musqueam) and s l ílw ta (Tsleil-Waututh) First Nations. Therefore, any historical anniversary celebration of the City of Vancouver would have had to first and foremost acknowledge the city's existence on 'stolen native land.'[3] It was only in 2014, three years after the celebration of Vancouver's 125th anniversary that

> Vancouver city council formally acknowledged (…) that the city was founded on land that still belongs to three First Nations communities (…). Vancouver's planning, transportation and environment committee unanimously passed a motion […] that these territories were never ceded through treaty, war or surrender.[4] (Coutts 2014)

Despite these complexly fraught conditions, the collaborators in the *Mapping the Everyday. Neighbourhood Claims for the Future* project decided to partake in the year of anniversary celebrations pointedly to make public and raise awareness for the claims for the future made by women throughout the history of the DEWC. Critically, this was done in order to counteract prevailing 'epistemic violence' and its resultant structural silencing (Spivak 1988, p. 280).

The Downtown Eastside Women's Centre
and the Audain Gallery

In what follows, I will provide contextualization for both of the involved institutions: the Downtown Eastside Women's Centre (DEWC) and the Audain Gallery. 'The DEWC is a self-initiated and self-organized space. (...) In many ways, it is an example of bottom-up feminist urbanism. In its day-to-day operation, the centre primarily represents Indigenous and older Chinese women, as well as other women of the Downtown Eastside community.'[5] On the occasion of *Mapping the Everyday. Neighbourhood Claims for the Future*, project partner Cecily Nicholson—a coordinator at the DEWC—described the founding moment via documents revealed through the research at the Centre as follows:

> A friendly drop-in centre with social services and recreational programs available. Women, young and old, with or without children, are welcome. The centre has a homey atmosphere for women to meet one another, talk things over, or get information for specific needs. We encourage women to become aware of their own strength, and provide the resources to help themselves. We are five community workers, including a Native, and Chinese worker. (Nicholson 2011, email to the author)

Founded and incorporated in 1978, the Centre was established in the Downtown Eastside neighbourhood which, since the late 1950s, had witnessed

> gradual marginalization of this community: the streetcars stopped running in the area; the main library moved to a location outside the Downtown Eastside; (...) The lack of affordable housing in other parts of Vancouver drove low-income people to the Downtown Eastside, as did the deinstitutionalization of thousands of psychiatric patients in the 1970s who found no other community willing to accept them (...) It is a culturally diverse community with 48 percent of its population representing visible minority groups, including residents of Chinatown, a large number of First Nations people from across the Americas, and many new immigrants to Canada.[6]

The neighbourhood is renowned for high rates of poverty, drug addiction, high levels of mental illness, prevalence of HIV-AIDS and the disappearance and murder of indigenous women. This district of Vancouver is invariably proclaimed as the 'poorest postal code in Canada' (Bitter 2011, p. 1). The Downtown Eastside area is marked by uneven development and massive gentrification pressures. There are high numbers of Aboriginal and homeless residents, many of them struggling with their vulnerabilisation and their everyday exposure to violence. At the same time, the neighbourhood boasts a long history of community activism—including groups such as the Western Aboriginal Harm Reduction Society, the Survival Sex Workers and the Vancouver Area Network of Drug Users—and also community centres, such as the Carnegie Community Centre or the Gathering Place. The Downtown Eastside Women's Centre is one such group, committed to support and activism.

The 1970s and the following decades witnessed a number of locally specific and complexly interrelated crisis transformations and emancipatory oppositional struggles. During this period, the Downtown Eastside saw deep structural urban transformations. These are Vancouver's local response to global currents of neoliberal urbanization—their capital-centric, developer-driven, and accumulation-oriented version. At the same time, the decades since the 1970s have given rise to a myriad of strong, vocal movements: indigenous political campaigns and claims, women's and feminist organizing, anti-poverty and housing struggles and a large number of different cultural, social and political mobilizations dedicated to producing 'oppositional consciousness' and instigating transformative change (Sandoval 1991). The DEWC is a safe space of everyday support to women in crisis under neoliberal urbanization conditions, and the Centre critically contributes to oppositional consciousness raising. Such support includes warm and nutritious meals just as much as legal or medical counselling, and healing practices like singing or poetry readings. The space allows for women to seek shelter from the violence on the streets just as much as it enables political subjectivization through the sharing of personal experiences, which leads to critical analysis and public claims-making.

Neoliberal urbanization and restructuring always take root locally. The everyday experiences of many of the women who are part of the DEWC are marked by the neoliberal globalized restructuring that reshapes the Downtown Eastside neighbourhood with rising property values and rising house prices driving out low-income and socially vulnerable long-time residents. 'Paradoxically, much of the contemporary political appeal to the "local" actually rests upon arguments regarding allegedly supra-local transformations, such as globalization, the financialization of capital, the erosion of the national state, and the intensification of interspatial competition' (Brenner and Theodore 2002, p. 341). The consequences of globalized neoliberal urban restructuring play out locally. The effects of this bear impact on questions of urban life and survival. It comes at the expense of lives and bodies made increasingly more vulnerable and exposed to structural dispossession and violence rooted in fierce competition over housing rights and access to the neighbourhood's resources.

In 2006, the Power of Women Group at the DEWC organized their first Women's Housing March, which has since taken place annually. On the occasion of the first march, the women put together a factsheet which included the following information:

> The number of homeless people has doubled to approximately 2,174 people in 2005. (…) 30% of those who are homeless are indigenous people. Recent immigrants and refugees have been termed the 'hidden homeless', dispro-portionately living in crowded, sub-standard conditions. Given their uncer-tain legal status and lack of familiarity with Canada, they are the most likely to 'fall between the cracks of welfare' and housing provisions. Women are also among the 'invisible homeless', over-represented in shelters and transi-tional housing.[7]

Many other community groups, labour groups and organizations joined in the march. The research by the group also revealed that 'cuts to income assistance, legal aid, women's centres, attacks on women's advo-cacy and support services, lack of childcare support, rising costs of living and low-income work' have all had devastating impacts on women. According to the Greater Vancouver Regional District (GVRD) Homelessness Count in 2005, there has been 'an increase of 60% in the number of homeless women since the 2002 Count (…).'[8] In their research-based activism and the arguments put forward, the Power of Women Group directly connect the structural victimization and increase in the numbers of homeless women to 'Indigenous Women Struggle against Colonialism, Violence, Racism and Poverty' as well as to 'Women Working in the Sex Trade.'[9]

The Power of Women group are a continuing part of long-term local women's activism. 1970s indigenous women's activism and struggle in Canada was provoked by the traumatic consequences stemming from the 1876 Indian Act. 'In Canada, the 1876 Indian Act redefined Indigenous identity in ways that disenfranchised and dispossessed large numbers of women (…)' (Huhndorf and Suzack 2010, p. 5). Therefore, the long-term implications of colonial dispossession and its legislation have proven to be one of the axes around which Aboriginal women's struggles and indigenous feminism in Canada pivot. As stated on the Canadian *Indigenous Foundations* website:

> The Indian Act has been highly criticized for its gender bias as another means of terminating one's Indian status, thus excluding women from their Aboriginal rights. Legislation stated that a status Indian woman who married a non-Indian man would cease to be an Indian. She would lose her status, and with it, she would lose treaty benefits, health benefits, the right to live on her reserve, the right to inherit her family property, and even the right to be buried on the reserve with her ancestors.[10]

The dual oppression by patriarchy and by colonialism informed indigenous women's resistance and counter-oppression activism. 'In the 1970s, Aboriginal women began organizing to battle the discriminatory legislation.'[11] The traumas of the 1876 Indian Act also include the imposition of sexual colonial politics and their long-term harmful impact on women's lives. 'The sexualization of Indigenous women, (…) an integral part of colonization, worsened the effects of governmental politics and left women particularly vulnerable to violence' (Huhndorf and Suzack 2010, p. 5).

The factsheet assembled on the occasion of the first annual housing march links poverty and homelessness to the enduring structural impact of both the historical and the amended current versions of the Indian Act. 'Poverty amongst indigenous people stems from a legacy of colonial conquest. This has led to massive dispossession of traditional territories, lack of autonomy, and annihilation of cultures and traditions. (…) Almost 60% of Indigenous people now live in urban settings with the erosion of their land base. The majority of Aboriginal women – 72% – live in non-reserve urban areas.'[12]

Many of the women at the DEWC are also actively involved with the annual Feb 14 Women's Memorial March. Between 1978 and 2001, over 60 women disappeared from the Downtown Eastside, many of them sex workers and Aboriginal. 'With over 60 women still missing from Vancouver's Downtown Eastside and the trial of William Pickton, the public has become increasingly aware of the issue of violence against sex workers, reflecting a larger pattern of violent assaults against women, particularly indigenous women.'[13] For years, the missing and murder cases of indigenous women and the trial of serial killer Robert William Pickton was mismanaged. The Women's Memorial March Committee raises awareness with regard to the systemic nature of violence that particularly targets sexualized and racialized women. They organize locally, nationally, and internationally. 'The first women's memorial march was held in 1991 in response to the murder of a Coast Salish woman on Powell Street in Vancouver. (...) Out of this sense of hopelessness and anger came an annual march on Valentine's Day to express compassion, community, and caring for all women in Vancouver's Downtown Eastside, unceded Coast Salish Territories.'[14] The practice also extends to the national raising of awareness, with other memorial marches held across Canada, besides international activism. On the occasion of the 2012 memorial march, the organizers also set out to seek justice internationally. 'The Feb 14th Women's Memorial March Committee and DTES Women's Centre have recently made submissions under Article 8 of the Optional Protocol of the UN Committee on the Elimination of Discrimination Against Women, and are now seeking justice internationally.'[15]

In a 2013 text—at once poem, political activism, and theory—Cecily Nicholson, quotes from the 'Communiqué' written by *Idle No More and Defenders of the Land*, a network of Indigenous communities in land struggle: 'Actively resist violence against women and hold a national inquiry into missing and murdered Indigenous women and girls, and involve Indigenous women in the design, decision-making, process and implementation of this inquiry, as [a step toward] initiating a comprehensive and coordinated national action plan.'[16]

Even though the DEWC is a staunch supporter of women's struggles and women's activism, feminism and feminist practice remain contested territory for many indigenous women. 'As (...) women of colour, both scholars and activists, have long contended, feminism as a political movement and academic practice originated as a means to address the social problems of the white middle classes' (Huhndorf and Suzack 2010, p. 2). Feminism and indigeneity is a contested territory. '(...) the label "Aboriginal feminist" [is] fraught' (Green 2012, p. 16). Feminist practice therefore has to 'acknowledge the fraught historical relationship between Indigenous women and mainstream feminism as it opens discussions about the ways Indigenous women can construct a theory and practice specific to their interests' (Huhndorf and Suczak 2010, p. 5). Yet, it is not only the fraught relationship between feminism and indigeneity that such a project like *Mapping the Everyday. Neighbourhood Claims for the Future* has to be aware of and resistant to, but the equally fraught relationship between capitalism and mainstream feminism which Nancy Fraser has theorized extensively (Fraser 2013, pp. 209–226). 'The urgent task that she [Fraser] sets for feminists is to find the points where neoliberalism and feminism do not so easily converge, and to disrupt the easy passage of feminist critique into its neoliberal double. To her mind, this requires feminists to more fully reconnect their analyses to critiques of capitalist economic processes and with social movements' (Pratt 2013, pp. 120–121). The DEWC's activist research, the women's public manifestations, and their political activism on local urban, federal, cross-Canadian national, and internationally oriented global scale demonstrate that the DEWC connects their struggles not only to critiques of capitalist economic processes, but equally to its entanglement with the histories of colonialism. The DEWC women's investment, in oppositional consciousness raising and in solidarity alliance-building, aims for individual and collective transformative effects.

The Audain Gallery, where the *Mapping the Everyday. Neighbourhood Claims for the Future* exhibition took place, is part of the massive gentrification pressure marking the Downtown Eastside. Significantly, new university infrastructures just as much as contemporary art spaces, redefine image and status of entire neighbourhoods and contribute to rising property values and house prices. In the fall of 2010, the Simon Fraser University School for the Contemporary Arts and the Audain Gallery moved to a downtown campus located at the Woodward's Building. This is a landmark building attended with historical significance, struggles and occupation. Originally built in 1903 for the Woodward's Department Store, the building stood empty after Woodward's bankruptcy in 1993. In fact, it was the 2002 housing occupation—known under the name of Woodsquat—that actually triggered the redevelopment. In 2004, the city of Vancouver selected Westbank Projects/Peterson Investment Group as developers for the project; the architectural design work was assigned to Henriquez Partners Architects. It included market housing units as well as non-market housing units, and an addition to Simon Fraser University's downtown campus. Critical scholarship on gentrification has paid close attention to the contemporary art and higher education institutions as drivers of urban redevelopment and gentrification processes. Therefore, the specific situation of the Audain Gallery—in bringing together both the contemporary art and the campus component in the midst of a major process of gentrification—warrants doubt and provokes conflicts regarding the politics and the ethics of alliance-building with its neighbours.

Sabine Bitter, the Audain Gallery's then director, stated that due to Simon Fraser University's downtown move, 'questions of gentrification, representation, site-specificity, and research ethics have become crucial' (Bitter 2011, p. 1).

CLAIMS FOR THE FUTURE

It is against these complex conditions wrought by the structural effects of historical colonialism and present-day neoliberal urbanization dynamics that the women at the DEWC have sustained their everyday survival practices and their long-standing commitment to activism regarding indigenous rights, housing rights, land rights and women's rights. The newsletters the Centre has issued since its inception are a repository, an archive of the women's work and, most importantly, of their claims. Following my suggestion to work with the Centre's history in order to demonstrate their persistence and their work towards futurity—which can be best understood from their claims—a series of workshops with an ad hoc group[17] at the DEWC provided the research necessary to map the claims from the newsletters, to select them and organize them chronologically for the exhibition. The list of claims were transformed into a text-based wall installation spanning the Audain Gallery's exhibition space as a horizon line. This key feature of the exhibition consisted of the extensive list of claims organized chronologically, going around the walls, in several lines of text on top of each other. All the claims that were presented are included in this text, so they can be read, and heard, again:

Take Back the Night (1979–)
Stop Violence Against Women (1980–)
Our Hearts Go Out (1980–)
In Loving Memory (1980–)
Battered Women's Support Group (1980–)
Banner Making Party (1982)
You are Not Forgotten (1982)
Create a Powerful Force of Change (1984)
East Meets West Social Party (1984)
Know Your Rights workshop (1984)
Hope for the Family (1984)
Support One Another (1985)
Role Models (1985)

Positive Parenting (1985)

Working Women's Drop-In – Ring Buzzer (1985)

A Chance for Women (1985)

We are the Seers, the Healers, the Warriors (1985)

The Common Woman is as Common as a Common Loaf of Bread and Will Rise (1985)

Gather Together (1986)

Free Soup and Bannock (1986)

Take Back Your Power (1986)

Ongoing Social Action (1986)

No drugs or alcohol in the Centre. We don't want a reason for the cops to come here! (1986)

See Some of the Strengths That You Did Not Know You Had (1985)

All Women Band A Benefit Performance—all proceeds to raise money for musical instruments for our Sisters in Oakalla. Women's Event—At the Centre. Free if you are broke

Condoms, street Talk and Badtrick Sheets Available (1986)

Gather Together (1986)

Take Back Your Power (1986)

Share Your Memories (1987)

Decrease the Grief (1987)

Bad Trick Sheets (1987)

Assertiveness with a Beat (1987)

Spruce You Up! Tie-dye to 50s music (1987)

Festival for Foods Parade (1987)

Grassroots Fundraising (1987)

Information and Support Sharing (1987)

No Way to Live (1988)

Take the Next Step (1988)

We Announce Our Solidarity (1988)

The Needs of Women Come First (1988)

Welfare Rates Under Attack (1988)

Tenants Rights Workshop (1988)

Becoming yourself through writing (1988)

Fight for Welfare Rights (1989)

Women's Right to Choose (1989)

Women's Forum (1989)

Willing and Able (1989)

No Homophobia (1989)

No Racism (1989)
Projects Collective (1989)
Fight City Hall (89-present)
On December 19th, approximately 2000 people gathered at City Hall to
  protest rising rents and growing homelessness (1989)
Red Road Warriors (1989)
Menopause Support Group (1989)
Clean and Sober Group meeting (1989)
Recovery (1989)
Family Clean and Sober Group (1989)
Please do not take things that are not yours (1989)
Hold Your Ground (1990)
Sleeping Hummingbirds (1990)
We've Survived the Long Winter (1990)
Always Play Safe (1990)
Impossible Takes a Little Longer (1990)
Their Spirits Live Within Us (1990 –)
Justice for Missing and Murdered Women (1990s)
Justice for Residential School Survivors (1990)
We are also always in need of clothes for women (1990 –)
Campaign to Get Welfare Raised (1991)
Reclaiming Your Power (1991)
Aboriginal Celebrations and Ceremonies (1991)
Sisters in Spirit (1990 –)
The February 14th Women's Memorial March Committee (1992 –)
We are committed to justice (1992 –)
Tools for Change (1994)
A Safe Place for Women (1994)
Grief and Loss Support (1995)
Visualizing Workshops (1995)
Stop the War on the Poor! (1996)
Raise the Rates (1998)
Bad Date Sheets (1998)
Psychiatric Day Program (1999)
Healing Circle (1999)
Make a Wild Woman Out of You (1999)
Popular Education (1999–2003)
End Legislated Poverty (1999–2004)
The Learning Group (2000–02)

Learn how to make something from nothing (stone soup) (2000)
Today in One Circle (2001)
Welcome Home (2001)
We Must Stand Together for Peace Justice, Freedom and Equality (2001)
Honour our Sisters and Grandmothers (2001)
Join Us Women (2001)
Sisters Resist (2001)
Breaking the Silence (2001)
Positive Body Images (2001)
Appropriate Programming (2001)
There is joy in the struggle (2002)
There is joy in the struggle (2002)
Outings Rock Our World (2003)
University Access: Institute of Indigenous Government Canada's First
    Nations College, in Partnership with the DEWC – Tuition Free (2003)
Stop Police Violence (2003)
DTES, I Love (2004)
Stop Attacks on Women (2004)
Rise Up (2005)
Love and Support (2005)
Imagine the woman who honours the face of the goddess in her own
    changing face (2005)
Fight to get power back into women's hands at the Women's Centre (2005)
Donations Committee asking for your help (2005)
Pow Wow (2005)
Celebrate a New Beginning (2006)
Build Community (2006)
[first annual] Women's Housing March (2006)
Our Own Voices: of Pain and Hope (2007)
Vigil and March to Honour Women (2007)
Stop All Forms of Violence Against Women: End Patriarchy! (2007)
Power of Women (2007)
Safe Housing for Women (2007)
An Open Letter to Mayor Sam Sullivan and City Council from Women in
    the Downtown Eastside (July 2, 2007)
DTES Community Meeting at DEWC – Men Welcome. Open to All
    Concerned DTES Residents and Community Members (2007)
March for Women's Housing and March Against Poverty! Elders, Youth,
    Men Welcome Bring Drums and Your Friends (2007)

Stop Child Apprehension, Support Mothers (2008)
We Demand an Inquiry into the Missing Women (2008)
People Are Dying (2008)
Social Housing, Healthcare and Childcare Now! (2008)
No More Evictions and No More Condos! (2008)
Stop Criminalizing the Poor (2008)
End Global Hunger and Poverty (2008)
Affordable and Safe Housing Now! (2009)
Stop Ticketing and Arrests Under Project Civil City (2009)
Fight Rapid Hotel/SRO Closures and Evictions (2009)
Stop Police Brutality (2009)
Housing Now (2010)
In Our Own Voices (2010)
No Olympics on Stolen Native Land! (2010)
People Before Olympic Profits (2010)
Survival, Strength, Sisterhood: Power of Women in the Downtown (2010)
Our Lives, Our Voices: Downtown Eastside women find healing through
    narrative (2010)
Respect Your Elders (2011)
We will be marching to demand action on women's safety (2011)
Women's Coalition of the Downtown Eastside: Women's Safety 24/7
    Women's Coalition of the Gone but not Forgotten (2011)
Downtown Eastside is a newly formed network of women-serving organi-
    zations and women's groups in the Downtown Eastside of Vancouver,
    Coast Salish Territories (2011)
Stop the Pantages Development (2011)
Boycott Sequel 138 (2011)
Gentrifuckation (2011)
Housing for All (2011)
Social Housing, Child Care and Health Care for All! (2011)
No more evictions and no more gentrification in the Downtown Eastside!
    (2011)
Stop criminalizing the poor! (2011)
DTES is Not for Developers (2011)
Many Paths of Our Resistance (2011)
Participant Groups in the Missing Women's Inquiry Pressure Premier
    Clark to Ensure Access and Justice (2011)
Committee Announces Non Participation in Sham Inquiry (2011)

Conclusion

Anniversary celebrations held by cities form part of the official rituals and political routines; they simply reinforce established hegemonic historical claims. However, through the collaboration between the women at the DEWC, the Audain Gallery and myself, claims to the future by indigenous and mostly elderly Chinese immigrant women active at the centre were presented and given attention within Vancouver's 125th anniversary celebrations. This action was made against a backdrop of the sheer complexity of fraught conditions surrounding the anniversary celebration and Vancouver's history, critically given the fact that Vancouver today remains as unceded Coastal Salish territory. When such claims form part of commemoration practices, they become constitutive to resistant historical narratives just as much as they have to be moved forward towards ensuring future change. 'The claims and demands, both current and historical, address issues of poverty, violence and insecurity, social exclusion, the deferral of rights, and the legacy of colonialism.(...) They are also expressions of conviviality and solidarity between women, between women and their neighbourhoods, and between the women of the Centre and their global context' (Krasny 2011, p. 2). Claims for the future imply that there is, in fact, a future to be claimed. Therefore, it is important to consider the act of putting forward claims as an act towards futurity. As the women collectively voice their claims, they enact modes of political subjectivization. Through their claims-making they perform their rights to and their rights of citizenship.

Notes

1. Canadian Pacific Railway, date accessed January 2, 2017.
2. No2010, date accessed January 2, 2017.
3. No2010, accessed January 2, 2017.
4. Coutts, 2014, accessed January 2, 2017.
5. Art and Education Net, date accessed January 2, 2017.
6. Learning Exchange, date accessed January 2, 2017.
7. Carnegie Centre, date accessed January 2, 2017.
8. Carnegie Centre, date accessed January 2, 2017.
9. Carnegie Centre, date accessed June 5, 2016.
10. Indigenous Foundations, date accessed January 2, 2017.
11. Indigenous Foundations, date accessed January 2, 2017.
12. Carnegie Centre, date accessed January 2, 2017.

13. Carnegie Centre, date accessed January 2, 2017.
14. Women's Memorial March, date accessed January 2, 2017.
15. Women's Memorial March, date accessed January 2, 2017.
16. Due to Injuries, date accessed January 2, 2017.
17. This ad hoc group included Stella August, Muriel Brunelle, Dalannah Gail Bowen, Shurli Chan, Pat Haram, Audrey Hill, Suzanne Kilroy, Karen Lahay, Terri Marie, Joan Morelli, Ramona, Sandra, Sara Dell, Sue Lee, Stirling Sexton, Beatrice Starr, Debbie Ventury, Bernice Verde and Deanna Wong (translation).

References

Art and Education Net. http://www.artandeducation.net/announcement/mapping-the-everyday-neighbourhood-claims-for-the-future/. Accessed 2 Jan 2017.

Bitter, S. 2011. Mapping the Everyday. Neighbourhood Claims for the Future. In *Mapping the Everyday: Neighbourhood Claims for the Future*, ed. Audain Gallery., Brochure Published on the Occasion of the Exhibition Held 17 November 2011–25 February 2012. Vancouver: Simon Fraser University.

Brenner, N., and N. Theodore. 2002. *Spaces of Neoliberalism: Urban Restructuring.* Oxford: Wiley-Blackwell.

Canadian Pacific Railway. http://www.cpr.ca/en/about-cp/our-history. Accessed 2 Jan 2017.

Carnegie Centre. http://www.carnegie.vcn.bc.ca/womens-housing-march-draws-large-support?Func=previousthread#id1uxppukq5vsewxuqfjhcjq. Accessed 2 Jan 2017.

Coutts, M. 2014. Vancouver Council Formally Acknowledges City Was Built on Unceded First Nations Territory. *Daily Brew*, June 26. https://ca.news.yahoo.com/blogs/dailybrew/vancouver-council-formally-acknowledges-city-built-unceded-first-220234880.html. Accessed 2 Jan 2017.

Due to Injuries. http://duetoinjuries.com/response-cecily-nicholson/. Accessed 2 Jan 2017.

Fraser, N. 2013. Feminism, Capitalism and the Cunning of History. In *Fortunes of Feminism. From State-Managed Capitalism to Neoliberal Crisis*, 209–226. London/New York: Verso.

Green, J. 2012. *Making Space for Indigenous Feminism*. Winnipeg: Fernwood Publishing.

Huhndorf, Shari M., and Cheryl Suzak. 2010. Indigenous Feminism: Theorizing the Issues. In *Indigenous Women and Feminism. Politics, Activism, Culture*, ed. C. Suczak, S.M. Huhndorf, J. Perreault, and J. Barman, 1–20. Vancouver: UBC Press.

Indigenous Foundations. http://www.Indindigenousfoundations.arts.ubc.ca/home/government-policy/the-indian-act.html. Accessed 2 Jan 2017.

Krasny, E. 2011. Mapping the Everyday. Neighbourhood Claims for the Future. In *Mapping the Everyday: Neighbourhood Claims for the Future*, ed. Audain Gallery, Brochure Published on the Occasion of the Exhibition, Held 17 November 2011–25 February 2012. Vancouver: Simon Fraser University.

Nicholson, C. 2011. E-mail Correspondence with the Author.

No2010. http://www.no2010.com/no-olympics-on-stolen-land/. Accessed 2 Jan 2017.

Pratt, G. 2013. Unsettling Narratives: Global Households, Urban Life and a Politics of Possibility. In *Rethinking Feminist Interventions into the Urban*, ed. L. Peake and M. Rieker, 108–124. London/New York: Routledge.

Sandoval, C. 1991. *Feminist Theory Under Postmodern Conditions: Toward a Theory of Oppositional Consciousness.* Santa Cruz: University of California.

Spivak, G.C. 1988. Can the Subaltern Speak? In *Marxism and the Interpretation of Culture*, ed. C. Nelson and L. Grossberg, 271–313. Urbana: University of Illinois Press.

Suczak, Cheryl, S.M. Huhndorf, J. Perreault, and J. Barman, eds. 2010. *Indigenous Women and Feminism. Politics, Activism, Culture.* Vancouver: UBC Press.

Women's Memorial March. https://womensmemorialmarch.wordpress.com. Accessed 2 Jan 2017.

Spaces of Citizenship

Sergio Tamayo

INTRODUCTION

Today, one way to understand the relationship between politics and culture, particularly in Latin America, is by observing how 'spaces of citizenship' are maintained. This concept emerges from empirical analyses I developed, focusing on Mexico. This opens a further area of research: How is one to reconstruct the formative process of social relations? How might 'spaces of citizenship' be reformulated so that new social subjects might emerge? These questions may appear obvious, but they pose a radically different way to conceive of societies globally—not only through the lens of Western traditions of knowledge in industrialized countries, but also from the perspective of the other 'half' of the world. The efforts of Latin-American scholars have not yet gone far enough in rethinking the social in a different fashion, or at least in a complementary approach taken from established Anglo- and Eurocentric positions.

As Bryan Roberts (1999) argues, struggles for rights of citizenship in Latin America have become the main engine for achieving change in social and political affairs. Nevertheless, in Latin America, this is an entirely new phenomenon. For decades, citizenship did not hold any weight: neither in politics, nor in the national imaginary. Many scholars from Latin America

S. Tamayo (✉)
Metropolitan Autonomous University, Campus Azcapotzalco,
Ciudad de Mexico, Mexico

© The Author(s) 2019   127
P. Hildebrandt et al. (eds.), *Performing Citizenship*, Performance
Philosophy, https://doi.org/10.1007/978-3-319-97502-3_9

therefore reviled this term, considering the emphasis on citizenship to be an ideological weapon deployed by elites to deflect attention from more pressing social inequalities.

However, the economic, technological, political and social changes attending globalization have created an adverse effect. These shifts over-value a handful of concepts in order to provide an absolute explanation for new social realities. Terms such as civil society, citizenship, and democracy are used to replace expressions such as class formation, social inequality, social movements, nationalism, 'the people' or socialism.

We understand that this question sets up a dialectic perspective. As argued by Roberts, the concept of citizenship can easily be subsumed to private or elitist interests, helping render inequalities invisible. However, the concept of citizenship and its specific practices also harbors its own dynamic that has escaped the control of the elites and the state. Citizenship builds on unstable practices, and these produce an unequal battlefield. Furthermore, although the institutional results of these citizenship prac-tices can be defined from above, the social struggle for citizens' rights might also create opportunities from below.

The concept of 'spaces of citizenship' faces this problem directly. In epistemological terms, it can be understood to arise from the uncoupling of the structural dynamics of the world system and historical processes, between system and lifeworld, between structure and agency, between global and local, between universalism and particularism, between objec-tivity and subjectivity. These dichotomies are in fact interfaces of the ten-sion of the social world and not only mere polarizations (see Wallerstein 1987; Habermas 1989; Bourdieu 1989; Wacquant 2002; Giddens 1995; Cohen 1987, 1996; Touraine 1993, among others). Indeed, 'spaces of citizenship' constitute struggles that arise because of the existence of sev-eral levels of action and settings that point out the need for mediation. The balance between such extremes can occur through social action, com-municative action, *habitus*, culture, historical analysis, and the construc-tion of the social subject.

My personal understanding of this takes its starting point from a series of empirical studies, undertaken since 1990, concerning the construction of citizenship in Latin America and Mexico. The concept of citizens' spaces—or 'spaces of citizenship'—has been brought about, not as a theo-retical hypothesis about the social, but rather as the theoretical result of empirical studies (Tamayo 2010). These studies examine the relationship between several pieces of a puzzle: city and citizenship; collective action and citizen participation; the impact of globalization on Latin-American economies and citizen revolts; the contentious politics of several citizenship projects; and the identity formations resulting from these diverse citizenship projects. Such projects often led to a level of social cohesion among specific groups, while excluding others. Indeed, 'spaces of citizenship' can be understood as a battlefield that testifies, sometimes dramatically, to the resistance of domination, inequality and injustice. It is a political, real and metaphoric space; it is the domain where social struggle takes place.

In this article, we will consider three categories that have shaped this approach: citizenship, space and the relationship between citizen practices and the city—bonded to the issues of community and political space. What follows is a definition of 'spaces of citizenship'.

CITIZENSHIP

Latin-American people are experiencing a tremendous identity shift: from proletarian and 'the people', to 'citizen'. The emergence of this new social subject in the era of globalization raises the following question: How has a citizen-based political practice historically transformed and affected cultural conceptions and forms of social organization? Of key importance is the context in which this question emerges. As a semi-peripheral country, Mexico has come abruptly and violently into a new model of growth. Several collective and relevant actors are trying to deal with this new social reality—notably, the state, entrepreneurial organizations and grassroots movements. The answer may be simply that citizens change and affect society through the formation of 'spaces of citizenship'.

In a strict sense, the terms 'collective identity', 'participation' and 'practices of citizenship' are essential in developing this hypothesis, offering a distinctive way to explain the changes that occur at specific points of social formation. Being a citizen comes hand-in-hand with a whole process of identity formation. In his text on citizen culture and consumerism in Latin America, García Canclini (1995) defines citizenship as the fact of sharing social and cultural experiences that provide a sense of belonging to a community. This cultural understanding takes into account the fact that citizen identity is best expressed through solidarity. However, accurate data points out that this cohesion is strengthened by the stigmatization of the foreigner and the *la lutte pour la reconnaissance* (Honneth 2000). Consequently, when we talk about identity, we do not think of an innocent ethical value, but we do assume that it reveals contradictory cultural practices and is born from an unavoidable tension between the included and the excluded. The study of citizen identity has to do with the making of a social subject, but it moves beyond the conceptual mistake of assuming this identity is pre-given or stable. We cannot only explain citizen identity through integration, inclusion and homogeneity, from a single and compact vision. Within a collective identity, citizens confront themselves with difference, exclusion and diversity—both from outside and from within. This tension qualifies different modes of identity and, accordingly, distinctive citizen practices.

To employ Melucci (1996), when individuals fight to change or enlarge citizenship, they are playing out a symbolic questioning of dominant codes. Through this they create a space of struggle, which we consider to be a further way to define 'spaces of citizenship'. This space of struggle is the particular focus of this work.

In a context of inequality and tension, the community defines the rules of participation. This means that various types of citizenship are reflected in social inequalities, the lack of social justice, the allocation of resources, the limits of individual liberties, and the struggle for power (Bauböck 1994). However, the concepts of citizenship and related ideologies (Shafir 1998; Reiner 1995) strive for equality; attainment of this is their utopia. In real terms, this label promoting universal rights serves to simply render inequalities invisible. As Marx explains—later elaborated on by Marshall (1950)—citizenship is just 'a skin of a lion': it can cover up differences among classes, but it can never negate them. One can be a citizen in being a soldier, a trader, an entrepreneur, a worker and/or a student. Such roles become the qualifier of a citizen and define the specificity of the practices and experiences of making citizenship. Thus, citizenship is not unique or fixed. Instead, it means different things for different actors, producing unequal social practices. Citizenship is a shifting process. It is a means, rather than an end, which operates to transform social relations.

Citizenship is unstable because it is thought out, figured out, longed for, and worked out in several ways. Social groups build different citizenship projects that oppose one another, such as political parties or social organizations. These citizenship projects are based on *social practices*, and *different ideas* of citizenship (Dagnino et al. 2010). Some scholars define this as a 'substantive citizenship', in contrast to institutional or formal citizenship (García and Lukes 1999).

The case of Mexico offers further reaffirmation of the three very closely linked dimensions that build citizenship, which together determine existing citizenship projects. These three dimensions define practices and ideas with regard to citizenship. The first dimension is the relationship between the state and civil society; this involves concepts such as nation and nationality, as well as the legal and cultural membership of a community. The second dimension is the process that defines—and redefines—citizen rights that are related to membership and serve to regulate social behavior. Marshall (1950) points out that citizen rights denote the imbalance of social, civil and political citizenship, and the more recent introduction of the cultural dimension of rights by theorists. The third and final dimension is participation, understood as the political process through which one may take part in a community and be involved in the decision-making process: one path toward democratization in a society (Tamayo 2010).

Struggles for citizenship can offer clear depictions. Firstly, they illustrate the social struggle between the state and well-organized groups from civil society. Secondly, citizenship specifically elucidates the struggle between those who demand an increase in rights, and those appealing for the abolition of others. Thirdly, it can show the balance between the regulation of citizen participation, the intensification of the democratization process, and political independence. Struggles for citizenship search for political hegemony (Mouffe 2003); they look for the feasibility of a citizen project, representing a clash of class interests. Furthermore, citizen projects are inevitably under the scrutiny of social actors according to their own vision of the state-civil society relationship, citizens' rights, and the limitations placed on participation.

The case of Mexico offers evidence regarding the nature of changes in political culture and is sourced from the interaction of three social actors: the political elite, the entrepreneurs, and the grassroots movement—all confronting each other based on their own claims and interests. All these actors undertake individual processes to draw on the views of social movements—some from below and the others from above—deriving from the vision of the governing elite and entrepreneurial class, in order to build their citizen projects.

The perspective from below defines citizenship as collective and nationalist, demanding an increase of social rights and promoting broader political participation. By contrast, the perspective from above—of traditional

Social Actors	70-82	82-94
Politic Elites	social	civil-social
	political-civil	political
Economic elite	civil-political	civil-political
	social	social
Social movements	social	social-civil-political
	civil-political	

Fig. 1 Vision and hierarchy of citizen rights and strategy changes during the 1968–1988 period in Mexico, according to social actors. (Source: Tamayo 1999)

liberal conception—looks for an individualistic citizenship. Evidence demonstrates that citizenship means different things for different social actors.

This dynamic can be observed in Fig. 1, showing these changes schematically in Mexico. From 1970 to 1982, the government defined and increased (although under certain limitations) the social rights of the population, privileging them over political and civil rights. In fact, the state intentionally minimized and abandoned civil rights—witnessed in presidential speeches as well as in daily practice—and achieved extreme limits on political rights through the use of corporate control and the absence of democracy within electoral processes. From 1982 to 1994, the emphasis was on civil rights—mostly those linked to private property—freedom of speech and religious liberty. The state tried to have less direct involvement in economics, denying the benefits of its populist predecessors' social policy and supporting demands linked to individual property. There was a general move to restrain social welfare programs.

As for entrepreneurs, they immediately reacted to those changes promoted by the state, compelled by the structural disturbance of the economy. For the first time, they moved politically and as a united class. In constituting for themselves what Touraine (1988, 1981) defines as 'the birth of a social movement', it naturally follows that social policies were the last ones they chose to support. From 1982 to 1992, the strategy and argument of the entrepreneurial class remained largely the same, as did the support for the Mexican bourgeoisie that was contained in their foundational principles. This finally led to an ideological proximity to the government's neo-liberal ideas, each party advocating individual rights without any constraints (Roberts 1995, 2010; Tamayo 1999).

Finally, Fig. 1 shows that the working class and grassroots movement were forced to defend rights that were attained decades ago. This explains why social groups of the 1970s focused on the centralization and prioritization of social and labor rights. With the onset of the economic crisis of the 1980s, their demands become more pressing. The movement fought for land, credits, education, social welfare, and better wages. Social citizenship overlapped dialectically with both civil citizenship—especially human and women's rights (Tamayo 2000)—and political citizenship, especially under electoral participation (López Monjardín 1989, 1986). This scenario led to an open debate in which the grievances of the population were expressed alongside social, civil and political concerns.

Empirical data suggests that several social sectors formed a wide social, democratic and nationalist movement (Tamayo 1999). Their struggle tried to combine and forecast demands from different sectors—including peasants, workers, residents, women, young people and students. With their help, the movement came up with the detail of a broad and nationwide plan that provided for, in the first instance, a huge range of actions. The struggle brought about what is termed a 'space of citizenship'.

As demonstrated, through the survival of a variety of practices and ideas of citizenship, it is not possible to talk about the existence of only one kind of citizenship. However, I do not believe it is accurate to talk about citizenships in a plural way, as some analysts with a postmodern bias do. I consider that there is a citizenship rooted in institutional models and social controls that determine the social and legal behavior of individuals, both on an international and on an intra-national level (Bäubock 1994, 1999; Kymlicka 1996, 1999). Nevertheless, we would do well to pay attention to *practices of citizenship* with reference to all the above-mentioned distinctive collective experiences.

In this regard, there is support for the perspective of Giddens (1995; see also, Cohen 1987) over the way citizenship is constituted. Building on the work of these analysts, citizenship may be articulated in three realms: agency, praxis, and context. Agency refers to those structural attributes of social systems; praxis, to the name of articulated patterns of social interaction; and context describes the situational aspect of these interactions in time and space.[1] Thus, we can say that practices of citizenship are a synthesis of the social experience and struggle of citizens to achieve particular visions of citizenship, and the socio-historical context in which they unfold.

SPACE

The concept of space is essential to the development of the theoretical argument that follows. In political sociology, the immediate reference to space is that given to the public sphere (Habermas 1993; Honneth 1996, 2000; Voirol 2003; Braig and Huffschmid 2009). This is an analytical and abstract concept of the communicative interaction among social actors. 'Spaces of citizenship' have an abstract and metaphorical intention but, alongside this, the space of citizenship exists in both its social and physical dimensions (Bourdieu 1989; Giddens 1995; Wildner 2003; Wildner and Tamayo 2002).

Despite the wide variety of perspectives pertaining to space from many different fields of knowledge,[2] I consider Giddens' view to be the one that affirms the contribution of historical geography to the study of cultural space. The analyst here picks up the contributions of Hägerstrand from geography in the analysis of day-to-day life, suggesting that, in everyday life, individuals associate with each other through entities that emanate from scenarios of interaction. These entities are other agents, indivisible objects (the solid material qualities of the environment of action), divisible matter (air, water, minerals, food) or domains. Domains imply something that Giddens calls a regionalization of a space-time: the movement of life-paths through scenarios of interaction that exhibit various forms of spatial differentiation.

From this outline, Giddens explains the theoretical and methodological meaning of the space-time concept within his notion of agency, praxis, and context in his theory of structuring this. For the specific case of space, the author focuses on the psychological qualities of social agents—as well as interactions to be found in face-to-face situations—both locating those actors in contexts of interaction and extending the inquiry into the inter-weaving of these contexts. In other words, he places interactions in time and space at different levels and scales.

In this complex relationship, our own vision of the function of space is not one of a passive support of objects. Instead, space becomes more of an actor, created through the dynamic relationship between those objects with the power of affecting socialization. Therefore, space is a social prod-uct and it becomes an active and critical part of social organization. Individuals act and think in ways which are always located in time and space. They are beings that inhabit and occupy a place and, in doing so, they become subjects of their own space. According to André Frémon

(1988, quoted in Di Méo 1998), individuals are active, thinking and rational subjects and cannot be considered mere inert objects. They act over space but, at the same time, space conditions sometimes determine their behaviors. An inseparable and permanent relationship exists between living beings and space, which is both real and imaginary (Di Méo 1998, p. 73). Yet, in considering space as a social product, its perception—imaginary, as well as interpreted though the social—is differentiated. This is due to the fact that it represents a society that is not homogeneous in its constitution, nor in its practice. The social, cultural and political position of individuals and groups informs images of space that, furthermore, determine the fashion of its visibility as only partially conceivable, as a collection of many pieces.

The concept of space is useful in re-evaluating expressions of culture in Mexico City. Case studies made in urban contexts constitute a way to continue the exploration of citizenship practices between 1968 and 1988 (Tamayo 1999). Since this time, research has become more spatially defined, contained by the perimeters of the city. The process involves the selection of political events and situations of social interaction in order to observe the collective behavior of citizens in public space. This forms an innovative method to introduce ourselves to the means of portraying the political culture (Tamayo et al. 2015; Tamayo 2016).

There are numerous examples of this; for instance, the influence exerted on the inhabitants of Mexico City by the armed indigenous rebellion from Chiapas, organized by the Zapatista Army of National Liberation (EZLN) in 1994. At the time, civil society demonstrated its stance of non-violence in several ways, and was significantly hard-pressed to reorient political events and governmental authoritarian policies. What happened there was something that I refer to as a *virtual bridge of struggle and communication*, formed by relevant actors of the Lacandona Jungle and the city. Diverse collective actors constituted a space of citizenship in dispute (Tamayo 2002).

After that—between 1995 and 2000—the people of the city began to express themselves in crowded events within the urban space, filling streets and squares. These public demonstrations had their own demands, depicting the political orientation of citizen practices—social rights, civil rights and political rights—around social welfare, justice and electoral transparency. All these issues generated a broad argument about the borderlines of citizen participation, giving birth to a conflictual space of citizenship (Tamayo 2010).

In the later years, this metropolis became the site of strong confrontation between different social and political projects, each of them sustaining a different utopia and a different vision of both city and nation. The city became then a receptacle for nationwide cultural dramas and social or political conflicts; national unions, regional organizations, political movements and indigenous rebellions became manifest, along with other demands from urban local organizations and civic associations. During the first decade of the twenty-first century, political parties centralized this effervescence within electoral campaigns—for example, to elect the President of the Republic and the new Governor for Mexico City—and the grassroots movement intensified huge public protest rallies around the claims of EZLN and other students and social movements.

Thus, public space changed due to several processes (Braig and Huffschmid 2009): a larger political dispute through the vote of the citizens, an organized debate from the legal political parties, an increasingly decisive intervention of the mass media and the ideological handling of public opinion surveys. Public space manifested in the way citizens openly took part in public affairs, even outside of institutional channels. This situation could be observed by the way citizens behaved collectively during public events in relation to several electoral preferences and by the degree of ideological persuasion in the collective imaginary of those political projects. Indeed, several groups and social classes in dispute produced, transformed, and politically appropriated public space.

The study of practices of citizenship shreds the political analysis of the public sphere and brings attention to the meaning of the physical space in relation to politics. Spatializing the public sphere has allowed us to remark on the relationship between the political components of arguments about several city and nation projects; furthermore, about the political (and necessarily physical) ways to appropriate urban space.

With this theoretical basis, I have studied specific cases through ethnographic approaches to the space of citizenship in Mexico. My object of study has focused on two types of case: first, the elections in Mexico have been full of conflict and fraught with violence; second, social protests have multiplied, witnessed in demonstrators taking to the streets of cities (Tamayo 2012).

On the one hand, electoral rallies reflect the articulation of citizenship projects toward popular culture of citizens. Political culture is expressed through interactions and meanings. In short, the elections synthesize symbolic forms of the struggle for power. The situational analysis of the forms of social and symbolic appropriation of public space, both physical and metaphorical, reveals interactions and identities that unfold as a field of deliberation and political confrontation. It is possible to emphasize the above if we compare the forms of political appropriation between political parties, both right and left. The mobilization of citizens takes place around these political projects (Tamayo et al. 2015).

On the other hand, I have studied cases of social protest. I am interested in explaining them as experiences of citizenship. I analyze the way in which protest builds collective identities through the dynamics of contestation, the repertoires of mobilization, and the forms of symbolic appropriation of public space. The larger national demonstration of the EZLN Indians, who went from the jungle to Mexico City, was an exemplary case. This protest produced spaces of political significance at the geographical, urban and ethnographic level. In this way, the Zapatistas constructed a space of citizenship in their passage through the country, and in their arrival to Mexico City. Both these differentiated and connected spaces were reflected in the way they were physically and symbolically appropriated to public space (Tamayo 2016).

SPACES OF CITIZENSHIP

The term 'spaces of citizenship' refers to the conflictual relationship between practices of citizenship and the constitution of the community. Community is understood as an identity produced by people in time and space, as well as a set of interactions among individuals moving at different scales. 'Spaces of citizenship' can be established on an international community level or on a regional or community-based level, such as through the European Union or the North America Free Trade Agreement (cf. Habermas 2001; Bauböck 1994, 1999). 'Spaces of citizenship' are also established at the level of the nation-state within its own territorial boundaries (Brubaker 1992). It is possible to consider a community on an ethnic scale: nations and villages inside a multi-ethnic state (Kymlicka 1996, 1999). The city is another scale of community: the polis as a community of residents (Hill 1994; Isin 1999a, b). Finally, it is possible to consider a community coming from elements of the urban structure—such as the ghettos, neighborhoods and villages of a multicultural city (Rogers 1995).

A community is anchored to processes of identity formation, traditions, culture, language and history. However, it can also be grouped around judicial affairs and certain rules that determine collective behaviors. The main ingredient of community is its political legitimacy. In order to legitimize itself, the community requires an inclusive concept of society that simultaneously allows a radical enactment of exclusion for those who do not belong. Citizenship is a community—like an association—with regulations and norms applied to all. It can only be institutionalized within territorially controlled borders and on the terms of its own membership structure. However, at the heart of its cohesion is culture. Culture implies permanence, belonging and common practices. Accordingly, it involves being physically present within the territorial space. It requires a spatial limit: the boundaries of citizens' struggles.

The city, the community and the nation-state all become the context and the environment of citizen practices. They form the battlefield—the site of several struggles for citizenship. City, national territory or world regions all represent spaces of confrontation in which the distinctive projects of city, citizenship and nation are played out.

More precisely, the city acquires a different connotation in the analysis of citizenship. The city is a primary space where community is formed. As a space, the city is a relational product of its components: architecture, facilities, images and landscapes, materiality and citizens. The city can also be thought of as a container for activity, a three-dimensional context for social action. However, at the same time, it is much more than that. It becomes, as a fundamental part of daily life, where the demand for citizenship can be made manifest as a result of political action.

The city is a place to stay. The city obtains significance when it is perceived, used, practiced, interpreted and qualified. Whether a city is large or small, beautiful or ugly, conservative or liberal, violent or safe, it is the context in which social identities are formed and expressed. A community begins, and can be qualified as a collectivity where resources and power are allocated.

As we have seen, projects of citizenship are collective aspirations which generate citizens' actions, ideas and utopias about the future of the social. Space, either within the city or the nation, becomes the battlefield for such aspirations, transforming them into 'spaces of citizenship'. This battlefield is not always visible, for it is not an institution in itself, but a situation of tension and conflict. This is a space of transition and transgression.

In Mexico, a broadened space for citizenship was created over a twenty-year period: from 1968—when the student movement rose—until 1988, when the elected President Carlos Salinas de Gortari initiated the neoliberal Mexican project. The most important feature of this transition was the presence of deep changes in the political economy that modified older relationships with other countries, creating new international circuits on the level of larger cities. According to Giddens (1995), this change was not only a result of the structural properties of the social system, but of articulated patterns of social interactions and the situational specificity of these interactions.

Objective factors caused this crisis, but the social response and resistance had an eminently subjective character (Mandel 1980). The space of citizenship created then was outlined as a transition for transgressing institutions understood as the very essence of the organization of social life. 'Spaces of citizenship' as an emerging movement invaded day-to-day life in a creative, euphoric fashion, through continuous social effervescence and explosive energy. The changes that took place were sometimes suggested or enforced by institutional commands, but they were always a result of social antagonisms uncontrolled by the system (Mouffe 2003; Norris 1999).

Let us go back to the original idea of space at its levels of city and national territory, and try to link it to the Mexican experience. There is the fact that citizen space was a political realm, created through appropriation—by citizens—of public space. Citizens interacted and expressed themselves within the physical space. Accordingly, citizens built a relational space that acquired new meanings for the population. It does not matter how different social groups express themselves in various cities; if the objectives are the same, the communicational flows multiply. Thus, a network of actions is produced from the concrete space of a locality. An intermediate-level space is constituted (the so-called mesolevel networks), developing broadcasting processes, in a sense more historical and geographical.[3] The citizen, in his or her political action, inhabits and appropriates public space collectively and politically on an interpersonal level, but individuals are also capable of thinking globally.

Public space acquires meaning because it is symbolically charged with the ideas and representations of groups of citizens; but it also is significant because it is a concrete, practiced space, established by citizens. In this space, several citizen identities can be formed and displayed. It is the scene for the achievement of citizens as political beings. The city or the community, talking about space, is just that: a space that is qualified by its characteristics and practices of citizenship.

This idea of citizen space is comparable with Pierre Bourdieu's concept of 'social space' (1989). Let us say that social space represents the social world constituted by objective material elements, as well as by subjective representations; by the social status of classes within that social space, as well as its cultural expressions. Thus, citizen space is that world of citizenship made of objective material elements—the political and symbolic appropriation of a square, public demonstrations on streets, the repertoire of social mobilizations (see also Tilly 1995 and McAdam et al. 2003)—as well as the representations, perceptions and ideas of citizenship. Hence, citizen spaces are objective as well as subjective. They are objectively constituted on two levels: first, the social appropriation of the physical space involving objects, architectures, regions, city networks and individuals who legitimize such a space; second, the city, the region, the community and the nation become objects to be claimed by citizens—the right to the city, to self-determination, the right to sovereignty and the right for cultural autonomy.

On the other hand, collective actors build spaces of citizenship subjectively because they perform, imagine and interpret them. As a result, spaces of citizenship are built in a social and in a political fashion. They are changing all the time, and they are dependent on the result of social confrontations. They are simultaneously both spaces of interaction and spaces of argumentation (Alejandro 1993).

FINAL REMARKS

The concept of 'spaces of citizenship' is useful in order to understand various citizen-based practices generated within communities and in cities. On the one hand, 'spaces of citizenship' represent spaces produced by the idea of political community, such as the polis. On the other hand, we understand the city as the immediate place for the exercise of citizen rights.

Spaces of citizenship are the result of social struggles. For this reason, they do not respond to fixed and untouched attributes. Spaces of citizenship are a product out of actions and imaginaries of individuals acting on the social.

The concurrence between city (or community) and citizenship provides a way to understand the social and symbolic production of citizen spaces. The analysis of spaces of citizenship can indicate the complex correspondence between city as space and citizenship as political, social and cultural practice.

NOTES

1. This triadic relationship has very important methodological connotations. In the latest works, a different methodology has been applied, based on the experience of the Manchester School (cf. Hannerz 1986) and Thompson's depth ethnography (1993). Both authors underline the link between the objective and subjective aspects through context. In empirical matters, it can be expressed in this way: the relationship between ethnographic space, hermeneutics, and the socio-historical context (see Tamayo and López-Saavedra 2012).

2. The notion of space has been defined by Physics, Mathematics, Landscape Architecture, Geography, Architecture, Urban Studies, Music, Dance, Art, and so on.

3. A good example of this relational level can be found in the analysis made by Hedströn et al. (2000), recovering the notion of mesolevel networks to broadcast the social movements and political party ideologies.

REFERENCES

Alejandro, Roberto. 1993. *Hermeneutics, Citizenship, and the Public Sphere.* New York: State University of New York Press.

Bauböck, Rainer. 1994. *Transnational Citizenship: Membership and Rights in International Migration.* Aldershot: Edward Elgar.

———. 1999. Liberal Justifications for Ethnic Group Rights. In *Multicultural Questions,* ed. Christian Joppke and Steven Lukes, 133–157. Oxford: Oxford University Press.

Bourdieu, Pierre. 1989 [1984]. *Distinction, a Social Critique of the Judgement of Taste.* Cambridge, MA: Harvard University Press.

Braig, Marianne, and Anne Huffschmid, eds. 2009. *Los poderes de lo público. Debates, espacios y actores en América Latina.* Madrid: Iberoamericana/ Vervuert.

Brubaker, Rogers. 1992. *Citizenship and Nationhood in France and Germany.* Cambridge, MA: Harvard University Press.

Cohen, Ira J. 1987. Structuration Theory and Social Praxis. In *Social Theory Today,* ed. A. Giddens and J.H. Turner. Stanford: Stanford University Press.

———. 1996. *Teoría de la estructuración, Anthony Giddens y la Constitución de la Vida Social.* México: UAM; [orig. Engl. Cohen, Ira J. 1989. *Structuration Theory: Anthony Giddens and the Constitution of Social Life.* London/New York: Macmillan/St. Martin's Press.].

Dagnino, Evelina, Alberto J. Olvera, and Aldo Panfichi, eds. 2010 [2006]. *La disputa por la construcción democrática en América Latina.* México: FCE, CIESAS and Universidad Veracruzana.

Di Méo, Guy, ed. 1998. *Geógraphie sociale et territoires.* Paris: Nathan Université.

Frémont, André. 1988. *France, géographie d'une société.* Paris: Flammarion.

García, Soledad, and Steves Lukes, eds. 1999. *Ciudadanía justicia social, identidad y participación.* Madrid: Editorial Siglo XXI.

García Canclini, Nestor. 1995. *Consumidores y ciudadanos, conflictos multiculturales de la globalización.* México: Editorial Grijalbo; [orig. Engl. García Canclini, Nestor. 2001. *Consumers and Citizens, Globalization and Multicultural Conflicts.* Minneapolis: University of Minnesota Press.].

Giddens, Anthony. 1995. *La Constitución de la Sociedad, bases para la teoría de la estructuración.* Buenos Aires: Amorrortu, reimpresión 1998; [orig. Engl, Giddens, Anthony. 1984. *The Constitution of Society, Outline of the Theory of Structuration.* Berkeley: University of California Press.].

Habermas, Jürgen. 1989. *The Theory of Communicative Action, Volume II, Lifeworld and System: A Critique of Functionalist Reason.* Boston: Beacon Press.

———— 1993. *L'espace public.* Trans. Marc B. De Launay. Paris: Payot; [orig. Ger. Habermas, Jürgen. 1962. *The Structural Transformation of the Public Sphere: An Inquiry into a Category of Bourgeois Society.* Trans. Thomas Burger. Cambridge, MA: The MIT Press. English Translation 1989.].

————. 2001. Por qué Europa necesita una constitución. *New Left Review,* No. 11. Madrid; [orig. Engl. Habermas, Jürgen (2001). Why Europe Needs A Constitution. *New Left Review,* No. 11, 5–26.].

Hannerz, Ulf. 1986. *Exploración de la Ciudad.* México: Fondo de Cultura Económica; [orig. Engl. Hannerz, Ulf. 1980. *Exploring the City: Inquiries Toward an Urban Anthropology.* New York City: Columbia University Press.].

Hedström, P., R. Sandell, and Ch. Stern. 2000. Mesolevel Networks and the Diffusion of Social Movements: The Case of the Swedish Social Democratic Party. *American Journal of Sociology* 106 (1): 145–172.

Hill, Dilys M. 1994. *Citizens and Cities Urban Policy in the 1990s.* London: Harvester Wheatsheaf Publishing.

Honneth, Axel. 1996. La dynamique sociale du mépris. D'où parle une théorie critique de la société? In *Habermas, la raison, la critique,* ed. Ch. Bouchindhomme and R. Rochlitz. Paris: Cerf.

————. 2000. *La lutte pour la reconnaissance.* Paris: Cerf.

Isin, Engin F. 1999a. Introduction: Cities and Citizenship in a Global Age. *Citizenship Studies* 3(2): 165–171. London: Carfax Publishing.

————. 1999b. Citizenship, Class and the Global City. *Citizenship Studies* 3(2): 165–171. London: Carfax Publishing.

Kymlicka, Will. 1996. *Ciudadanía multicultural* [Multicultural Citizenship]. Barcelona: Editorial Paidós Ibérica S.A.; [orig. Engl. Kymlicka, Will. 1996. *Multicultural Citizenship: A Liberal Theory of Minority Rights.* Oxford: Clarendon Press.].

———. 1999. Nacionalismo Minoritario dentro de las democracias liberales. In *Ciudadanía justicia social, Identidad y participación*, ed. García Soledad and Lukes Steven. Madrid: Editorial Siglo XXI.

López Monjardín, A. 1986. *La lucha por los ayuntamientos: una utopía viable*. México: siglo XXI Editores e IIS-UNAM.

———. 1989. Las mil y una micro-rebeliones. *Ciudades* 2: 10–18.

Mandel, Ernest. 1980. *Long Waves of Capitalist Development. The Marxist Interpretation*. New York: Cambridge University Press.

Marshall, Thomas H. 1950. *Citizenship and Social Class and Other Essays*. Cambridge: Cambridge University Press.

McAdam, D., S. Tarrow, and Ch. Tilly. 2003 [2001]. *Dynamics of Contention*. Cambridge: Cambridge University Press.

Melucci, Alberto. 1996. *Challenging Codes, Collective Action in the Information Age*. Cambridge: Cambridge University Press.

Mouffe, Chantal. 2003. *La Paradoja Democrática*. Barcelona: gedisa editorial [orig. Engl. Mouffe, Chantal. 2000. *The Democratic Paradox*. London: Verso.].

Norris, Pippa, ed. 1999. *Critical Citizens, Global Support for Democratic Governance*. Oxford: Oxford University Press.

Roberts, Bryan. 1995. *The Making of Citizens*. London: Arnold.

———. 1999. Presentación. In Los veinte octubres mexicanos, ciudadanías e identidades, ed. Sergio Tamayo. México: Universidad Autónoma Metropolitana-Azcapotzalco [orig. Engl. Roberts, Bryan. 1994. Presentation. In *The 20 Mexican Octobers: A Study of Citizenship and Social Movements*, ed. Sergio Tamayo. Austin: University of Texas at Austin.].

———. 2010. ¿Ciudades manejables? La urbanización latinoamericana en el nuevo milenio. In *Sistema Mundial y nuevas geografías*, coords. Alfie Miriam, Iván Azuara, Carmen Bueno, Margarita Pérez Negrete, and Sergio Tamayo, 251–294. México: Universidad Iberoamericana, Universidad Autónoma Metropolitana, unidad Cuajimalpa y unidad Azcapotzalco.

Rogers, Alisdair. 1995. Cinco de mayo and 15 January: Contrasting Situations in a Mixed Ethnic Neighbourhood. In *The Urban Context. Ethnicity, Social Networks and Situational Analysis*, dir. Alisdair Rogers, and Steven Vertovec. Oxford: Berg Publishers.

Shafir, Gerson, ed. 1998. *The Citizenship Debates. A Reader*. Minneapolis: University of Minnesota Press.

Tamayo, Sergio. 1999. *Los veinte octubres mexicanos, ciudadanías e identidades colectivas*. (The Twenty Mexican Octobers). México: Universidad Autónoma Metropolitana, Azcapotzalco; [orig. Engl. Tamayo, Sergio. 1994. *The 20 Mexican Octobers: A Study of Citizenship and Social Movements*. Austin: University of Texas at Austin.].

———. 2000. La ciudadanía civil en el México de la transición: mujeres, derechos humanos y religión. *Revista Mexicana de Sociología* 62 (1): 61–97.

———. 2002. Los doce días que conmovieron la ciudad de México: impacto político y persuasión simbólica de los neozapatistas. *Secuencia* 54: 88–113.

———. 2010. *Crítica de la Ciudadanía.* México: UAM.

———. 2012. Cuando la sociología se encuentra con la etnografía. Una metodología multidimensional del análisis situacional. In *Apropiación Política del Espacio Pública. Miradas etnográficas de las campañas electorales en México 2006*, eds. Sergio Tamayo, y Nicolasa López-Saavedra. México: Instituto Federal Electoral IFE y Universidad Autónoma Metropolitana, Azcapotzalco.

———. 2016. *Espacios y repertorios de la protesta.* México: Red Mexicana de Estudios de los Movimientos Sociales; CONACYT; Universidad Autónoma Metropolitana, Azcapotzalco; Editorial Colofón.

Tamayo, Sergio, and Nicolasa López-Saavedra. 2012. *Apropiación Política del Espacio Pública. Miradas etnográficas de las campañas electorales en México 2006.* México: Instituto Federal Electoral IFE y Universidad Autónoma Metropolitana, Azcapotzalco.

Tamayo, Sergio, Nicolasa López-Saavedra, and Kathrin Wildner. 2015. *Siluetas y contornos de un sufragio.* México: Universidad Autónoma Metropolitana, unidad Azcapotzalco.

Thompson, John B. 1993. *Ideología y cultura moderna. Teoría crítica social en la era de la comunicación de masas.* México: Universidad Autónoma Metropolitana, Xochimilco; [orig. Engl. Thompson, John B. 1990. *Ideology and Modern Culture: Critical Social Theory in the Era of Mass Communication.* Cambridge: Polity Press.].

Tilly, Charles. 1995. Los movimientos sociales como agrupaciones históricamente específicas de actuaciones políticas. *Sociológica* 10 (28): 13–36. UAM/Azcapotzalco.

Touraine, Alain. 1981. *The Voice and the Eye: An Analysis of Social Movements.* Cambridge: Cambridge University Press.

———. 1988. *Return of the Actor: Social Theory in Postindustrial Society.* Minneapolis: University of Minnesota Press.

———. 1993. *Crítica de la Modernidad.* México: Fondo de Cultura Económica.

Voirol, O. 2003. L'espace public et les luttes pour la reconnaissance. De Habermas à Honneth. In *Le public en action. Usages et limites de la notion d'espace public en sciences sociales*, ed. C. Barril et al. Paris: L'Harmattan.

Wacquant, Loïc. 2002. De l'idéologie á la violence symbolique: culture, classe et conscience chez Marx et Bourdieu. In *Les Sociologies critiques du capitalisme*, ed. Jean Lojkine. Paris: Presses Universitaires de France, PUF.

Wallerstein, Immanuell. 1987. World System Analysis. In *Social Theory Today*, ed. A. Giddens and J.H. Turner. Stanford: Stanford University Press.

Wildner, Kathrin. 2003. *Zócalo – Die Mitte der Stadt Mexiko: Ethnographie eines Platzes.* Berlin: Reimer.

Wildner, Kathrin, and Sergio Tamayo. 2002. Orte der Globalisierung, eine architektonische und ethnologische Betrachtung der Stadt México. *Asien, Afrika Lateinamerika* 13: 251–268.

Urban Citizenship: Spaces for Enacting Rights

Kathrin Wildner

In autumn 2015, one of many demonstrations in Hamburg caught my particular attention. It was not so much the size of the 'Never Mind the Papers'[1] demonstration that was impressive, it was the dynamics: the broad range of participants, the diversity of languages, posters and signs. It was the first sizeable demonstration that came at the end of the 'long summer of migration' (see Hess et al. 2016). The protest was organized by a coalition of the refugee movement and its supporters, including many newcomers, refugees and migrants who lived in Hamburg. After the first month of a collapsing border regime with people continuously arriving—crossing the Mediterranean Sea and national borders in Eastern Europe (Hess et al. 2016, p. 6)—a fairly intense state of emergency was present in most big cities within (northern) Europe. Receiving thousands of people daily led to a lack of shelter and basic provisions. At the same time, an incredible mobilization of voluntary support and solidarity substituted or supplemented the failing local institutions (Mokre 2015). By November 2015, the situation was slowly changing; the initial days of emergency were left behind and everyday life had to be faced. The newly arrived began organizing with other groups of refugees and migrants and engaging

K. Wildner (✉)
HafenCity University Hamburg, Hamburg, Germany
e-mail: wildner@hcu-hamburg.de

© The Author(s) 2019
P. Hildebrandt et al. (eds.), *Performing Citizenship*, Performance
Philosophy, https://doi.org/10.1007/978-3-319-97502-3_10

more directly with the city. This also involved claiming their rights to social and political participation. Political participation in this compilation is discussed as one of the conditions for citizenship; this is precisely how I would like to frame it here: citizenship not as a formal, institutional and normative arrangement made by national governments, but as an active process of doing and negotiating, performed by diverse groups claiming the right to participate (see Isin 2017; Cvejic and Vujanovic 2015; Lebuhn 2013).

At the time of the refugee struggle, I was involved in a project on urban learning. The *metroZones school of urban action*[2] was a self-organized, model project for political education and critical urban reflection; a think-tank for perception and discussion, for theory and urban debates, for practical tools and urban interventions. Focusing on questions surrounding the production of urban space, the refugee movement was an important aspect—looking at the ways in which new forms of appropriation, negotiation and citizenship in urban space were invented and, in diverse ways, leading to a re-politicization of the urban debate (Hess and Lebuhn 2014, Lanz 2015, p. 487).

Based on the hypothesis that citizenship is a performative act (Isin 2017, p. 501ff.), I would like to have a closer look at the spatial conditions for acts of citizenship: How and which kinds of urban situations can facilitate or prevent accessibility to the city? Are there possible spaces where citizenship might be provided or invented? How can citizenship be performed? Are there certain tools, skills and expertise required in performing citizenship? And if there are certain spaces which might facilitate practices of citizenship, how can citizenship be enacted in those spaces? How can citizenship as a practice be learned?

What role could the *metro Zones school for urban action* play in providing space and tools for debates and interventions to politicize the urban?

In order to reflect on some of these questions, I will focus on a certain moment and discussion of the *metroZones school for urban action*. The text is a compilation of questions and ideas connected to each other; it is not a finished analysis. In the same way, the drawings by artist Eric Göngrich are to be read as graphic *comments*, in dialogue with the text (Fig. 1).[3]

THE METROZONES SCHOOL FOR URBAN ACTION

The *metroZones school for urban action* was born out of cooperation between the Hamburg-based initiative *dock europe* and *metroZones – center of urban affairs* from Berlin. Over a period of two years, a wide range of

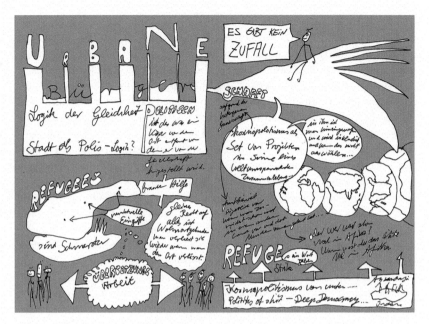

Fig. 1 This work by Eric Göngrich comments on the diverse claims of a cosmopolitical city and the right to public space, interpreting the everyday practices of refugees as political protest. (*metroZones school for urban action*, November 2015)

urban actors, activists and other urban citizens met in Berlin und Hamburg to discuss, and put into practice, a number of conceptual ideas and methodological tools from critical urban studies for the purpose of urban explorations and interventions beyond academia.[4]

Therefore, the school actively oriented itself towards those urban dwellers and activists who were curious to think about urban practices in dialogue, to learn from one another in order to connect various urban skills, experiences and expertise. Understanding the city as a cosmo-polis, made up of people arriving from very different global contexts, we asked ourselves how negotiate spaces of acting and belonging. Urban action here is understood in the sense of the German term *Handeln*; it refers to the act of negotiating, to be distinguished from working or producing. In the meaning of Hanna Arendt's concept of *Handeln*, acting is understood as a process of communication and primarily as a political interaction which takes place in public space (Arendt 1998).

For six months, the participants of the *metroZones school* met continuously—at events such as public lectures, reading circles and discussion 'salons', partaking in practical exercises in workshop sessions and attending a four-day summer camp. The combination of theoretical and practical approaches, conceptual as well as methodological tools, exercises and performative enactments in public space, produced various formats and situations for collective reflection on urban experiences and practices. The questions and discussions revolved around issues of production and configuration of urban spaces on different scales: the effect of collective perceptions and actions on everyday life as well as the invention of strategies and tactics as modes of [urban] citizenship.

Crossing boundaries between disciplines—in the reclaiming of those border zones of context between everyday practices and activism, art and science, political and urban education—the *metroZones school* experimented with diverse formats of urban learning. We understand urban learning as meaning practices and interactions through which knowledge is created, contested and transformed (McFarlane 2011). This production of knowledge, which takes place beyond academic, cultural or education institutions, is seen as a collaborative process of self-empowerment. Densities, diversities and unsettledness—considered to be predominantly urban—are made productive. Therefore, urban learning needs to address different speeds, ways of speaking and body languages. Precisely *through* disruption—of routines, critical reflection on situations usually taken to be self-evident, attempts at de-normalization and alienation—potential for (social) change might emerge. This way, urban learning and knowledge production—useful in everyday practices as well as political action—become urban strategies in and of themselves.

Aside from questions of the potentials and limitations of the format of a school—with its corresponding hierarchies between lecturer and learner, classroom and public space—one of the main questions arising from our experiment was: how the school could position itself within pre-existing political structures, or as a political structure in its own right. Could the school provide a space to act as (urban) citizens?

THE DEMONSTRATION 'NEVER MIND THE PAPERS'

In November 2015, the alliance 'Right to the City – Never Mind the Papers' initiated a demonstration in Hamburg, focussing on the everyday situation and the necessity of political participation for the newly arrived.

The call for the demonstration asserted that the basic condition of political participation was a human right equal to the right to adequate shelter, the right to work, access to education and medical care.[5] Under the slogan 'Refugees Welcome means Equal Rights for All!', about 7000 people took part.

Months before the demonstration, the coalition of self-organized migrant groups and supporters concentrated on mobilizing people. Beside a series of networking and organizing meetings of the involved initiatives, inside the refugee camps, claims were discussed, slogans invented and posters created; speech workshops were organized to practise the use of microphones as well as shuttle buses to transport people from their accommodation so they might participate actively in the demonstration.

The demonstration 'Never Mind the Papers' in November 2015 coincided with the workshop weekend of the *metroZones School for urban action* in Hamburg. As the subject matter of the weekend involved reflection on public space and urban intervention (see Wildner 2003; Yudice 2005), the demonstration seemed to be a perfect source (and cause) to discuss and rehearse diverse aspects of urban action. Such questions arising

Figs. 2 and 3 Erik Göngrich visualizes public space as a fragmented space of negotiation, art in public space is seen as a box composed of practices, places, activities, situations, and stories. (*metroZones school for urban action*, November 2015)

as: What is public space? What kind of tools and instruments might be helpful to intervene in public space? How can they be practised and implemented? (Figs. 2 and 3)

SPACES AND STRATEGIES OF ENGAGEMENT

By means of theoretical inputs and lectures, we started to have a closer look at various spatial settings and events, looking at discussion in public space as a mode of negotiation between contradictory positions (Delgado 1999; Wildner 2003). We identified the demonstration as a well-established means of public political intervention, whereby civil society practices collectivity on the streets and dissent is made visible. Alongside the discussion of concepts, a main focus for the school lay in identifying tools and practices to intervene or generate visibility in public space (Fig. 4).

At the school workshop, we split into three groups to work with different perspectives. One group decided to take the perspective of observation. Under the guidance of the cultural scientist Anne Huffschmid, this group prepared a series of questions and a variety of formats of notation (photography, mapping, use of note-taking, sound recording, in order to

Fig. 4 Eric Göngrich depicts urban intervention as a rehearsal stage, a possibility or a city marketing process. (*metroZones school for urban action*, November 2015)

carry out participant observation at the demonstration. Spatial settings of the route and material elements (sound trucks, banners, posters) as well as slogans and shouting were registered—producing a kind of archive of collected of elements of protest culture, looking at participating groups and different ways to perform participation at the demonstration.

Who is giving a speech? About what, and where? Who is invited to talk? And who claims the right to speak?

The idea of this approach was to create a register that later could be used for a discourse-analytical observation, going beyond the concrete situation of the demonstration in Hamburg. The register of elements become a manifested inventory of politics of participation that is to be analysed in the contexts of ongoing conceptual debates on the potential and limits of urban citizenship (Lebuhn 2015) (Fig. 5).

A second group worked on the topic of performative speech-acts as interventions in public space.[6] In this workshop, choreographer Liz Rech and mediator Petra Barz reflected on the performative aspects as corporal interventions in public space. Using examples of artistic urban interven-

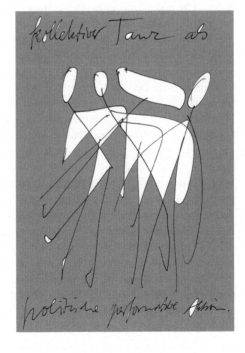

Fig. 5 The drawing by Eric Göngrich evokes a mutual body, naming the collective dance as a political performative action. (*metroZones school for urban action*, November 2015)

tion, they discussed the diversity of performances and activism conducted in public space. By way of practical input, they provided technical and vocal training. Some of the participants of the workshop were unused to speaking out loudly and, during the workshop, experienced their own voice in this way for the first time.

At the demonstration, some of the group took a closer look at the sound truck and the moderator group. This group not only moderated the well-prepared speeches by members of the diverse communities but, during the march, a mobile microphone was also used, allowing people on the street to participate by actively speaking of their situations—being given a voice and being heard. Through the school's exercise at the demonstration, participants experienced the importance of speech and bodily presence when participating politically in public space. Alongside achieving an experience of collectivity, this moment supported the individual presence in public space as an important moment of participation.

A third group on this weekend was guided by Erik Göngrich.[7] As an architect and artist, Erik was especially interested to develop tools that utilized writing and drawing as material elements to intervene into public space. The workshop began with some drawing exercises, producing simple protest boards that participants then carried into the outside space.

What do I want to say? What happens if I carry my protest board—a slogan as a statement—into public space? How visible or vulnerable do I become?

Initially, the boards were tested out in the garden and streets around the workshop space, a cultural centre in Wilhelmsburg on the periphery of Hamburg. That Friday evening, the neighbourhood was characterized by everyday life, with no apparent reason for protest or demonstration. This meant that the action became something of an artistic intervention, which left some participants (a number of whom did not want to take their boards into public space) feeling even more vulnerable. This situation produced discussion full of controversy around the question of how the *metroZones school* could and should take part in the demonstration the next day. In particular, the meaning of intervention was discussed: What kind of slogans could be invented, which message would be appropriated— and, in particular, would it be a misuse of the refugee cause to make an intervention as a part of the *metroZones school*? Finally, some members of the group decided to go to the marketplace in the neighbourhood, talking to the people about the demonstration and the situation of the refugees, offering to write a message on a board composed by their conversation partners and bring it to the demonstration in the city centre the next day. Motivated by positive responses, eventually, the school's participants did indeed take part in the demonstration, bringing messages from the periphery of the city to the centre. Again, questions surrounding accessibility, visibility and possible acts of participation became subjects of discussion.

URBAN CITIZENSHIP ENACTED

The different examples of the *metroZones school*, in the context of the demonstration, showed certain conditions of negotiating urban space as moments of performing citizenship. Taking into account the idea that people become citizens through their participation in the conception, construction and negotiation of space (Irazabal 2008, p. 15), certain configurations of public space and elements for citizenship were pointed out.

We agree: People become citizens when they act as political subjects. One of the fundamental characteristics of a political subject is to make claims for rights (Isin 2017, p. 501).

Hannah Arendt's phrase 'the right to have rights' (Arendt 1998), which addresses the right to be part of a political community, is here pushed further. The right to make claims for rights goes beyond the surface concessions of 'integration'. Instead, it marks an active positioning of the subject by way of *doing* things, such as claiming rights (Isin 2017).

In this sense, citizenship is not understood as a top-down arrangement made by national governments—so called 'paper citizenship'—but as an active process of doing and negotiating, in the sense of a *performed* citizenship (Isin 2017, p. 504). Re-conceptualizing the notion of citizenship means shifting its centre from the state to the people; stressing pluralist models; and including participatory, inclusive and insurgent definitions of citizenship (Miraftab and Wills 2005, p. 202). This understanding of citizenship unfolds over time. Since we understand the moment of acting or engaging as a fundamental moment in which citizenship comes into play, we can define citizenship as a time-based and ongoing process of negotiation (see the introduction to this volume). Citizenship here is not a formal—but a substantive position—with bearing on an array of civil, political, social economic rights, including rights to shelter, water, education, and so on (Miraftab and Wills 2005, p. 201). At the same time, this concept of citizenship is not focused on an endpoint—the achieved status—but is a permanent debate, a temporary and changing condition, acted out in time and space.

To understand the act of citizenship as a performative act, we have to look carefully at the time and space in which these performances are acted out, or in Isin's words, 'look at the performing acts through which people become citizens in exercising or claiming rights and duties' (Isin 2017, p. 520). A demonstration represents a temporary space in which citizenship is enacted as a right to speak and be heard, to participate, to be part of a multitude. The demonstration that came out of the refugee movement—discussed above—'Never Mind the Papers', provided such a space for those who are excluded from the basic rights of state citizenship. By performing speaking-acts on the street, they 'transform conventions by enacting provocative acts' (Isin 2017); the refugees' struggles for rights are made public. In this moment, re-politicizing the urban debate (Lanz 2015, p. 487), they become citizens through their actions.

Here, public space comes into play: through the demonstration, participants collectively become manifest in urban space, turning the streets into a stage for their claims, visible for everybody to see, 'transform[ing] them into temporary places of urban citizenship' (Lanz 2016, p. 489). The appropriation of the streets by masses of people, right in the middle of Hamburg's downtown shopping district, waving colourful banners, shouting slogans and eliciting reactions from passers-by, succeeded in creating—despite the heterogeneity of the participants—at least a momentary sense of common struggle and collectivity.

Among urban practices, the demonstration is a ritualized and sometimes spectacular event. Following Engin Isin's argument for 'acts of citizenship as quotidian enactments, which might lack the visibility of certain performative acts but nevertheless can be consequential' (Isin 2017, p. 509), we might look in more detail to the collective appropriation of urban public spaces; for example, in the playing out around the tent of the 'Lampedusa in Hamburg' group at the central station, or the dynamics of the former self-organized refugee protest camp at Oranienplatz in Berlin (Fontanari 2016). In these cases, the everyday production of space in the city reflects a heterogeneous and diverse society, seemingly tying together those central elements of everyday practice that constitute possible versions of a continuous urban citizenship (Lanz 2015, p. 489). With the *metroZones school for urban action*, a situation was created to reflect upon urban spaces and urban citizenship as a localized practice. The school became a space to exchange experiences, reflect on activities, and discuss self-empowered political engagement, as well as a performative space for enacting urban citizenship.

Notes

1. 'Never Mind the Papers' is a Hamburg-based network of refugee activists, supporters, the 'The Right to the City' movement, Union activists and other left-wing initiatives, all fighting for an accessible and just city for everybody. https://nevermindthepapers.noblogs.org, date accessed 13 March 2018.

2. The *metroZones school of urban action* is a two-year public founded project (2015–2016) conducted by the Berlin-based group *metroZones – center for urban affairs* – www.metrozones.info, date accessed 2 February 2018—and the Hamburg-based NGO *dock europe*—www.dock-europe.net, date accessed 2 February 2018.

3. For each workshop of the *metroZones school*, an artist was invited to protocol and comment the discussions by a kind of graphic record, see https://schoolbook.metrozones.info, date accessed 2 February 2018. For this paper, I selected some drawings by the Berlin-based artist, Eric Göngrich. His drawings have a specific focus and narration, presenting his position as an observer of some moments of the *metroZones school* as well as an active participant of the situation: 'It is not so much about learning, but I try to understand through my drawings [...] I try to summarize the situation in a subjective and provocative way.' Eric Göngrich, https://vimeo.com/209878106, date accessed 2 February 2018 (translation by author).

4. The *metroZones Schule für städtisches Handeln* was financed for two years (2015–6) as a model project by the German Federal Institution Bundeszentrale für politische Bildung, see www.metrozones.info, date accessed 11 February 2018.

5. http://hh-mittendrin.de/2015/11/demo-fuer-gefluechtete-zeigen-dass-alle-menschen-in-hamburg-gleiche-rechte-haben, date accessed 10 January 2018.

6. For further information about the workshop, see Liz Rech (2015) 'Körper und Öffentlichkeit – zur performativen Dimension städtischen Handelns' in *metroZones Schule für städtisches Handeln: 'Von der Situation zur Intervention — Zugänge und Stationen'*, https://www.metrozones.info/wp-content/uploads/2016/08/mZ-Schule-fuer-staedtisches-Handeln-Dossier-2015.pdf, date accessed 10 January 2018.

7. The artist Erik Göngrich was invited to organize a workshop on drawing and artistic intervention in public space through objects. Additionally, he was invited to comment on the school workshop by taking minutes through the action of drawing; the graphic comments in this text thus arose in the framework of the *School for urban action* in the autumn of 2015.

References

Arendt, Hannah. 1998. *The Human Condition*. Chicago: University of Chicago Press.

Cvejic, Bojana, and Ana Vujanovic. 2015. *Public Sphere by Performance*. Berlin: b_books.

Delgado, Manuel. 1999. *El Animal Public: Hacia una antropología de los espacios urbanos*. Barcelona: Anagrama.

Fontanari, Elena. 2016. Looking for Neverland. The Experience of the Group "Lampedusa in Berlin" and the Refugee Protest of Oranienplatz. In *Witnessing the Transition: Moments in the Long Summer of Migration*, ed. Gökce Yurdakul et al., 15–35. Berlin: Assoziationen A.

Hess, Sabine, and Henrik Lebuhn. 2014. Politiken der Bürgerschaft. Zur Forschungsdebatte um Migration, Stadt und *citizenship*. *Sub/urban* 2 (3): 11–34.

Hess, Sabine, et al. 2016. *Der lange Sommer der Migration* [The Long Summer of Migration]. Berlin: Assoziationen A.

Irazabal, Clara. 2008. Citizenship, Democracy, and Public Space in Latin America. In *Ordinary Places, Extraordinary Events. Citizenship, Democracy, and Public Space in Latin America*, ed. Clara Irazabal, 11–35. New York: Routledge.

Isin, Engin. 2017. Performative Citizenship. In *Oxford Handbook of Citizenship*, ed. Ayelet Shachar, Rainer Bauböck, Irene Bloemraad, and Maarten Vink, 500–523. Oxford: Oxford University Press.

Lanz, Stephan. 2015. Refugees und die Stadt. In *The Dialogic City – Berlin Wird Berlin*, ed. Arno Brandelhuber, Florian Herzwech, and Thomas Mayfried, 487–495. Berlin: Walter König.

Lebuhn, Henrik. 2013. Local Border Practices and Urban Citizenship in Europe. *City: Analysis of Urban Trends, Culture, Theory, Policy, Action* 17 (1): 37–51.

McFarlane, Colin. 2011. *Learning the City. Knowledge and Translocal Assemblage*. Oxford: Wiley-Blackwell.

Miraftab, Faranak, and Shana Wills. 2005. Insurgency and Spaces of Active Citizenship. The Story of Western Cape Anti-Eviction Campaign (AEC) in South Africa. *Journal of Planning, Education and Research* 25: 200–217.

Mokre, Monika. 2015. *Solidarität als Übersetzung. Überlegungen zum Refugee Protest Camp Vienna*. Vienna: Transversal.

Wildner, Kathrin. 2003. *Public Space as a Space of Negotiation*. http://eipcp.net/transversal/1203/wildner/en. Accessed 15 Nov 2017.

Yudice, George. 2005. The Heuristics of Contemporary Urban Art Interventions. *Public* 32: 9–21.

A Space of Performing Citizenship: The Gängeviertel in Hamburg

Michael Ziehl

A performative perspective on citizenship allows us to overcome conventional views of citizenship and points a spotlight on the question of how people articulate claims as rights (Isin 2017). In this chapter, I will focus on this question by using the example of the Gängeviertel—the abandoned quarter in the middle of Hamburg that was occupied by an activist initiative in 2009. Since then, the Gängeviertel activists continue to publicly articulate claims concerning the self-management of the place and the right to the city. They apply these practices in situ, and therewith continuously produce a space of performing citizenship. I will illustrate some of these practices and point out how they contribute to an effective articulation of claims with the help of a spatial entanglement of the public to the place. With reference to Lefebvre's concept of the production of social space, I will show thereby that place-specific conditions play a particular and important role.

M. Ziehl (✉)
Graduate Program Performing Citizenship, HafenCity University Hamburg, Hamburg, Germany
e-mail: kontakt@urban-upcycling.de

© The Author(s) 2019
P. Hildebrandt et al. (eds.), *Performing Citizenship*, Performance Philosophy, https://doi.org/10.1007/978-3-319-97502-3_11

HISTORY, MATERIALITY AND CHARACTERISTICS

The Gängeviertel is a historic ensemble of thirteen houses, situated in the city center of Hamburg. Although it is heritage-protected, the city of Hamburg sold the abandoned quarter and permitted substantial amounts of demolition, largely to enable the construction of luxury flats, offices and commercial space. While the demolition was being planned, two artists' collectives were using storefronts in the Gängeviertel as studio spaces. When they heard about the plans they decided to mobilize against it. As a result, in August 2009 about 200 artists, cultural workers and activists occupied the Gängeviertel in protest against the neoliberal policy of the city government. They demanded the creation of affordable working and residential space in the city, the preservation of the historical buildings, as well as a more participative urban development policy. The occupation— or cultural appropriation[1] as the activists prefer to call it—gained huge publicity and a lot of people sympathized with the activists. Due to public pressure, and after intense negotiations, four months later, the Senate of Hamburg decided to buy the Gängeviertel back from the investor. This was the start of official cooperation between the occupiers and the city administration of Hamburg; both began to acquire a development concept for the Gängeviertel. In essence, the new idea provides for the gradual renovation of the thirteen buildings and the creation of publicly funded social housing, studios, and cultural spaces on about 7500 m² of floor space. The entire cost of the renovation was earmarked at 20 million Euros.

However, the occupiers did not wait until an agreement with the city government was achieved; they already began to refurbish and to adapt the thirteen houses informally. On the upper floors studios and workshops were established, while rooms on the ground floors were prepared for semi-public usage—such as cafés, galleries and venues. Today, the Gängeviertel is a vibrant and non-commercial urban space that functions on the basis of openness, voluntary work, collectives and grass-root democratic structures. Everybody who is capable and interested can be involved in the decision-making processes and the organizing of groups, take-on tasks, start a new undertaking or apply for free rooms. These characteristics depend on the self-management[2] of the place and became established after the occupation. Since the renovation began, the Gängeviertel activists increasingly fear that it is the aim of the city government to normalize the place and its management by cleaning up its unique appearance and installing a professional housing administration. Furthermore, they criticize the fact that cooperation is not carried out openly and honestly by the municipality and that the mandated redevelopment agency gives too little regard to their demands concerning the renovation measures. The municipality largely ignored these problems and proceeded as scheduled in order to remain on-time with the renovation process. Consequently, the Gängeviertel refused further collaboration and, in February 2015, the cooperation was close to failure. All project planning stopped and the two parties started to negotiate over the implementation of further renovations, as well as the continuation of the proposals for self-management from the initiative.[3]

CLAIMS, CONFLICTS AND CITIZENSHIP

Notions of citizenship are diverse, as critical citizenship studies have shown. As Engin Isin points out, 'citizenship, while typically understood as a legal status of membership in the state, if not the nation-state, became increasingly defined as practices of becoming claim-making subjects in and through various sites and scales' (Isin 2008, p. 16). Thus, citizenship derives not only from someone's status of having rights but also from someone's performance in *claiming* rights. This performative take on citizenship 'allows us to appreciate that how people perform citizenship plays an important role in contesting and constructing citizenship and attaching meanings to rights' (Isin 2017, p. 501). Before examining more closely how the Gängeviertel activists perform their claims, I will consider the question of how far these claims are connected to issues of citizenship. Accordingly, it is helpful to distinguish formal and substantive citizenship, as James Holston and Arjun Appadurai did with regard to ongoing renegotiations of citizenship within cities. As they put it, '*formal* refers to membership in the nation-state and the *substantive* to the array of civil, political, socio-economic, and cultural rights people possess and exercise' (Holston and Appadurai 1999, p. 4) [emphasis of the author]. The struggle of the Gängeviertel activists—who mostly are *formal* citizens of Germany or other nation-states—is about *substantive* citizenship whereby they articulate several claims concerning two distinctive scales.

On the local scale of the Gängeviertel, the activists demand the continuation of self-management for the time following the renovation. For them, self-management is a necessary requirement so that the Gängeviertel functions as an open and cultural place to live and work. Furthermore, they see it as the only guarantee that the place cannot be sold later on. Concerning the renovation, they urge more participation; they wish to take more responsibility and make greater contribution within the process because they are not satisfied with outcomes concerning usability of the buildings and aspects of heritage protection. To actually meet these claims, the city government would have to adjust the existing renovation concept and to assign property rights to the Gängeviertel cooperative.[4] That would entail a relinquishment of control over the place and its development. Contrary to this, the city government seeks to keep control to ensure the finalization of the renovation and the long-term development of the place. City representatives argue that they cannot adapt the proposed renovation procedure due to administrative directives and are obliged to verify the accurate application of public investments. Additionally, the government would have to accept a shortfall in receipts, as the activists of the Gängeviertel are not willing and not able to pay the actual market value. City representatives assert that giving such advantage is not compatible with the principle of equal treatment. Altogether, claims of the Gängeviertel activists on a local scale challenge governance practices, municipal directives, and property rights concerning the place.[5]

On the city scale of Hamburg, the Gängeviertel activists claim the right to the city as a universal right for all urban dwellers.[6] To put this claim into practice they contest the policy of the city government and work against its growth-oriented and enterprise-friendly agenda. Moreover, they are proactive in supporting self-organized social and housing projects; they campaign against the privatization of public property, real estate speculation, as well as for the rights of refugees. Alongside many initiatives of the 'Right to the City Network' in Hamburg, the Gängeviertel is part of a political voice in the city.[7]

SUCCESSES AND PUBLIC RELATIONS

The activists of the Gängeviertel have achieved some remarkable successes on both local and city scale. Only a few days after the occupation, they signed a contract allowing them to use the abandoned houses temporarily without paying rent. Four months after the occupation, they achieved the buy-back of the Gängeviertel. Shortly thereafter, the city government announced the abolition of the *Höchstgebotsverfahren*, according to which public real estate was sold to the highest bidder without regard to the concept of usage. In 2010, an association and a cooperative were founded

by the activists, as legal structures for self-management, making legal entities available as contracting partners with the municipality. In 2011, the
activists of the Gängeviertel enforced a cooperation agreement stating
terms of rights and duties during the renovation process,[8] and in 2015,
they enforced a general rental agreement for the first three renovated
buildings. Notably, the agreement to halt the planning process can be seen
as an achievement for them, because it was their aim to stop the ongoing
process in order to allow for adjustments and further negotiations.

These successes are the result of intense debates, a huge amount of
organization and paper work, the advice of experienced consultants, solidarity among the 'Right to the City' network, and huge support and backing from a substantial part of the public. From the cultural appropriation
until today, the Gängeviertel activists act with respectful regard to public
opinion. They know that, in negotiations with the municipality, the public
sits at the table and that media and social networks play an important role
as distributors and co-creators of public opinion. Thus, actions of claim-
making are designed with a careful view to media coverage and public
relations.[9] As Gesa Ziemer pointed out, with reference to Nancy Fraser,
the activists of the Gängeviertel never aimed to create a counter-public as
is typical for many occupiers (Ziemer 2014). Rather, they understand the
public sphere 'as a vehicle for marshaling public opinion as a political
force' (Fraser 2007). To mobilize a wide range of the public sphere, they
argue that the self-management of the Gängeviertel is to the benefit of
many people in Hamburg, primarily because its structural openness and
cultural program form an enrichment for city dwellers generally—not only
for those who are interested in art and culture or would like to become
active in self-organized structures. They highlight that the Gängeviertel is
accessible for marginalized urban dwellers, and that they take care to force
the municipality to put heritage protection in place. By doing so, to some
degree, they enact themselves as representatives of social and cultural public interests and ask the question: who is in position to represent these
interests—politicians, as elected representatives of those who have the
right to vote? Or activists like themselves, who proactively get involved in
public issues? In the following, I introduce some practices to illustrate how
demands of the Gängeviertel activists are performed publicly, particularly
at the place in question.

Practices of Performing Citizenship

Cultural appropriation of the Gängeviertel can be seen as the starting point for the development of place-specific practices of performing citizenship. It was organized by a core group of activists who planned the appropriation, explored the place, and secretly prepared exhibitions and installations in the houses. The 'happening' was announced as a courtyard festival throughout the city, and thousands of people came to celebrate in the narrow passageways among outdoor bars and exhibitions. One by one, activists opened doors to the visitors but made sure to stay unidentifiable as responsible persons. Instead of barricading the houses, they were made accessible and everybody was invited to become a part of the appropriation process. This generated a positive response from a broad spectrum of Hamburg society and the media. After reports in the local media, the international press also picked up on the subject. Following the first reports, politicians began to speak up. Most expressed their understanding for the reasons behind the action and signaled their willingness to engage in speaking for the concerns of the initiative. Out of this experience the

Fig. 1   Gängeviertel 2nd anniversary. (Photo: Franzi Holz, August 2011)

activists constantly progressed in arranging cultural events. One can say that they continued with the cultural appropriation but stabilized this process while establishing organizational structures. Currently, exhibitions, concerts, film showings, readings and public discussions take place somewhere in the Gängeviertel nearly every day. Hundreds of visitors come every week and take advantage of the mostly free and open-to-all events and activities. The cultural program is the key means for the Gängeviertel activists to keep the place vibrant, gain sustained public awareness and increase the popularity of the place (Fig. 1).

During the G20 summit in July 2017, the Gängeviertel was converted into a 'Free Oasis' with outdoor concerts, exhibitions and rest areas, together with an infrastructure to supply protesters with food, first aid and information about ongoing police and protest action. Demonstrations in the Gängeviertel were prohibited by the court during the G20 summit because it was located in the official safety zone, where the right to free assembly was suspended; police forces had the area surrounded over and over again in order to prevent blockades that might obstruct diplomatic convoys passing nearby. Nevertheless, hundreds of activists from all around Europe used the place to organize peaceful protests and to recover from actions in the streets of Hamburg. Shortly after the summit, the Gängeviertel activists publicly declared their solidarity with activists of the Rote Flora, who were blamed by politicians as being responsible for violent confrontations between radical left activists and the police force. As a consequence, local politicians moved to cut official funding for the Gängeviertel, and its activists feared that the administration could stop the negotiations about further renovation. Despite this, the Gängeviertel activists maintained their declaration of solidarity and sustained critique on the G20 Summit. Many creative protest actions were supported and organized by them, raising their public profile—like a rave demonstration with around 20,000 protesters and a zombie-like performance called '1000 Gestalten' that gained wide attention in international media.

The anniversary of the cultural appropriation is celebrated with a large program over several days. For this event, the place is transformed into a festival area with installations, temporary bars and stages. The organization is partly chaotic, but works on a foundation of experience and spontaneity together with a sense of responsibility from most of the visitors. With this yearly spectacle, the Gängeviertel activists publicly demonstrate their popularity and general backing in the city society. When the cooperation process with the municipality was close to failure in 2015, the

Gängeviertel organized a solidarity concert with the Goldenen Zitronen—an experimental punk band famous for its progressive music and critical lyrics. The band played in one of the passageways to underline the demand for self-management by the Gängeviertel activists and marked the starting point of a solidarity campaign that was undersigned by hundreds of artists and cultural workers from all around the world.[10]

There is a continual practice of hosting conferences, public workshops and discussion events concerning political and social issues. Some are self-organized, others are arranged by non-profit organizations and activist groups. In this way, the activists of the Gängeviertel attract a critical audience, promote political dialogues and demonstrate its connectedness to political activist networks and scholars. Inspired by such events, in April 2015, I organized a symposium as a practical part of my research about the Gängeviertel cooperation process. A workshop, conducted with city representatives and activists, took place to get insight into the aims and interests of the stakeholders, and to figure out common ground so to further improve the process. It became clear that both sides have different aims and ideas concerning the future development. City representatives see it primarily as a determined construction process with a clear ending, resulting in affordable spaces for cultural production and living in the city center. In contrast, the Gängeviertel activists want to maintain the political significance of the place and maintain its openness for spontaneous developments. After the workshop, a public debate took place titled 'Cooperations between Municipalities and Citizen Initiatives'. It was my aim to involve the city representatives in a public debate about the cooperation and development process, but they refused to take part as panelists. Those who did come to the discussion highlighted that they took part as citizens and did not speak publicly. It seems that city representatives fear the nature of the public the Gängeviertel creates and prefer to avoid public debates on-site.

PLACE, STAGE AND SCENE

To connect these practices to the concept of performing citizenship, as it is promoted in this chapter, I again refer to Engin Isin. He contrasts '"activist citizens" with "active citizens" [...]. While activist citizens engage in writing scripts and creating the scene, active citizens follow scripts and participate in scenes that are already created' (Isin 2008, p. 38). If we apply this principle to the Gängeviertel one can say that the activists of the Gängeviertel created a scene out of the cultural appropriation of the place and then used this as the stage to continuously recreate the scene. Out of an 'act of citizenship' (Isin 2008) diverse practices of performing citizenship were developed. With the help of these practices, they address their claims to the public and at the same time incorporate parts of the public sphere into the scene. To better understand this process, I refer to sociologist Erving Goffman, who argues that all social interactions between groups can be understood as performances on specific 'stages' that consist of:

> front regions where a particular performance is or may be in progress, and back regions where action occurs that is related to the performance but inconsistent with the appearance fostered by the performance. (Goffman 1956, p. 82)

Furthermore, there is a third region that encompasses all places other than those defined as 'front' or 'back':

> The notion of an outside region that is neither front nor back with respect to a particular performance conforms to our common-sense notion of social establishments, for when we look at most buildings we find within them rooms that are regularly or temporarily used as back regions and front regions, and we find that the outer walls of the building cut both types of rooms off from the outside world. (Goffman 1956, p. 82)

According to this model, the assignment of people to the three regions determines their role within social interactions. In case of the Gängeviertel, people from the outside region are invited to become part of the front and back region due to the openness of the place and its relatively inclusive decision-making structures. Borders between inside and outside are blurry and, therewith, social functions of activists, visitors and the public become entangled. Consequently, claims are not only articulated to, but also with and through the public; the Gängeviertel is the particular stage where these social interactions work successfully. Thereby place-specific aspects play a notably important role. In order to deepen our understanding about how people articulate claims successfully, we must take the conditions of the stage into account where new scenes of citizenship are created. Here, it is pertinent to refer to Lefebvre's concept of social space.

A Space of Performing Citizenship

Henri Lefebvre's conceptualized space is an ongoing process of social production and reproduction, characterized by the interrelations of three equivalent dimensions: spatial practices, representations of space and spaces of representation (Lefebvre 1991). Lefebvre developed his theory out of the observation of long-term macrosociological processes. Nevertheless, his concept is applicable to smaller scale processes that take place within shorter timeframes—like the struggle over the Gängeviertel.[11] If we apply his spatial triad to the articulation of claims in the Gängeviertel, one can understand all the practices of performing citizenship as a part of spatial practices. This dimension refers to the material foundation of space—like walls, buildings and streets—and also encompasses the everyday usage of material structures. Concerning the articulation of claims in the Gängeviertel, its many venues, galleries bars and cafés, the open building structure and the overall situation in the inner city of Hamburg are of particular importance. They weave the place into the fabric of urban life and so make it possible to reach a wide range of the public throughout the city. Moreover, the small-scale configuration of buildings supported the appropriation of the thirteen houses and the maintenance of self-management structures that, still today, facilitate the many practices of performing citizenship in situ.

Representations of space refer to conceptualizations and planning, as well as the creation of images with the help of words, pictures and signs. Thus, all planning and concept work concerning the renovation and the development of the Gängeviertel should be seen as representations of space; additionally, publications, media reports and—on a more abstract level—the public discourse about the Gängeviertel, all refer to this dimension. It is far less based on the physical characteristics of the place because representations of space are largely produced outside of the Gängeviertel—in planning offices, editorial departments, the public sphere and so on. Spaces of representation concern subjective imaginations that are connected to the space, along with the attribution of significance and associations of symbolic meanings to material objects. In case of the Gängeviertel, this dimension plays a particularly important role. The historic significance of the Gängeviertel appears to visitors through the building's historic materiality. Provisional outbuildings, art installations, street art and overall repair of the buildings all contribute toward an esthetic that gives expression to the self-management of the space. The walls of the Gängeviertel are carriers of meaning and stand in clear contrast to the appearance of the surrounding highly-priced and formalized real estate downtown. Thus, they function as a unique stage set for the ongoing performance happening within the place.

In the case of the Gängeviertel, the production of social space depends to a high degree on practices of performing citizenship that actually take place. The production of space intensively interrelates with the process of performing citizenship in all dimensions. Public articulations of demands contribute to the symbolic significance of the place. Politics of the city government and municipal development plans are crucial for the intensity and the design of practices of performing citizenship. Architectural planning of the renovation to some degree predetermines the esthetic of the place and its subjective perception by visitors. I assume that such spatial interrelations are of particular importance in understanding how practices and acts of claim-making unfold effectivity. This applies in particular to struggles with strong connection to specific places. The Gängeviertel activists are by now successful in asserting themselves against the city government because of the space they continue to create and hold. Here, they articulate claims to, with, and through the public. At the same time, they perform the rights they demand to some degree as they realize the self-management of the place. In this way, they articulate their demands as the right to the city and put it into practice simultaneously.

As the case shows, to perform citizenship successfully might depend on the ability of citizens to open up and maintain a stage where they enact claims publicly, and effectively interrelate them with the preconditions of the place of claim-making, thus creating a space of performing citizenship. To have transformative impacts on the execution and design of rights, such spaces of performing citizenship have to establish a local social system that clearly differs from the society it is intertwined with. Such a space can unfold the power to challenge and question particular rights that shape society as it manifests a new social reality within a particular place.

Notes

1. 'Cultural appropriation' in this chapter stands for the peaceful appropriation of the abandoned houses with the help of cultural performances and artistic means. It fundamentally differs to current notions within the critical discourse on 'whiteness'.

2. I use the term *self-management* following Henri Lefebvre's understanding (Lefebvre 1976, p. 120). As Neil Brenner puts it, self-management for Lefebvre connotes 'a political orientation through which various sectors of social life – from factories, universities, and political associations to territorial units such as cities and regions – might be subjected to new forms of decentralized, democratic political control through the very social actors who are most immediately attached to them' (Brenner 2008, p. 240).

3. For more information about the Gängeviertel and a more detailed description of the cooperation process, see Ziehl 2016.

4. The cooperative was founded by the activists in 2010 in order to undertake the management of the houses from the municipality and the redevelopment agency. Members of the cooperative are required to make a minimum subscription of at least one share (500 Euro). Membership of the cooperative is not limited to the activists; supporters can also become members and participate in decision-making.

5. For more information about the protest of the Gängeviertel activists and their entanglement with the urban development policy of Hamburg, see Novy and Colomb 2013 and also Fraeser 2017.

6. Henri Lefebvre conceptualized the right to the city as follows: 'The right to the city, complemented by the right to difference and the right to information, should modify, concretize and make more practical the rights of the citizen as an urban dweller (citadin) and user of multiple services. It would affirm, on the one hand, the right of users to make known their ideas on the space and time of their activities in the urban area; it would also cover the right to the use of the center, a privileged place, instead of being dispersed and stuck in ghettos (for workers, immigrants, the "marginal" and even for the "privileged")' (Lefebvre, in Kofman and Lebas 1996, p. 34).

7. To fully meet the claim for the right to the city, it would not be enough to fundamentally change the current policy of the city government. Rather, a fundamental transformation of social, political, and economic structures would be necessary, with far-reaching consequences for processes of democratic decision-making and also the current notion of citizenship. Thus, claims concerning the right to the city often are connected to a national, if not global, scale. For a critical discussion of the relation between the right to the city, citizenship and representative democracy, see Purchell 2002. For more information about the 'Right to the City' network in Hamburg in the context of local urban development, see Birke 2016.

8. The cooperation agreement between several senators and the Gängeviertel activists is the fundament for the cooperation process and a unique piece of paper—there is no other example in Germany of a contract like this

between a city government and organizations that developed out of an occupiers' movement.

9. For a press review of the Gängeviertel, see http://das-gaengeviertel.info/medien/pressespiegel.html, date accessed 29 January 2018.

10. For the list of supporters, see http://das-gaengeviertel.info/nc/b/soli.html, date accessed 29 January 2018.

11. It is not my aim to analyze the spatial production process that takes place in the Gängeviertel in all its aspects; rather, I am briefly outlining the relations of the practices of performing citizenship and Lefebvre's three dimensions of space. Furthermore, within the limits of this chapter, I cannot go into detail about Lefebvre's complex concept; it has been discussed by several scholars in recent years. For a profound discussion see, for example, Schmid 2008.

References

Birke, P. 2016. Right to the City– and Beyond. The Topographies of Urban Social Movements in Hamburg. In *Urban Uprisings – Challenging Neoliberal Urbanism in Europe*, ed. M. Mayer, C. Thörn, and H. Thörn, 203–232. New York: Palgrave Macmillan.

Brenner, N. 2008. Henri Lefebvre's Critique of State Productivism. In *Space, Difference, Everyday Life – Reading Henri Lefebvre*, ed. K. Goonewardena, S. Kipfer, R. Milgrom, and C. Schmid, 231–149. New York: Routledge.

Fraeser, N. 2017. Fantasies of Antithesis – Assessing Hamburg's Gängeviertel as a Tourist Attraction. In *Protest and Resistance in the Tourist City*, ed. C. Colomb and J. Novy, 320–339. London: Routledge.

Fraser, N. 2007. Transnationalizing the Public Sphere: On the Legitimacy and Efficacy of Public Opinion in a Post-Westphalian World. http://eipcp.net/transversal/0605/fraser/en. Accessed 29 Jan 2018.

Goffman, E. 1956. *The Presentation of Self in Everyday Life*. Edinburgh: University of Edinburgh Social Sciences Research Centre.

Holston, J., and A. Appadurai. 1999. *Cities and Citizenship*. London: Duke University Press.

Isin, E.F. 2008. Theorizing Acts of Citizenship. In *Acts of Citizenship*, ed. E.F. Isin and G.M. Nielsen, 15–43. London: Zed Books.

Isin, E. 2017. Performative Citizenship. In *Oxford Handbook of Citizenship*, ed. A. Shachar, R. Bauböck, I. Bloemraad, and M. Vink, 500–523. Oxford: Oxford University Press.

Kofman, E., and E. Lebas. 1996. Lost in Transposition: Time, space, and the City. In *Writings on Cities*, ed. E. Kofman and E. Lebas, 3–60. Oxford: Blackwell.

Lefebvre, H. 1976. *The Survival of Capitalism: Reproduction and the Relations of Production*. New York: St. Martin's Press.

————. 1991. *The Production of Space*. Oxford: Blackwell.

Novy, J., and C. Colomb. 2013. Struggling for the Right to the (Creative) City in Berlin and Hamburg: New Urban Social Movements, New Spaces of Hope? *International Journal of Urban and Regional Research* 37 (5): 1816–1838.

Purchell, M. 2002. Excavating Lefebvre: The Right to the City and its Urban Politics of the Inhabitant. *GeoJournal* 58: 99–108.

Schmid, C. 2008. Henri Lefebvre's Theory of the Production of Space: Towards a Three-Dimensional Dialectic. In *Space, Difference, Everyday Life – Reading Henri Lefebvre*, ed. K. Goonewardena, S. Kipfer, R. Milgrom, and C. Schmid, 27–46. London: Routledge.

Ziehl, M. 2016. Cooperation with Resistance: The Development of the Gängeviertel in Hamburg. In *City Linkage – Art and Culture Fostering Urban Futures*, ed. T. Haupt, C. Rabe, and M. Ziehl, 75–85. Berlin: Jovis.

Ziemer, G. 2014. Urbane Öffentlichkeiten zwischen Kunst und Nichtkunst. Kollektive Dynamiken im Lauf der Zeit – am Beispiel des Gängeviertels. In *Versammlung und Teilhabe. Urbane Öffentlichkeiten und performative Künste*, ed. R. Burri, K. Evert, S. Peters, E. Pilkington, and G. Ziemer, 317–331. Bielefeld: Transcript.

PART III

Citizenship and (Non-)Performance: Premises/Critique/Speculations

Performance as Delegation: Citizenship in 'Lloyd's Assemblage'

Moritz Frischkorn

With an annual turnover of 7734 million Euros in 2016, Hapag-Lloyd is one of the world's biggest container carriers. Its business activity, first and foremost, is logistics. This large-scale transportation company is based in Hamburg. In 2012, the city of Hamburg itself held nearly 37 percent of the company in shares. This, in fact, makes Hamburg citizens one of the company's major owners.[1]

Logistics can be interpreted as one possible conception of the art, science and practice of moving things. It is like 'choreograph[ing] a ballet of infinite complexity played across skies, oceans and borders' (UPS 2010), claims the well-known UPS commercial of 2010. However complex and expansive it may be, this choreography of things remains largely invisible and unnoticed – similar to what Keller Easterling states in her notion of infrastructure space. The term describes spatial infrastructures that manage and control the relation and movements of objects and thereby govern human behaviour: 'Contemporary infrastructure space is the secret weapon of the most powerful people in the world precisely because it orchestrates activities that can remain unstated but are nonetheless consequential. Some of the most radical changes to the globalizing world are

M. Frischkorn (✉)
Graduate Program Performing Citizenship, HafenCity University Hamburg,
Hamburg, Germany

© The Author(s) 2019
P. Hildebrandt et al. (eds.), *Performing Citizenship*, Performance
Philosophy, https://doi.org/10.1007/978-3-319-97502-3_12

being written, not in the language of law or diplomacy, but in these spatial infrastructural technologies [...].' (Easterling 2014, p. 15).

In as much as logistics is part of spatial and choreographic infrastructures of this kind, its very quality lies in an unnoticeable efficiency – the fantastically frictionless secrecy of operating underneath the radar of a general public concerned with seemingly more important matters. All the while, it is on the basis of these largely invisible choreologistic infrastructures that Western liberal subjects act as apparently free and autonomous citizens.

Thinking of Hapag-Lloyd, one might mention the fact that in the mid-19th century the name 'Lloyd' was used as a general term for a shipping company. Yet, it also points to an actual place and person: Edward Lloyd, who, in 1688, opened a coffeehouse on Tower Street in central London. One could argue that this forefather of modern choreologistics, by opening a coffeehouse, took part in the foundation of an important spatial technology of citizenship; for in both the Habermasian discourse on *The Structural Transformation of the Public Sphere* and in Richard Sennett's *The Rise and Fall of Public Man*, the coffeehouse holds a key position in the emergence of a modern bourgeois public sphere. Concurrent to the realms of power of the state and economics, the public sphere is posited as a normative ideal of inclusive deliberation and thereby allows for new and different practices of citizenship (Habermas 1962).[2] Richard Sennett explicitly highlights the performative dimension of the 18th century public sphere (Sennett 1974; Cvéjic and Vujanovic 2012). And the coffeehouse, as Craig Calhoun argues, is important to this specific performance of citizenship as part of its 'institutional base' and as 'a new infrastructure for social communication' (Calhoun 1992, p. 291).

'But where does the coffee come from?', post-colonial scholar Nikita Dhawan asked in a recent talk in Hamburg (Dhawan 2016), referring to the coffee sold and consumed at Lloyd's and other coffeehouses all over Europe, that fostered the emergence of a modern public sphere? It is obvious what she hints at: beginning in the 17th century, coffee is industrially produced in Asian and South American colonies, based on exploitative slave trade and work. Both the luxury crop and the workforce needed to plant, maintain, harvest and refine it are taken from West Africa (and Ethiopia, where coffee supposedly originated from), made eminently transportable, and forcibly exploited. Only in as much as coffee thus becomes affordable as a mass product can it fuel the performance of the coffeehouse as spatial infrastructure of the public sphere. But what are the implications of this entanglement of a bourgeois public sphere with colonial enterprise? Is there a structural, or *only* a historic dilemma at the heart of modern liberal citizenship? Who is allowed to perform in what role and function? And who is forced to work at the invisible choreologistic base of what Arendt terms 'the space of appearance' (Arendt 1958, p. 199), unnoticed and never to appear themselves?

In the following, it is argued that citizenship is always situated in multiple assemblages that include divergent sets of invisible – often exploitative – infrastructures and choreologistic modes of abduction. In as much as any act of citizenship can only exist based on these infrastructures, it employs modes of delegation that, voluntarily and involuntarily, stay invisible. Citizenship is then necessarily based on other delegated performances.[3]

Thinking about the constitutive dilemma inherited from the 18th century coffeehouse and the (exclusive) performance of citizenship it allowed for might be a way of challenging an easy conception of delegation that is central and constitutive of modern politics.

In political terms, delegation is that specific form of outsourcing that explicitly implies transfer of legitimation or authority to someone else, or a body of higher order, while at the same time implementing modes of accountability. The following definition is given in the *International Encyclopedia of Political Science*:

> [...] delegation occurs in politics whenever one actor or body grants authority to another to act on behalf of or to carry out a function for the first in the political process. In such general terms, delegation is ubiquitous and a defining feature of politics beyond individual actions. Voters delegate to elected officials in representative government; governments delegate to ambassadors in foreign affairs; legislatures delegate to committees the authority to study policy issues and report bills and to the authority to make policy. (*International Encyclopedia of Political Science*, 2011, p. 548)

Yet, when looking at the logistical choreographies that emerge in the name of Lloyd's, we can shed light on another, more problematic dimension of delegation, one that is not based on voluntary transfer of legitimation or authority, but rather on practices of exploitation and abduction. Generally speaking, we here deal with delegated performances and exploited bodies located in epistemological, ontological and geographical realms and regions that are actively negated, and therefore excluded from the practice and legal framework of citizenship itself. How do we account for all of that? Or do we potentially have to move beyond counting, accounting, and accountability, beyond credit and credibility, to deal with this largely invisible, yet highly political dimension of citizenship and delegation?

In order to tackle these questions, we here sketch out how one specific choreologistic network – that will be called 'Lloyd's assemblage' – is at the heart of the modern performance of citizenship. Lloyd's, we here speculate, could be the point of departure for understanding the entanglement of the notion of bourgeois public sphere, coffeehouse culture, coffee-plantations, colonialism, slave trade and, finally, insurances, financial trade and risk management. Can a notion of performance as delegation help us to take the emergence of 'Lloyd's assemblage' into focus?

Performance as Delegation

Generally, a performative is a discursive, gestural or bodily act that participates in the generation of a social situation. A performative 'does' what it names, it enacts what it means. Nonetheless, any such performative creation or production is bound by conventional social procedures that have to be iterated (Austin 1982; Derrida 1988). A performative is thus always composed both of moments of repetition and of drift, or shift. Within the arts and cultural sciences, the notion of performance is often linked to the promise of experimentation or transformation (Fischer-Lichte 2008). It entails the possibility of altering conventions because it does more than to merely represent them. Concurrently, it can be read as the imperative to become effective, governed by convention and context from its beginning and thereby fostering dangerous neoliberal regimes of 'self-responsibility' (McKenzie 2001; Butler 2015, pp. 5–12).

In its history, the concept of performance is most often related to two central notions: execution and embodiment. When talking of performance as execution, we claim that an action matches an already existing quantifiable standard or that it follows a pre-written social script. Talking of performance as embodiment, we highlight the physical-material presence and the taking into service of bodily capacities. In performance, a material body is put on the line: it becomes visible, it exposes itself, gains voice and agency, all the while being rendered subject to contextual judgements, norms and conventions.

In linking performance and delegation, we argue for a shift away from the old opposition of performance and representation – where it is performance that exceeds practices of representation. This reflection might serve as counter-argument against easy celebratory claims of the 'transformative power' of performance, sometimes articulated within artistic theories of performance. As Lepecki reminds us in his most recent book (Lepecki 2016), we have to take into consideration how performance is constituted by a 'structural paradox': it 'can be read as both experimentation and normativity' (McKenzie 2001, p. ix). By contrast, we here want to focus on actual and real-worldly distributions of agency that performance enacts, shifts or sustains.

It is in the vein of Adam Smith, maybe, that we can then talk of performance as delegation and thus as a specific mode of a 'division of labour' (Smith 1993): performance always entails the possibility to delegate work, in the sense of making someone else execute a task. This is what choreographers normally do – they hire dancers, highly trained bodies that can successfully execute virtuosic movements. Regarding the social realm, the nexus of script and delegated execution is developed further in Judith Butler's theory of gender: While we are interpolated by a hetero-normative regulatory matrix that shapes our behaviour, this matrix becomes effective only insofar as we actually perform it in our daily routines (Butler 1990, 1993).

But let us deepen, or rather turn around the logic that is analysed here. As Bruno Latour and others have argued, in executing an action – contained within my daily performances (that are surely highly pre-scribed in social terms) – I always rely upon a heterogeneous field of co-operating entities, a milieu or network that enables these actions. Within this theoretic framework, to perform means to become the delegate of a wide array of enmeshed, inter-connected bodies, human and non-human. Already in 1992, Latour explicitly speaks of delegation to non-humans when analysing the socio-political power of technology (Latour 1992). But most explicitly, the aspect of delegation is expressed in his model of mediators, which is at the base of his understanding of agency. In mediated agency, Latour argues, 'action is [...] shifted or *delegated* [my emphasis] to different types of actors which are able to transport the action further through other modes of action, or types of forces altogether.' (Latour 2005, p. 70).

Latour's concept of delegation as transfer or translation of agency makes apparent how any form of expression, including performance, is predicated upon the take-over of a potential that is – at least partly –

located in the surrounding milieu. Interestingly, in a text from 2010, Judith Butler develops a similar idea in relation to performativity. Here, she speaks about the performativity of economics that, according to her, necessarily relies upon organizations of human and non-human networks, including technology. In her analysis of pricing patterns, a performative always activates a broad network of entities, human and non-human alike:

> Hence, even when Bernanke speaks, it is not simply that a subject performs a speech act; rather, a set of relations and practices are constantly renewed, and agency traverses human and non-human domains. What this means, though, is that performativity implies a certain critique of the subject, especially once it is severed from the Austinian presumption that there is always *someone* who is *delegated* [my emphasis] to speak or that performative discourse has to take the form of discrete verbal enunciation. (Butler 2010, p. 150)

The concept of a 'sovereign' speaker is lost, for one presumes that agency itself is dispersed. At the very crossing point of performance and delegation, we are thus able to formulate an extended notion of performance. Here, performance names the historic and artificial process in which a set of relations between bodies – their practices of moving and reacting with one another, the institutional structures that thus emerge and their technological and choreologistic dimension – is constantly renewed.

In short, a system of relations, that one could also term assemblage, re-generates itself over time, performatively and through its performance. Any such assemblage exists only insofar as it is built from interacting components, yet at the same time acts both as a resource and a constraint to those components. As forms of co-functioning and co-evolution of divergent parts, assemblages both enable potential movement and action, as well as inhibiting other movements or action-possibilities of their components. Indeed, Manuel De Landa – whose conception of *agencements* might be deemed rather technical but is used here for its abstracted clarity – writes: '[...] a whole provides its components with *constraints and resources*, placing limitations on what they can do while enabling novel performances.' (De Landa 2006, pp. 34–5).

Within an assemblage, agency is distributed and will thus constantly be taken over by other components; it is delegated upwards, downwards, but most notably, delegated sideways or transversally. This means that for the performative to become effective, the whole network has to be activated. With this notion of performance as delegation within assemblages, one can now explicitly account for the fact that acting or performing is not only a voluntary act of appearance, but always involves an involuntarily component. One becomes a delegate of an assembled field of differently abled bodies, of heterogeneous networks too manifold and too big to be made fully transparent. In as much as one takes over agentic potentials, thus one acts beyond being able to pay back what we will here call one's 'agentic debts'.

In arguing for an understanding of performance as delegation (and vice versa), we have outlined a possible use of the concept that is different compared to the political conception of delegation mentioned above. While delegation is a prevalent and necessary mode of transferring authority and legitimation in modern politics – a transfer of authority that constantly has to be checked, monitored and balanced by means of instituting modes of accountability – in this model, delegation always begins with a distribution of agency. As agency is always predicated on the activation of manifold sets of relations and comprises material, technological, animal and human entities, in as much as I perform, I thus become the delegate of a distributed field of agency without necessarily having been legitimized to do so and beyond being fully accountable.

When assimilating these arguments into our discussion of citizenship, what becomes apparent at this convergence point – the point where performance can finally be understood as a takeover, as borrowing, reception, acquisition, and transfer of agency – is a structural dilemma. Citizenship necessarily begs for transparent and well-balanced modes of exchange of legitimation and authority regulated by delegation and its counterpart of accountability. Yet, as performance – that is in its dimension as practice – it always implies the collaboration, the usage or using, the mediated transfer, or, even more so, the exploitation of a wide field of other and differently abled bodies and entities, and maybe does so beyond fantasies of full transparency or accountability. These forms of exploitation will often include modes of choreologistic abduction, even if they may not be limited to those.

Lloyd's Assemblage

When Edward Lloyd established his coffeehouse in 1688, it was quickly frequented mostly by men: sailors, merchants, ship-owners and business-men in the shipping industry. Lloyd – because he was at the centre of the information flow – was able to provide them with reliable shipping news that also took shape in the form of a newspaper named Lloyd's, published thrice weekly. For this reason, it was here that important agents of the growing shipping industry gathered to discuss insurance deals. The deal-ing that took place eventually led to the establishment of insurance mar-kets such as Lloyd's of London, Lloyd's register and several related shipping and insurance businesses.

Compellingly, at the very moment in history when the slave trade is being established on an ever-bigger scale, we find (among other things) the very coffeehouse of Lloyd's (and its infamous offsprings) at the centre of the gigantic colonial enterprise. As Eric Williams, the famous early anti-colonial historian, reminds us in *Capitalism and Slavery*: 'Lloyd's, like other insurance companies, insured slaves and slave ships, and was vitally interested in legal decisions as to what constituted "natural death" and "perils of the sea".' (Williams 1944, pp. 104–5).

While only able to briefly sketch these entanglements here, what we can take into focus when looking at what may then be termed 'Lloyd's assem-blage', is the installation – performatively and as performance – of a whole new set of relations, practices and technologies. Elucidating 'Lloyd's assem-blage', we begin to see that the 17th century on the one hand witnessed the emergence of a bourgeois spatial technology of citizenship – namely the cof-feehouse which helped to spawn its nowadays emphatically welcomed off-spring, the public sphere. On the other hand, these structures are inherently entangled with entirely different sets of materials, practices and technologies. They include the foundation of the Atlantic slave trade and its related legal frameworks – which are hinted at in the above citation, and which can easily be linked to what Achille Mbembe terms 'necropolitics', that is, modes of sovereignty that reside 'in the power and the capacity to dictate who may live and who must die' (Mbembe 2003, p. 11). Furthermore, 'Lloyd's assem-blage' is constituted by new techniques of accounting for risk: the concept of insurance or, more generally spoken, risk management, which is, at least in its early form, born from within the shipping industry (aside from fire insurances). In his fantastic and alarming book, *Specters of the Atlantic*, Ian Baucom narrates the terrifying events on board of the slave ship *Zong*, where, in September 1781, 133 slaves were thrown overboard for the Liverpool owners of the ship to be able to file an insurance claim for their lost cargo. And, indeed, Baucom closely links these events to the workings of insurance companies such as Lloyd's and a newly flourishing market for financial trade based on speculation established in the 18th century (Baucom 2005).

What becomes apparent, first of all, is how the modern performance of citizenship has never been a national affair in the first place. Political theorist Aihwa Ong has argued that citizenship – which used to be a relatively coherent assemblage of rights, entitlements, a nation state and its territory – today becomes more and more disarticulated from its original entanglement with the nation state and is thus reconfigured:

> We used to think of different dimensions of citizenship – rights, entitlements, a state, territoriality, etc. – as more or less tied together. Increasingly, some of these components are becoming disarticulated from each other, and articulated with diverse universalizing norms defined by markets, neoliberal values, or human rights. (…) The space of the assemblage, rather than the territory of the nation-state, is the site for new political mobilizations and claims. In sites of emergence, a spectrum of mobile and excluded populations articulates rights and claims in universalizing terms of neoliberal criteria or human rights. (Ong 2006, p. 500)

Ong's argument can be extended. Modern citizenship has always comprised multiple and international infrastructures of domination and a largely invisible and exploitative choreography of logistics. In its peculiar choreologistic logics, 'Lloyd's assemblage' turns everybody (and everything) it transports into liquid quanta – to be shipped, insured and eventually disposed of as 'cargo'. As Fred Moten and Stefano Harney, in their essay 'Fantasy in the Hold' remind us, it is through the shipping of slaves that practices such as 'containerization' – the technology for the capture and transportation of this paradigmatic 'commodity that speaks' – lay the foundation for modern logistical capitalism and world-spanning systems of domination and exploitation of whoever or whatever cannot be counted or categorized as 'person' or fully-human. For that matter, 'modern logistics is founded with the first great movement of commodities, the ones that could speak. It was founded in the Atlantic slave trade, founded against the Atlantic slave.' (Harney and Moten 2013, p. 92).

If, in fact, as we want to suggest, a modern performance of citizenship is predicated on the cooperation and exploitation of multiple bodies, bodies that are actively or unknowingly excluded from the Western public sphere by being rendered mere material of choreographic modes of abduction, what consequences does that have for the notion and practice of citizenship? Today, one could think of the super-exploitative conditions under which the tablets and smartphones are produced that actually provide the material infrastructure for some of the highly mediatized public protests of the last years (Dhawan 2016). How can we identify the inherent logics of these choreologistic assemblages?

What is installed in 'Lloyd's assemblage' primarily is a way of accounting for risk, accounting for the risk of cooperation as bourgeois citizens – which is a cooperation that is predicated on mediated agency, not to say domination. It happens at sea, and, as Burkhardt Wolf tells us: 'The land is full of dangers, whereas the sea yields risks' (Wolf 2013). Now, dangers can be overcome, but risks can only be calculated, they have to be counted and accounted for. And is this not the mode of operation of 'Lloyd's assemblage', of logistics in general? Its logic resides in the desire to manage, that is, to quantify and render quantifiable the risk of capturing, transporting and speculating on all these different commodities that speak, these mute or muted objects that ask for participation nonetheless, and that we involuntarily become delegates of in our daily performances, political or not. How is it that we want to account for these movements, these other performances, this work and generativity, these local and global, human and non-human forces that our performance as citizens bases itself upon, but which might, at least partly, stay oblique, beyond transparency, beyond critique? How can our sense of delegation, as risk that needs to be calculated and governed in the name of (financial) speculation, be complemented with another take on delegation – one that welcomes it as debt that cannot be paid back?

'The [...] transport of things remains, as ever, logistics' unrealizable ambition,' Harney and Moten remind us (Harney and Moten 2013, p. 92). With this claim in mind, and thinking back to a conception of logistics as 'infinitely complex choreography', I wonder how to propose an even more speculative notion of choreography, one that overtly affronts the choreologistic modes of abduction and exploitation outlined in this text. How to think of choreography as a mode of documenting, as a practice of care and trust, as a certain giving up on agency? Is it the art of listening to other, nonlinear, unmanageable movements, never to be captured fully? And, while performance used to carry the meaning of freely placing one's own body in the spotlight, on the line, on the street – could it become the practice of taking responsibility of one's entanglements beyond what one can rationally account for? How could *we* do so? *We* citizens (of Hamburg, or other cities), who come to realize that we have been and still are, more than ever, silent accomplices of choreologistics, every day, not only as share-holders of Hapag-Lloyd.

NOTES

1. The city has less bearing on the company today, as it sold some of its shares and also because of a planned merger of Hapag-Lloyd AG with its competitor UASC (United Arab Shipping Company) in 2017. Yet the three biggest shareholders of Hapag-Lloyd AG – the Chilean shipping company CSAV, the City of Hamburg and Kühne Maritime – still have an agreement to pool 52 per cent of the shares in Hapag-Lloyd in order to take key decisions together (Welt 2016; Hapag-Lloyd 2016; World Maritime News 2016; Onvista 2016).
2. It is important to mention Nancy Fraser's critique of the Habermasian notion of bourgeois public sphere which puts into question the normative ideals implied for the public sphere from a gender perspective (Fraser 1990).
3. I take the notion of delegated performance from a lecture by André Lepecki, given at the Museum of Modern Art in Warsaw, February 2013 (Lepecki 2013). In the lecture, he uses the notion of delegation in relation to work by Bruce Nauman and Santiago Sierra to designate an entanglement of practices of command, the production of subjectivity and an embodied dimension of performance. Furthermore, Claire Bishop published an article entitled 'Delegated Performance' in which she utilizes the term to describe artistic practices that are based on hiring non-professionals to perform (Bishop 2012, p. 91). In this paper I hope to give a somewhat different, more extensive meaning to this notion.

REFERENCES

Arendt, H. 1958. *The Human Condition*. London/Chicago: University of Chicago Press.

Austin, J.L. 1982. *How to Do Things with Words: the William James Lectures delivered at Harvard University in 1955*. 2nd ed. Oxford: Oxford University Press.

Badie, B., et al., eds. 2011. *International Encyclopedia of Political Science, Vol. 2*. London: SAGE Publications.

Baucom, I. 2005. *Specters of the Atlantic: Finance Capital, Slavery, and the Philosophy of History*. Durham: Duke University Press.

Bishop, C. 2012. Delegated Performance: Outsourcing Authenticity. *October* 140: 91–112.

Butler, J. 1990. *Gender Trouble: Feminism and the Subversion of Identity*. New York: Routledge.

———. 1993. *Bodies that Matter: On the Discursive Limits of 'Sex'*. New York: Routledge.

———. 2010. Performative Agency. *Journal of Cultural Economics* 3 (2): 147–161.

———. 2015. *Notes Towards a Performative Theory of Assemblages*. Cambridge, MA/London: Harvard University Press.

Calhoun, C. 1992. *Habermas and the Public Sphere*. Cambridge, UK: Cambridge University Press.

Cvejic, B., and A. Vujanovic. 2012. *Public Sphere by Performance*. Berlin: b_books.

De Landa, M. 2006. *A New Philosophy of Society. Assemblage Theory and Social Complexity*. London/New York: Continuum.

Derrida, Jacques. 1988. Signature Event Context. In *Limited Inc*, 1–24. Evaston: Northwestern University Press.

Dhawan, N. 2016. 'Saving the Female Migrant. Fleeing, Gender, and (Im)Possible Solidarity!', lecture given at HFBK, University of Fine Arts Hamburg, in the frame of 'What Time Is It on the Clock of the World', International Festival on Feminism and Public Space, 4–7 May 2016. https://vimeo.com/167930520. Accessed 3 Jan 2017.

Easterling, K. 2014. *Extrastatecraft: The Power of Infrastructure Space*. London/New York: Verso.

Fischer-Lichte, E. 2008. *The Transformative Power of Performance: A New Aesthetics*. London: Routledge.

Fraser, N. 1990. Rethinking the Public Sphere: A Contribution to the Critique of Actually Existing Democracy. *Social Text* 25 (26): 56–80.

Habermas, J. 1962. *Strukturwandel der Öffentlichkeit: Untersuchungen zu einer Kategorie der bürgerlichen Gesellschaft*. Neuwied: Luchterhand.

Hapag-Lloyd. 2016. *About Us*. https://www.hapag-lloyd.com/de/about-us.html#anchor_24ae92. Accessed 30 Dec 2016.

Harney, S., and F. Moten. 2013. *The Undercommons. Fugitive Planning and Black Study*. Wivenhoe/New York/Port Watson: Minor Compositions.

Latour, B. 1992. Where are the Missing Masses, Sociology of a Few Mundane Artefacts. In *Shaping Technology-Building Society. Studies in Sociotechnical Change*, ed. W. Bijker and J. Law, 225–259. Cambridge, MA: MIT Press.

———. 2005. *Reassembling the Social. An Introduction to Actor-Network-Theory*. Oxford: Oxford University Press.

Lepecki, A. 2013. 'Performance as the Paradigm of Art', a lecture given at the Museum of Modern Art, Warsaw. https://vimeo.com/60432032. Accessed 30 Dec 2016.

———. 2016. *Singularities. Dance in the Age of Performance*. London/New York: Routledge.

Mbembe, A. 2003. Necropolitics. *Public Culture* 15 (1): 11–40.

McKenzie, J. 2001. *Perform or Else: From Discipline to Performance*. London/New York: Routledge.

Ong, A. 2006. Mutations in Citizenship. *Theory, Culture & Society* 23: 499–505.

Onvista. 2016. *Insider Fusion von Hapag-Lloyd mit UASC verzögert sich*. http://www.onvista.de/news/insider-fusion-von-hapag-lloyd-mit-uasc-verzoegert-sich-50436415. Accessed 30 Dec 2016.

Sennett, R. 1974. *The Fall of Public Man*. Cambridge, UK: Cambridge University Press.

Smith, A. 1993. *An Inquiry into the Nature and Causes of the Wealth of Nations*. Oxford: Oxford University Press.

UPS. 2010. New UPS Campaign Delivers Without Brown Truck in *AdWeek*. http://www.adweek.com/brand-marketing/new-ups-campaigns-deliver-without-truck-157919/. Accessed 1 Apr 2017.

Welt. 2016. *Warum Hamburgs Einfluss bei Hapag-Lloyd schwindet*. https://www.welt.de/regionales/hamburg/article157139168/Warum-Hamburgs-Einfluss-bei-Hapag-Lloyd-schwindet.html. Accessed 30 Dec 2016.

William, E. 1944. *Capitalism and Slavery*. Chapel Hill: UNC Press.

Wolf, B. 2013. *Fortuna di mare. Literatur und Seefahrt*. Zurich/Berlin: Diaphanes.

World Maritime News. 2016. *Hapag-Lloyd's Shareholders Approve UASC Merger Terms*. http://worldmaritimenews.com/archives/200639/hapag-lloyds-shareholders-approve-uasc-merger-terms/. Accessed 30 Dec 2016.

(Re)Labelling: Mimicry, Between Identification and Subjectivation

Thari Jungen

When in 2015 the purported 'summer of migration' occurred, the question of how to deal with the pressure of assimilation within the discourse of citizenship became ubiquitous. Citizenship is not only a legal and bureaucratic tool of exclusion, it is comprised of cultural and social interaction. Furthermore, the unspoken and informal knowledge carried within the practice of citizenship leads to modalities of exclusion and participation. In this sphere, legal means are to a large extent ineffective. That gap within the daily practice of citizenship is plastic, providing for the racist, sexist and homophobic practices of 'othering', as well as production of a space for resistance. Within the triangle of habitus, status and origin, the social and cultural capital also produces the homogenous desire for normalcy. Although resistance does not depend solely on differently empowered realms, the question of agency in the practice of 'othering' occurs. Inside the labelling concept of Erwing Goffman (1986) and the theory of subjectivation of Michel Foucault (1988), the practice of 'othering' betrays its ambivalent basis.[1] Therefore the need of a tool, without high level of restraint, difficult approach or complicit methodology, may be answered in this essay, within exploring the practice of mimicry as a subversive tool of reflection.

T. Jungen (✉)
Graduate Program Performing Citizenship, HafenCity University Hamburg, Hamburg, Germany

© The Author(s) 2019

191

P. Hildebrandt et al. (eds.), *Performing Citizenship*, Performance Philosophy, https://doi.org/10.1007/978-3-319-97502-3_13

By referring to the concept of the postcolonial theorist Homi Bhabha (2004a), I will try to explain the ambivalence of mimicry practices in the following, between a repetition of the predominant discourse and the production of a reflective space through overstated repetition. While doing so, the historical figure of the jester – shown here in persona of Marthurine – gives an example of the ambivalence of the Janus-faced discourse of mimicry (cf. Lemaignan 2009). The carnivalesque fool, sanctioned around 1622, acts as a figure moving freely between the spheres of sovereignty and citizenry (cf. Lemaignan 2009). In March 2016, around 400 years later, a collective of so-called refugees, organized the *Carnival al Lajîn_ Al-Lajiàat*. This carnival shows a reformed traditional yet contemporary practice to react to labelling and stigmatization in precarious social situations. Referring to Michail Bakhtin, the notion of carnival includes a collective form of mimicry which he described as 'laughter from below', therefore I will question in the following if mimicry, as a practice of exaggerated humorous repetitions, gives one the chance to emancipate oneself from the unsaid and informal habits of labelling and stigmatizing.

Marthurine, le fou: The Emancipation of a Female Jester

Mimic parodies – as a pervasive method to play with language, combined with gesture – are historically determined due to the historical figure of the jester. As the following will illustrate, Marthurine, *le fou*, a famous jester from renaissance times, gives an example of how to play with self-defined rules (cf. Lemaignan 2009). She was a female jester at the court of King Louis XIII – regarded as *père du peuple* ('father of the people') – at the Louvre, Paris. Mathurine was one of few women to have the role of court jester – a position which was, above all, dominated by men. As mentioned in literature, she was a former head of an army canteen, sharp-tongued and smart. The alleged homosexual King Henry III was thrilled by her wisdom and humour, worshipping her burlesque costumes. Marthurine played a dual role in the French absolutist state; she embodied the figure of the court jester but was also writing a yellow press newspaper, brimming with secret information from the court. In this way, Marthurine's actions were Janus-faced, as simultaneous citizen and jester in the post-Gutenberg era.

Since she was in a powerful but delicate position, being in close contact with the inhabitants of Paris as well as being a member of the court, Marthurine was in a unique situation with regard to the exchanging of information between her, the people and the monarch. Nowadays she is remembered for two accomplishments: for her self-made costumes (she created several male and female characters, wearing outfits that she designed herself, such as fictional soldier's uniforms) and the trading of hidden messages in her newspaper *Les Caquets de l'Accouchée*.[2] Although the content of the paper was labelled as gossip, her yellow press supplied the inhabitants of Paris with internal confidential information. The paper was secretly printed at the king's court and was regularly distributed by Marthurine from the Pont Neuf, thereby gaining new information through her encounters.

MIMICRY AS A FOOL'S GAME

Marthurine, or more widely the figure of the jester, at once embodies a counter-figure of the predominant discourse, through the undermining of hierarchies. As a character, she conveys a reiteration of the theoretical discourse through the use of parody and jokes, here described as the practice of mimicry by Homi Bhabha (cf. 2004a, p. 85). Since Bhabha is speaking in his theory from a postcolonial perspective, I would like to broaden his approach. It is salient to note that, in addition to the 'othering' strategies of racist discourse, sexist and even homophobic practices also colonize their subjects within the predominant discourse. Therefore, my notion of a postcolonial theory does not strictly refer to the idea of migration and colonized people as the labelled *other* in purely racial terms, but also within the context of sexism and homophobia.

Within the performance of mimicry lies, on one the hand, the desire to become or produce an equality that clearly will never be reached; on the other hand, the obscurity of this performance gains the potential to process, to incorporate and even to absorb the alleged primal image, to indicate it is reflecting the alleged profound reality.[3] Here primal image and its imitation no longer exist, but a copy has absorbed the primal image. The imitation of the primal image becomes an accident of its imitation – an invisible accident, in consistent danger of being absorbed – and not conversely (cf. Didi-Huberman 2001, pp. 15–21). With the Freudian theory of the *doppelgänger*, the discussion about the strangely familiar, rather than just mysterious fear and uncanniness, became an interesting topic for psychoanalysis, philosophy and the discourse around race. When Sigmund Freud (2003, p. 267) stated, '[t]he prefix *un* in this term is the marker of repression', he is describing those actions that remain uncanny, even if the subject seems to be performing ordinarily. When speaking of *doppelgänger*, within the repetition of a subject, the primal image stays invisible – without separate existence, remaining bound to the whole. The similarity seems to be uncanny because of its random allocation of the signifier and the signified. The double takes the role of a crossover, a mash-up, indicated through the ambivalence of a ghostly afterimage. Bhabha explains mimicry as an overstated repetition that doesn't quite repeat but forces slippage; while the *doppelgänger* replaces the primary image, mimicry stresses and re-emphasizes it in order to have an impact on reflection.

Marthurine is an example of a figure that is capable of undermining hierarchies. She exploited her role as a jester to hold up a mirror to the king, because she was allowed to within this role. A jester, in an absolutist court, was the only person permitted to convey newly gained information and damaging news truthfully. She observed the atmosphere of the city and would gather word from public voices overheard while riding on her horse through Paris. When telling her jokes to the king, she often presented herself as a soldier in self-made regimental dress. In her spoof as a soldier, she was able to raise her voice on behalf of the citizens of Paris. In wearing the costume, she uses a sort of fool's cap as an implement of invulnerability and invisibility. The fool's cap symbolizes her independent agency by mocking the king and his politics, the inhabitants of Paris, as well as herself. With this form of mimicry, the narration of Marthurine discloses the ambivalence of the predominant idea of normalcy, when she is performing a position 'that is unmarked by the discourse' (Bhabha 2004a, p. 114).

Marthurine's paper is called *Les Caquets de l'Acouchée* – meaning cackling – and is a synonym for gossip (cf. Lemaignan 2009). Yellow press journalism uses fake interviews, misleading headlines, pseudoscience, and a parade of false learning from presumed experts; here this kind of journalism plays an essential role in degrading the power of the monarchy by using the technique of mimicry to carry Marthurine's insights into the court.[4] The paper suggests the idea that gossip could contribute to an emerging public sphere of political debate. Through her supply of an independent publication, Marthurine shaped a movement of empowerment, with the chance to speak with one own voice. Gossip plays an important role here: '*Les Caquets*' is an illustration of how the slippery, sloppy talkativeness of gossip might have operated as public critique, despite the attempts to silence it.

Homi Bhabha explains mimicry practices – such as the humorous and overstated reiterations of stigmatizing arguments, comments or situations – as routines that reflect the demand for identity – its slippage, its excess, its difference (Bhabha 2004a, p. 122) as a dual approach: 'As colonialism produces mimicry itself, mimicry "emerges as one of the most elusive and effective strategies of colonial power and knowledge"' (Bhabha 2004a, p. 121). Here, Bhabha illustrates the powerful nature of colonial mimicry, but leaves it there; there is ambiguity as to whom it gives power; consequently there is the suggestion that the colonized can use it to subvert the colonizer. Bhabha argues that colonial mimicry is 'the desire for a reformed, recognizable other, as a subject of a difference that is almost the same, but not quite' (Bhabha 2004a, p. 122). In that sense, the other becomes almost the same as the colonizer, but never quite fits in with the hegemonic cultural and political systems that govern both of them. The actions of mimicry reveals concurrent fascination and disgust, which is the experience of a decentralized figure of ambivalence. The process of mimicry represents the Janus-faced idea of colonialism and 'othering', with its desired and simultaneously stigmatized otherness of race, sex and gender. Bhabha continues to show that for (colonial) mimicry to work, it must continue to express its difference, which he terms ambivalence.

While Bhabha is speaking of an imperceptible strategy, mimicry opens a field for action and agency as a result of discourse as conscious resistance. Ultimately, because mimicry requires this 'slippage' to function, it gives power not only to the colonizer, but also becomes the subversive tool of the colonized. Albeit Bhabha intends mimicry as a subliminally utilized strategy, it seems to be an important addition to the toolbox of resisting commonplace racism, sexism and homophobia. The figure of the jester, embodied by Marthurine, exhibits the ambivalence of mimicry since she employs the double face of the situation.

The diverse mimicry practices that Marthurine uses can be seen as a probing of rules, habitus and status social systems of order when political commentary is insubstantial. Foolish ways of mimicry, such as Marthurine's cross-dressing, may produce arbitrary laughter, focusing on light relief. Additionally, Marthurine exploits the opportunity of dealing with conflict without using involved theoretical arguments or setting the scene for tragedy. Jokes, as Freud argues (1992 [1915]), are constructing a level for a playful game, allowing insights into conflict through emphasizing and taking resistance by surprise. Mimicry practices function as joyful doubles of reality. Legally, socially and culturally the community is exclusively regulated by citizenship regulations; hereby mimicry enables playful use of the rules and regulations for reinterpretation. The appeal lies in the disruption of the political framework, in trying to create new scenarios through repetition – a chance to revisit. Generally, practices of mimicry refer to social and political regimes, they are markers of the democratic processes. Through these practices, affiliation and exclusion become a visual and effective means to recover agency of formerly uncontrollable dictates. While Stuart Hall emphasizes that the very parts of institutional habits that cannot be destroyed are to be found in, '[...] informal and unsaid ways through daily practices' (Hall and du Gay 1996, p. 32). By detaching oneself from acquired cultural conventions and schemes, mimicry gains agency through taking a hybrid position. Bhabha's concept traces the production of a domain that doesn't utilize the theoretical arguments of the discourse around race and discrimination. Through humour, a distorting mirror reflects the colonist's desire for a reformed, recognizable 'other' as a subject of difference. The colonialist sees mimicry as double vision in which the disclosure of ambivalence toward colonial discourse also disrupts its authority.

CARNIVAL AL LAJIIN_AL-LAJIÀAT: CONTEMPORARY PRACTICES OF MIMICRY

In political, legal and humanitarian discourse, individual and practical activities –undertaken to gain agency – often remain unseen or even invisible. While still questioning what are the ways to gain agency in situations leading to stigma, how does one deal with labelling? Or, to ask this another way around: how can one relabel the stigmatized? On 20 March 2016, a group of so-called refugees, in collaboration with the campaign 'My Right is your Right' and several cultural institutions, organized the *Carnival Al-Lajiìn_Al-Lajiàat* (Arabic for 'female refugee/male refugee') in Berlin-Kreuzberg – one of the most famous and discussed Berlin quarters, proclaimed for the past 30 years as a multi-cultural district.[5] Here, carnival symbolizes the element of mimicry that reveals diversity, beyond the dominant discourse. Samee Ulaah, one of the organizers of 'My Right is your Right', told me that the *Carnival Al-Lajiìn_Al-Lajiàat* is inspired by

Michail Bakhtin's theory of carnival (cf. Bakhtin 1984). Carnival is a popular ancient heritage ritual where art and life meet within a collectively performed play, allowing moments of exaggeration and the grotesque. According to Russian philosopher Bakhtin, in blurring the borders between actors and spectators, carnival reveals a rich variety of voices that join to deny convention, disobey hierarchies and stimulate genuine human exchange – a currency leading to agency, that additionally is polyphonic. The carnival has many forms of expression (Fig. 1).

Happening on a grey weekend, in the middle of the 'alternative' *kiez* of Berlin-Kreuzberg, the procession of the *Carnival Al-Lajiin_Al-Lajiàat* seemed to be a combination of carnival and demonstration; a caravan of decorated vehicles and people wearing costumes, referring to their very different backgrounds and ideas of carnival. New images and costumes were introduced to the established guise of the fool within the western carnival. In welcoming all, the carnival offered many international ideas of the grotesque forms of mimicry. The initiative came from a small collective of refugees from their base in the studio of the *Maxim Gorki* theatre of Berlin. Backed up by a collective of city theatres (*Stadttheater*), such as the *Berliner Ensemble* and *Schaubühne*, as well as *Deutsches Theater*, the *Carnival Al-Lajiin_Al-Lajiàat* became a spectacle of impressive diversity.

Fig. 1 *Carnival Al-Lajiin_Al-Lajiàat* in Berlin-Kreuzberg. (Photo: Thari Jungen)

By focussing on the idea of the laughter of solidarity amongst the camou-
flaged, no logos of any political or cultural institution were shown. In
addition to the support of the theatres – loaning their costumes and stage
equipment – countless citizens, urban activists, and organizations of refugees became involved. The idea of carnival, with the original meaning as
'celebration of the flesh', was performed through the streets with the participation of more than 5000 people.[6]

When one of the costumed participants wanted to start the countdown
to a small performance in the back of a truck, he asked: 'Should we count
in the German language?' The gathered jovial group he was addressing
answered the question firmly with: 'No!' Instead, somebody proclaimed
loud and clear: 'Everybody should learn to count in Arabic!' – which was
then put into effect immediately after. By raising the voice within a spontaneous assembly of strangers, the very idea of assimilation and participation through language produced an unexpected response to the contrary,
thereby gaining agency by incidental comment on the political situation.
As Mikhail Bakhtin (1984) determines: 'Carnival contains a laughter from
below, directed to the privileged and the ruling order' (Fig. 2).[7]

Fig. 2   Many participants of the *Carnival Al-Lajiin_Al-Lajiàat* manifested their
solidarity and sympathy for so-called refugees through display of puppets and costumes. (Photo: Thari Jungen)

In a similar way to Marthurine, the so-called refugees not only brought about the carnival, they also published a newspaper: *Daily Resistance*.[8] Projects such as this are establishing public spaces of critique and self-empowerment by using mimicry and parody as one way of speaking out. Both of these projects – the newspaper *Daily Resistance* and the group 'My Right is your Right' – were inaugurated by people who have fled; they are dedicated to people *in* the refugee camps and made by people *from* the refugee camps. In both instances, they mock their own situation to break the isolation. They return from the imposed status of a supposed *Mängelwesen* (being a person without rights or agency) to being individuals with diverse wishes, needs and realities.[9]

In looking at the practice of labelling let us give insight into how attributions by others are formed, dependent on and regulated through habitus, politics and legal rights.

> Stereotyping is not the setting up of a false image which becomes the scapegoat of discriminatory practices. It is a much more ambivalent text of projection and introjection, metaphoric and metonymic strategies, displacement, over-determination, guilt, aggressivity; the masking and splitting of 'official' and phantasmatic knowledges to construct the positionalities and oppositionalities of racist discourse.[10] (Bhabha 2004b, p. 117)

Mimicry, as an approach of ethnology, reveals the dubiety of concepts such as identity and similarity; moreover the notion of mimicry discloses the most important categories of imitation as in 'belief and desire' (de Tarde 1979 [1890], p. 217), as shown in the very different practices within the regime of normalcy. Since mimicry can become an act of resistance, through joking, mocking, 'vogueing' or specific rites, it reveals the ambivalence of the homogenous desire for normalcy, assimilation and power within modern nation states. Mimicry practices using gaps within bureaucratic, social and political regulations to re-examine the practice of relabelling and subjectivation in daily life.

When the German 'Welcome Culture' (*Willkommenskultur*) emerged in 2017, Simone Dede Ayivi – a female black activist – wrote an article in the German newspaper *Die Zeit*, wherein she was referring to a black volunteer in one of the refugee camps who had been interrupted in her work when another helper said: '*Du musst nicht helfen. Wir helfen!*' ('You must not help. We help!', author's translation).[11] It is no surprise when even voluntary workers of the supposed 'Welcome Culture' themselves are not immune to labelling and stereotyping as racist practices. This example, however, shows how diverse constructions of labelling have become acceptable to us, as well as showing the ambivalence involved in the application of such labels. The practice of labelling has become ingrained within every day identification. Labelling involves the selection of particular characteristics by the labeller; these are exaggerated and simplified and so self-identity and behaviour may be determined or influenced by the terms used to describe or classify.

Those labels or fantasies of selected characteristics, that are gaining the effect of a 'natural' inscription, are unchangeable according to Homi Bhabha. 'Like fantasies of the origins of sexuality, the productions of "colonial desire" mark the discourse as "a favoured spot for the most primitive defensive reactions such as turning against oneself, into an opposite, projection, negation."' (Bhabha 2004b, p. 116) Racism, as Mark Terkessidis (1997, pp. 172–87) points out (and here sexism may be added in as well), is not a prejudice but rather very much of a part of the assembly of social values, as well as part of *collective knowledge*. "Labelling is referring to the modern nation state's heightened demand for normalcy" as I would equate with the predominant discourse (Goffman 1986 [1963], p. 7). Erwing Goffman states that today's stigmas are the result not so much of ancient or religious prohibitions, but of a new demand for normalcy. This demand does not only affect the colour of the skin, but specific cultural and social codes. Living in a divided world, according to Goffman, there are the forbidden places where the revelation of otherness means vulnerability and risk, where people of colour are sorely tolerated, and other places where people of colour are more easily accepted without need to dissimulate, to camouflage and hide in order to protect themselves (Goffman 1986 [1963], p. 13). 'What are unthinking routines for normals can become management problems for the discreditable' (Goffmann 1986 [1963], p. 88). Here, Goffman points out, the ambivalence and the plurality of the roles and patterns that exist and can change according to the very different situations. Within labelling, seen as an act of signification, lies a device that reduces, normalizes and fixes the difference of subjects and communities with their imposed identity. The conscious repetition of such practice belies a vital, very physical sense of discomfort, thus prompting the mind to reflect on the reasons behind the need to adhere to the use of labels. Performances – such as playing with language, highlighting, manifesting shifts and transformations – are usual forms of subversive (language) politics against the hegemonic and homogenous influence of western cultures.

The performance collective Kanak Attack engages in a wide range of subversive language politics; by electing to use an *ethnolect* known as 'kanakisch' they offer their own new interpretation of the abusive and racist origin of the term *Kanake*.[12] Their ethnolect uses a typically Turkish accent, full with exaggeration, providing a jokey response to the ubiquitous stereotypical labelling of the Turkish. Thus 'kanakisch' became a popular form of slang, even throughout the non-Turkish community in Germany. Mimicry creates the possibility to explore symbolic situations through provocative performance, in the copying and representation of social situations, personal individual characters or role models.[13]

Although stigmatized and labelled subjects do not actually represent a passive, homogenous collective at all, rather they are persons with agency, diverse wishes and competencies. In asserting their legal rights, they engage in different creative forms to achieve a better daily life within their differing statuses of citizenship. Conversely, this does not imply the ignoring of particular histories, trauma or fears. Additionally, it does not prompt an agreement based solely on the terms of the current legal or political situation.

In contrast to the external valuation made by Goffman of the labelling concept, Michel Foucault describes the idea of subjectivation, within technology of the self as a mental attitude. He conceives of the subject as a being, existing and therefore a quasi- complete subject, logically described as a 'final production'. Foucault suggests to negotiate the procedures of subjectivation as an object of analysis instead of defining the category of the subject itself. The central thesis of Foucault (1980) points out that what is done, the subject itself, defines the very moment of creating history – or saying it the other way around, erroneously we imagine practice defines itself out of creating and forming.[14] Through examining the historification of subjectivation, Foucault breaks with the notion of sovereign and constitutive subjects, while perceiving subjectivation according to becoming subject, and therefore gains the ability to decentralize the subject.

Mimicry sheds light on the variety of instruments, objects and methods, as practical methodological tools of analysis that makes labelling practices more visible. Imitation and mimicry are considered forms of performance itself that highlight differentiation in the modes of production of representation, politics and identity. The political dimension of imitation seems always to refer to a presumed *society of origin*, and by doing so it constructs an exclusive *fictional community* (Bielefeld 1997,

p. 99). The inevitable alliance of the origin and the mimicry itself seems to be concurrent with the predominant idea of the society of origin, moreover appropriated by imitation and, at the same time, re-emphasizing its antagonistic qualities; the falsification, the false, if not to say the fraudulent. These negative external ascriptions are common daily acts of stigmatization. The gap – between the process of identification and the person subjected to this process – enables one to emancipate and reflect on the truth through the means, or strategy, of mimicry.

By saying that this process of imitation is never complete, Bhabha argues that there is always something lacking. There are always cultural, historical, and racial differences which hinder one's complete transformation into a subject that is not subjectivated and not labelled from the outside. According to Nikita Dhawan and Maria do Castro Varela (2015, p. 221), I would formulate that the agency of the colonized lies in shifting the meaning. Every attempt at stereotype – with whom the colonized, stigmatized or labelled 'other' is determined as fixed to a definitive picture – is nevertheless inevitably fragmented in itself and self-contradictory. Here, Bhabha shaped the term *hybridity* that describes the cultural and psycho-social effects of colonialism, and also points to the inherent ambivalence of the discourse (meaning *every* discourse) within. By doing so, he attains a level of visibility, revealing the ambivalence of the dualism of orient and occident, as well as of colonizer and colonized, or the exclusive and inclusive (cf. Young 2004, p. 26).

CONCLUSION

Jokes, spoofs and parodies aim to reflect the sphere of emancipation and empathy through reiteration. In trying to reclaim the question of equality – through the creation of alternative views of daily life, and a utilization of the subject's vulnerability to linguistic and parodic mimicry – there emerges a discourse on debasement and reflection. Irony questions our ability to define ourselves in reference and deference to others. The theory and its practice reflects and retransfers – it sets up a 'live' perpetuating capacity for rethinking – whereas discourse, increasingly routinely criticized for its limitations, becomes an end in itself, existing purely to serve the needs of western academic discourse rather than seeing theory as a tool of intervention, or seeing theory as supplementary to practice.[15] Moreover, by actively highlighting the contradictions and objections of society though personal appropriation and exploiting the potential of humour to reach others, practices of mimicry can become acts of resistance. Furthermore, such performed technologies of the self, demonstrate the ambivalence of the homogenous desire for normalcy, assimilation and power in modern nation states.[16] Diverse subjectivation and labelling practices in everyday situations are calling for the intervention of jokes and humour, although mimicry practices are only minor supportive acts of self-empowerment that do not in themselves replace – or necessarily change – any legal or political situation. They refer to the ambivalent discourse of appropriation and assimilation as both practices and theory of mimicry. The carnival, in particular, perfectly expresses the idea that citizenship is more than a legal right; citizenship also consists of a demand for social, political and cultural agency.

NOTES

1. Erwing Goffman's theory on stigma deals with techniques of the self, by analysing the specific interactive practices of individualities with their pictures from outside, answering to the institutionalized scripts with regard to their respective external perception. While Michel Foucault's notion of the 'technologies of the self' references regulation and governmental practices within the perspective of flexible, normalized spaces for different possibilities of lifestyle attended to the individualities. Cf. Michel Foucault (1988) *Technologies of the Self*. Also, Goffman, Erving (1986) *Stigma: Notes on the Management of Spoiled Identity*.

2. Cf. Edouard Fournier: 'Feu de Joye de Mme Marthurine', in *Variétés historiques et littéraires*, (Paris, Jannet), 1855–1863, p. 274. See also: *La cholère de Mathurine, contre les difformez reformateurs de la France, À sa grande Ame*, (Paris), pp. 168–73.

3. Here, the term *performance* is used as an ephemeral concept – not necessarily attached to definitive categories as, for example, within the arts – but inside the alliance of acting as a conscious statement, practice or movement, referring to Michel Foucault's term of self-technology (Foucault 1988).

4. The term 'yellow press' or 'yellow journalism' appeared first in Ervin Wardman's New York Press in late January 1897, as a concise expression for 'new journalism'. Over the years, the term is used to describe misconduct in news-gathering. 'The term has served as a derisive shorthand for denouncing journalists and their misdeeds, real and imagined' (cf. Campbell 2001).

5. For more information about the collaborative project please see, www.myrightisyourright.de, date accessed 18 February 2018.

6. The meaning of the original Italian term 'carnevale' refers to *carnem* (meat) and *levare* (remove). The etymology embedded in its meaning is as a dared festival where the flesh of bodies is removed by costumes. Translated as 'flesh farewell' in the figurative sense, the term also marks the festivity as a Christian tradition when Lent begins, forty days before Easter.

7. Since the Bolshevik committee eventually took responsibility to release (belatedly) Bakhtin's famous study *Rabelais and his World* (1984), the question relating humour to government, power and discipline was first allowed to be asked publicly only after 30 years had passed by. The potential benefits of parody, spoofs and jokes as daily – not necessarily – political acts, is expressed within the dissertation of Mikhail Bakhtin, writing from a subversive classification. For further reading please see, Robin Andrews (2011) 'Bakhtin: Carnival against Capital, Carnival against Power' in *Ceasefire*, 09/ 2011, www.ceasefiremagazine.co.uk/in-theory-bakhtin-2, date accessed 26 January 2017.

8. www.dailyresistance.oplatz.net, date accessed 18 February 2018.

9. Arnold Gehlen points out that to rule the world a man, apart from the owned deficiencies (*Mängel*), must not only be able to take action, he has also to be capable of development. Gehlen emphasizes that the degree to which a human being is defenceless is commensurate with its surroundings, thereby he proposes to strengthen both institutions and organizations in both the state and private sectors (for further reading please see, Gehlen 2016 [1940]).

10. Comparing both terms – labelling as well as stereotyping – the practice of stereotyping forces, in Homi Bhabha's words, the codifying of whole communities while the discourse of labelling seeks to normalize individuals (for further reading please see, Bhabha 2004b, p. 117).

11. Simone Dede Ayivi describes in her article, entitled as '*Wir müssen über Rassismus reden*' ('We need to talk about racism', author's translation) her perspective as a black German citizen due to the period of the so-called 'summer of migration'. cf. www.zeit.de/kultur/2015-10/integration-rassismus-fluechtlingshilfe-10nach8, date accessed 18 February 2018.

12. Kanak Attak is a community of different people from diverse backgrounds who share a commitment to eradicate racism from German society; amongst others they are known for their *ethnolect 'getürkt'*. Their manifesto states: 'We sample, change and adapt different political and cultural drifts that all operate from oppositional positions' [author's translation], cf. www.kanakattak.de, date accessed 18 February 2018.

13. Oliver Marchart (2007, p. 80) points to the fact that Bhabha's theory of subversion, like every other theory of subversion, has a problem in proving its threat toward power – because it isn't revolution or open protest. He relegates to the fact that power structures themselves need a certain

amount of subversion in order to exert power, as well as preserve their stability, while also remarking a difference to other forms of protest. Contained within the subversion of mimicry, there aren't any defined claims and goals, thus cannot be proven or quantified, only be theoretically formulated.

14. For further reading and a more expansive overview of this discourse, the following is recommended: Paul Veyne (1997) 'Foucault Revolutionizes History' in Davidson, Arnold I. (ed.) *Foucault and His Interlocutors*, pp. 146–82.

15. Focussing on the gap between theory and practice: Elleke Boehmer (2013) 'Revisiting Resistance' in *The Oxford Handbook of the Postcolonial Studies*, pp. 307–21.

16. By referring to the concept of citizenship, as Seyla Benhahib (2008, p. 35) states, '[…] we face a paradox internal to democracies, namely, that democracies cannot choose the boundaries of their own membership democratically'. Although this state-centred perspective may be criticized, through the agreement that citizenship must also be defined as a social process through which individuals and social groups engage in claiming, expanding and losing rights (Isin and Turner 2002, p. 4). Since Engin Isin, amongst other theorists, speaks of the practice of 'acts of citizenship', they describe those moments and habits through which subjects actively produce citizens by governing themselves (Isin 2009, p. 367).

References

Anonymous. 1616. *La cholère de Mathurine, contre les difformez reformateurs de la France, à sa grande Amye.* Bordeaux: Jean Milot.

Bakhtin, M. 1984. *Rabelais and His World.* Bloomington: Indiana University Press.

Benhahib, S. 2008. *Another Cosmopolitanism.* New York: Oxford University Press.

Bhabha, H.K. 2004a. On Mimicry and Men: The Ambivalence of Colonial Discourse. In *The Location of Culture.* London: Routledge.

———. 2004b. *The Location of Culture.* London/New York: Routledge.

Bielefeld, U. 1997. *Das Eigene und das Fremde. Neuer Rassismus in der Alten Welt?* Hamburg: Junius Verlag.

Boehmer, E. 2013. Revisiting Resistance. In *The Oxford Handbook of Postcolonial Studies*, ed. G. Huggan. Oxford: Oxford University Press.

Campbell, W.J. 2001. *Yellow Journalism: Puncturing the Myths, Defining the Legacies.* Westport: Greenwood Publishing Group.

Castro Varela, M. do M., and N. Dhawan. 2015. *Postkoloniale Theorie: Eine kritische Einführung.* Bielefeld: Transcript.

de Tarde, G. 1979. *Les lois de l'imitation: etude sociologique.* Paris: F. Alcan.

Didi-Huberman, G. 2001. Das Paradox der Phasmiden. In *Phasmes*. Cologne: DuMont.

Foucault, M. 1980. *Power/Knowledge: Selected Interviews and Other Writings, 1972–1977*. New York: Vintage.

———. 1988. *Technologies of the Self: A Seminar with Michel Foucault*. Amherst: The University of Massachusetts Press.

Fournier, E. 1855a. Feu de Joye de Mme Mathurine (An Advertisement Placed) in *Variétés Historiques et Littéraires*. Paris: Jannet.

———. (ed.) 1855b. Les Caquets de l'Accouchée. In *Les Essais de Mathurine*, Paris: Jannet.

Freud, S. 1992. *Jokes and Their Relation to the Unconscious*. Trans. Joyce Crick. Harmondsworth/New York: Penguin.

———. 2003. *The Uncanny*. Trans. David McLintock. Harmondsworth/New York: Penguin.

Gehlen, A. 2016. *Der Mensch: Seine Natur und seine Stellung in der Welt*. Frankfurt am Main: Vittorio Klostermann.

Goffman, E. 1986. *Stigma: Notes on the Management of Spoiled*. New York: Touchstone.

Hall, S., and P. du Gay. 1996. *Questions of Cultural Identity*. London: Sage UK.

Isin, E.F. 2009. Citizenship in Flux: The Figure of the Activist Citizen. In *Subjectivity*, 29/S1. Basingstoke/New York: Palgrave Macmillan.

Isin, F.E., and S.B. Turner. 2002. An Introduction. In *Handbook of Citizenship Studies*, ed. E.F. Isin et al. London: Sage UK.

Lemaignan, M. 2009. Mathurine ou la question d'un tiers espace de l'hétérodoxie, dans La Confession catholique du Sieur de Sancy d'Agrippa d'Aubigné' in L'Atelier du Centre de Recherches Historiques. http://journals.openedition. org/acrh/1234#quotation. Accessed 10 Mar 2018.

Marchart, O. 2007. Der koloniale Signifikant. Kulturelle 'Hybridität'und das Politische, oder: Homi Bhabha wiedergelesen. In *Kultureller Umbau, Räume, Identitäten und Re/Präsentationen*, ed. M. Krönke et al. Bielefeld: Transcript.

Terkessidis, M. 1997. Woven into the Texture of Things. Rassismus als praktische Einheit von Wissen und Institution. In *Evidenzen Im Fluß: Demokratieverluste in Deutschland; Modell D – Geschlechte – Rassismus – PC*, ed. A. Disselnkötter. DISS: Duisburg.

Veyne, P. 1997. Foucault Revolutionizes History. In *Foucault and His Interlocutors*, ed. Arnold I. Davidson. Chicago: University of Chicago Press.

Young, R.J.C. 2004. *White Mythologies. Writing History and the West*. London/New York: Routledge.

Paralogistics: On People, Things and Oceans

geheimagentur and Sibylle Peters

A FIRST REPORT

This is a first report from a long-term research into paralogistics. It covers about seven years of inquiry and travel over the course of several projects that dealt with questions around Hamburg port, shipping, radical seafaring, cruise ships and seafarers' rights, with piracy and the right to the sea – most of them conducted by the performance collective *geheimagentur*.[1] At the beginning of this journey, I did not know that this research was about paralogistics. In fact, the whole concept of paralogistics, including the term itself, is a recent invention – or rather discovery – that allows me to put experiences, difficulties and insights of these last years and months into perspective.

What might be agency, based on our connectedness through the sea? Paralogistics provide answers to the question of how to act together in ever changing entanglements of people, things and oceans. Often, paralogistics are hiding under the radar, but once you find and connect to them, they turn out to be everywhere. Then they can produce a feeling of evidence that is ubiquitous and contagious and paralogical. One might

geheimagentur (✉)
Hamburg, Germany

S. Peters (✉)
FUNDUS Theater, Hamburg, Germany

© The Author(s) 2019
P. Hildebrandt et al. (eds.), *Performing Citizenship*, Performance
Philosophy, https://doi.org/10.1007/978-3-319-97502-3_14

suspect that paralogistics are related to logistics, as the paranormal is to the normal. In that sense, paralogistics talk to the ghosts of logistics and through them.

This is a report from an ongoing research process which intentionally manoeuvers between academic discourse on the one hand, and accounts from artistic experimentation and explorative travel, on the other. It traces paralogistical connections and movements more than formally investigates them, and it also includes dead ends and failing proofs. Ultimately, paralogistics are not just about how to hack logistics, but possibly also about how these hacks fail to be quite logical.

WHAT IS HYDRARCHY TODAY?

In 2010, a group of Somali pirates hijacked the cargo ship *MS Taipan* that was sailing under German flag. Dutch naval forces captured the pirates and brought them to Hamburg for trial. It was the first piracy trial in Hamburg since 1624.

At the time I was working at the Theatre of Research, a children's theatre that had been turned into an institute for transgenerational art-based research.[2] Given that there was no birthday party without a treasure hunt, and that a kid pirate called Captain Sharky was depicted on their toothbrushes, the children were curious: 'How come the pirates have escaped from the movies and why does nobody like them anymore, now that they are real?' The children were asking questions we all had, but no one dared to ask. Therefore, *geheimagentur* and Theatre of Research decided to invite them to dress up in their pirates' costumes and record their questions for real pirates on video.

Exploring the idea that everyone on this planet is connected to everyone else through no more than seven links, we asked friends of friends of friends if they knew any Somali pirates. After a remarkable odyssey we finally found the pirates in Eastleigh, the Somali part of Nairobi, in the club room of a hotel. The pirates were more afraid of us than we were of them. Watching the kids' videos made them relax. They opened up and really tried to give an account of what had happened, for the kids of Hamburg to understand:

> 'How did you become a pirate in the first place?'
> 'How do you like *Pirates of the Caribbean*?'
> 'Have you ever killed somebody and doesn't it hurt you in the heart?'
> 'Would you like your children to become pirates, too?'

Among the pirates we met there was an old man who had been part of that first group of fishermen who had thought of themselves as acting on behalf of the non-existent coastguard of the non-existent state of Somalia, trying to reinforce the three-mile zone which had been violated by corporate fishing fleets that had taken away the livelihood of Somali fishermen. There also was a fragile-looking guy of 17 who had just escaped from Somalia and whose body spoke of lifelong hunger. Because he was so light he had been forced to be the first of his crew to climb up that shaking ladder onto the deck of the containership with a machine gun hanging round his neck. His bosses, who had safely stayed ashore, gave him 10,000 dollars out of the million-dollar ransom. Money that soon after was taken from him again, when he was robbed on his way out. He had never been on a ship before and did not intend to set foot on one again.

Paralogistics is first and foremost a take on logistics, coming from outside of the logistical systems to hack and interrupt them for access.

Have you ever looked up the bow of a containership from a little boat floating next to it? Next time you do a harbour trip in one of the small tourist boats, envisage your only way to escape from oblivion was to climb onto that deck up there in the sky and claim that monster of a ship as yours. Imagine what an extraordinary kind of courage it takes to do that, the courage of those who had no part in the global order of things, until they realised that one of the major logistical lifelines of global capitalism was right there, on the horizon, within their reach.

While we brought the answers of the pirates, recorded on video, back to the children of Hamburg and transformed their dialogue into a stage performance, the Atalanta naval mission slowly managed to reinstate what has lately been called 'supply chain security'. The shipping industry of Hamburg founded a centre to train private anti-piracy forces for their ships. These forces, trained in a remote industrial zone of the city, were more than discreet; they never took prisoners and no one in Hamburg has ever heard of their actions again.

Considering that the shipping industry of Hamburg had made donations to the Theatre of Research in the past, we realised that by connecting children and pirates in this improbable dialogue we had enacted a link that had already been there, but which somehow was hidden from our sight. We understood that, being citizens of Hamburg, one of the biggest ports in the world, there were many links between us and other people somewhere else,[3] and that it was not by accident that these links remained hidden and remained offshore somehow. We understood that something crucial had happened to the logistics of the port during the last decades. And not just to our port; London, New York, Hong Kong – port cities around the world have moved their docks and terminals out into special zones with no connection to the urban space we live in.[4] Containerisation has brought the mass expulsion of labour from the ports. At Hamburg's Euro Terminal, no more than five people are needed to unload the biggest containerships in less than a day. Less than 20 people work on a big containership and none of them are from Hamburg. Instead, the captain and his officers are most likely from Russia and the crew is from the Philippines. Because they stay at the terminal for only one day at a time, they no longer get to visit Hamburg, not even the famous brothels of St. Pauli. For the first time since the city was founded, citizens of Hamburg do not sail the seas anymore.

From Peter Linebaugh and Marcus Rediker's book 'The Many-Headed Hydra',[5] we learned about the heritage of piracy. We learned about Atlantic piracy as an improbable alliance between liberated slaves from West Africa and a first form of the European working class which was forced into service on the ships of the European empires, effectively the first factories. Linebaugh and Rediker call this alliance 'Hydrarchy'. *geheimagentur* collective asked: What might *hydrarchy* be today?

A first step to finding out, we thought, would be to reclaim our right to the harbour as citizens of Hamburg. So, we tried. Some of us worked at the seafarers' mission, some of us kept a small historical steel ship afloat, some of us lived in an old shipyard. We did research about the boom of the cruise ship industry that had recently taken over big parts of Hamburg port. In summer 2015, *geheimagentur* collective temporarily opened an 'Alternative Cruise Ship Terminal' in the middle of the port, where for a few weeks different kinds of experiences of the port were facilitated and created.[6]

Learning by doing, we became knowledgeable about the power structure of Hamburg Port Authority (HPA) – a half-private, half-public organisation that owns the land and makes the rules in Hamburg port. We found that, in the name of safety and security, HPA keeps everyone out of the port who is not 'relevant for port economy'. Of course, only Hamburg Port Authority gets to decide who and what fits this criterion. Nobody can live in Hamburg port or to open, for instance, a café on a boat without the permission of HPA, which is very hard to get. In the port, it seems we are all illegal migrants.

THE LOGISTICAL TURN

Meanwhile, people all over the world were squatting the streets and squares of their cities in the name of real democracy. The Tahir Square Movement, the Syntagma Square assemblies, the Occupy Movement in the US, the Indignados in Spain, and many others – and *geheimagentur* started to work within a network of artists, activists and researchers to explore this new 'art of being many'.[7] We met people from Tunis, Cairo, Madrid, New York, Athens and Istanbul. And we asked ourselves if in some way, the pirates of Puntland Somalia were to be counted in. But we did not understand what the connection between these struggles was, until we read Deborah Cowen's book, *The Deadly Life of Logistics*,[8] in which she constructs a relation between Somali piracy and the Occupy movement:

> Much like 'The Many-Headed Hydra', the seemingly disparate lives of these movements are connected through the infrastructures of logistics space. Alongside profound differences in strategy, tactics, and the logistics of struggle, together with the very real distance (socially and spatially) between these collectivities, there has also at times been exchange between members and overlap in organizers, events, and ideas that point to the potential for a different occupation and organization of logistics space. (Cowen, p. 227)

Cowen, as well as thinkers like Keller Easterling,[9] Sandro Mezzadra and Brett Neilson,[10] or Fred Moten and Stefano Harney, argue that capitalism currently is taking a logistical turn.[11]

Logistics – the science of the supply chain – comes from warfare and, in warfare, has traditionally been a service dominated by the master discourse of warfare: strategy. Of course, logistics is also of crucial importance for trade, where it is also in a position of service to the system of production that has for the longest time been seen as the core of the economy. In this position of service, to either strategy or production, logistics has connected warfare to trade and trade to warfare for thousands of years. But when containerisation had its breakthrough – not least due to the U.S. Army's use of containers to keep supply chains open to their troops in Vietnam – something changed for logistics and made it rise up over its former masters. The free movement of capital around the globe, the digital revolution alongside the fact that the internet has become a gigantic catalogue to order from, crisis-driven migration between continents and the primary importance of energy systems: all of this contributed to the rise of logistics. Thus today, strategy follows logistics in warfare, and production took its position in a system of circulation, in a gigantic supply chain that more and more models society as such. In a paper on *Extraction, Logistics and Finance*, Sandro Mezzadra and Brett Neilson write: 'Stemming from military practices, logistics organizes capital in technical ways that aim to make every step of its "turnover" productive' (Mezzadra and Neilson, p. 5). Capitalism itself has become the movement of movements.

UPS,[12] global player of logistics, describes this as follows: 'Everybody loves something. We love logistics. We love its precision, its epic scale, its ability to make life better for billions of people. Each day, our customers count on us to choreograph a ballet of infinite complexity played across skies, oceans and borders. And we do. What's not to love?'[13]

Logistics seems humble. Its subordinate position turns out to be its strength. It focuses on operations which seemingly only build the platform, create the conditions for human life to happen. Customers count on it to supply what is needed in some other place, where life is supposed to happen. Logistics is not considered a part of that, it does not have to be thought of in terms of the public and the social. It is just a service. To really be of service it mainly has to be one thing: it has to be safe and secure. Or else, how is it supposed to provide what is needed in that other place where life is happening? But in its growth, global logistics takes the space where life was supposed to happen and turns it into logistical zones designed and defined by the safety of the supply chain.

Look at the things that surround us, such as clothing, furniture, technical equipment. Make a guess: how much of it has been shipped before it arrived where you find it right now?

Rose George turned the answer to that question into the title of her book, *Ninety Percent of Everything*.[14] In it, she cites the chief of the British navy: 'Today we suffer from sea blindness' (George, p. 4). George extrapolates, 'There are no ordinary citizens to witness the working of an industry that is one of the most fundamental to their daily existence' (George, p. 2). But citizenship needs witnesses. If there are no citizens to witness something, there is no citizenship in that which is not witnessed. George points out that citizen rights do not apply for everyone working on a containership. 'Imagine you have a problem while on a ship. Who do you complain to, when you are employed by a Manila manning agency on a ship owned by an American, flagged by Panama, managed by a Cypriot in international waters?' (George, p. 10).

Obviously, ports are crucial sites for – maybe even something like the DNA of – the logistical turn. And this goes for all kinds of ports: airports, the tiny ports that connect digital streams of information to local interfaces, and, of course, seaports. Therefore, to observe what happens in ports, and what does not, might provide us with some insight about what to expect from the logistical turn. Is there a chance to persist, to claim, to squat or inhabit it? How are we going to take part in the dance of logistics? In what ways are we already dancing in this ballet across skies, oceans and borders? What if precision and epic scale are not exactly our strong side, and what if we suck at ballet?

Looking at seaports as crucial sites of this development, what do we see?

We see that we see nothing. We see that we are blocked out, we are blinded. And even if we really try and manage to enter the port zone to investigate, we find ourselves confronted with a striking difficulty to name and to politicize anything that happens there. Sea blindness starts ashore.

Epic scale also plays a role in that. In the world of logistics everything has to be as big as possible: ships, terminals, rivers, everything. Global scale is not human scale, and logistics generally does not like people much; it likes algorithms that try to create circuits of movements that rely on human agency as little as possible. Standing at the gate of a containership terminal, dwarfed by a form of capital that resembles the sublime – something that is so huge it is not even entirely here, but always partly somewhere else. Too big to even form something like a locality. Too big to concern us local dwarfs.

Supply chain security is another important factor in this scenario. It is not new, but it is diversifying and by now can appear in the disguise of workers' rights or children's health considerations. It goes along with a closed system of insurance calculations, which make us all accountable for the security of the supply chain and make it almost impossible to intervene, to create new, alternative supply chains. Safety is just too expensive. It is so expensive that only corporate capital can pay for it. And thus, there is only corporate capital left in the port, and there are fences and gates and cameras to shut everything else out: for your own safety. There are only operators, no citizens, in logistical space.

For centuries, Hamburg port has created the connections and the means to sustain a city of free people. The concept of the free port as a special economic zone was partly invented here (Easterling, p. 27 ff.). Of course, exclusion, extraction and exploitation always had a part in this. However, relying on the free port, Hamburg declared itself independent of kings and territorial empires centuries ago. The zone of the free port has been the key to this independence; it has enabled the growth and persistence of the biggest European city that is not a capital and has also helped to establish something like a citizenship by the seas. What is happening to this tradition, to this form of citizenship, after the port itself has been turned into a logistical zone beyond citizenship? Can the use of paralogistics be a tactic to reclaim the ports?

THE BEACH OF BADAGRY

During the most successful years of Somali piracy, containerships stopped coming to Mogadishu port. Containerised sea trade came to a complete cessation there. But sea trade itself did not.

In their documentary *From Gulf to Gulf to Gulf*, the artist collective Camp from India show footage of a different kind of sea trade that works under the radar of the global logistical machine. It stems from a coastal zone in India, somewhere north of Bombay, where special environmental conditions allow people to build massive wooden boats without big machinery, based on traditional craftsmanship. Hundreds of these simple cargo ships are then used to transport cargo between India, Africa and the whole Gulf region – a trade that is governed by people from the Indian province, who employ their families, friends and neighbours. The documentary consists solely of edited footage that people on those ships shot with their own cellphones. These videos show hard working conditions, but also give the impression of self-determination, of companionship and of living with and by the sea.

When *geheimagentur* temporarily opened the Alternative Cruise Ship Terminal in Hamburg port during the summer of 2015, Shaina Anand from Camp from India came to visit. Together, we discussed the idea of building a ship like that in Hamburg. Could that reconnect us to a civil and self-determined kind of seafaring? To a practice that, once upon a time, was essential for our city and for the claim to citizenship? Or would that just be a romantic regression?

In summer 2016, we saw ships like this again elsewhere. Not as big, not for crossing the oceans, but nonetheless cargo ships made from wood, in a natural dry dock. It was our last day in Nigeria and after seven days of full-on research, day and night, on informal trade between Hamburg and Lagos port, we had only one wish: to get out of this 20-million-people-no-public-infrastructure-monster of a city. Get out of the traffic, get out of the crude oil hub, get out of that never-ending street market, that zone of EFRITIN, and go to the beach. The beach of Badagry. 20 miles of white sand. No international resort, nothing much but coconuts and fishermen and people driving their motorbikes along the shoreline because there they could go faster than on the bumpy road. The waves of the Atlantic were just perfect, a surfers' paradise that seemed untouched, unseen, unheard of. And then there were these huge boats made from tropical wood overarching the beach. Actually, this was not quite a beach. It was a shipyard. The ships were made right here, probably to serve as cargo ships for the informal trade with Benin, the border being just ten miles away.

When we saw them, we realized that we would not have found them if we had not followed the informal sea trade from Hamburg to Nigeria, created by migrants, and that we would not have understood what we saw if we had not watched Camp's documentary. And that we would never have watched it if we had not opened the Alternative Cruise Ship Terminal. And that we would not have done that if we had not been involved in the improbable dialogue between pirates and children. And next thing we could do, together with our Nigerian business partners, would be to find out about these cargo ships and try and buy one, and turn it into a little cruise ship for our Alternative Cruise Ship company. And then all would fit together in an extremely seductive version of a happy ending, that comes with the feeling that everything is connected, people and things and oceans. That they arrange themselves and each other, that they never stop arranging each other, floating, bending, and not only building machines, but bodies full of needs and desires. And that we, as part of these bodies, are constantly following the moon and the tides around the planet, riding and at the same time creating, the currents.

But some of those currents are quite old, and within them something is transported through time that will never find a happy ending. And thus, just when you feel happily connected with everything, the ghosts of logistics might come and speak to you, opening up a paralogistic dialogue.

Back in the city we got ready for the flight back, when a guy turned up at the bar of the hotel, just in time for last orders. 'My name is Memory', he said, 'like memory. Do you know the card game?' He asked me about my day, and when I told him about the beach of Badagry, he smiled: 'Did we know', he asked, 'that Badagry was ground zero of human trafficking? Did we know that that beach saw the very beginning of the Atlantic slave trade and that just a few miles from where we were, there was a famous and bloody stone that was called the stone of no return, because everyone who had passed that stone had turned into a thing to be shipped? No, we had not known that. But there was Memory standing right in front of us, raising his glass to our safe journey.

In *The Undercommons*, Stefano Harney and Fred Moten sometimes seem to speak with the voices of the shipped with the voices of those who had walked past that stone of no return. In their discussion of the logistical turn they argue that modern logistics was born there, that the Atlantic slave trade is the first model of modern logistics. This does not mean that all logistics involve the slave trade, but it does indicate that the position afforded to people in logistics tends to be that of the shipped. However, this is no position, no standpoint. At least not when it comes to the circuits of capitalism. Harney and Moten write:

> If the proletariat was located at a point in the circuits of capital, a point in the production process from which it had a peculiar view of capitalist totality, what of those who were located at every point, which is to say at no point, in the production process? What of those who were not just labour but commodity, not just in production but in circulation, not just in circulation but in distribution as property, not just property but property that reproduced and realized itself? The standpoint of no standpoint, everywhere and nowhere, of never and to come, of thing and nothing. (Moten and Harney, p. 100)

If this is what happens when logistics takes over, the question of what logistics might be from 'our point of view' cannot be answered, as logistics moves us and moves us around until we become the shipped, those who have no standpoint.

I asked Memory if he would agree that if Badagry is ground zero of the Atlantic slave trade, it also had to be ground zero of hydrarchy? As by producing the shipped, it also produced new alliances of the shipped, pirates' alliances, that crossed borders of continents and races and powers in a new planetary dimension? But Memory did not know that, and I had to get to the airport to fly back to Hamburg. Maybe I was too stoned to make myself clear.

THE SHIPPINGS OF THE SHIPPED

The weed dealers from our neighbourhood were the ones who finally cleared our heads and started to cure our sea-blindness beyond our projection of the Hamburg port. They added a most important piece to the puzzle. When we had opened the Alternative Cruise Ship Terminal we had postulated publicly that the citizens of Hamburg had lost their relation to their port and were not using it anymore, which is why the port was now sold to them as spectacle in festivals and cruises. And that might still be right, but then we found out that the non-citizens of this city do use the port. Not so much for transporting weed. No, they were using the port for the same reason they had started to sell weed in the first place; they had recently come here from West Africa. Hence, most of them had no citizen rights, which means no access to the market where they could sell their labour and become a properly exploited member of what is left of the proletariat. So, they tried to find access to the entanglement of people, things and oceans in a different way.

They told us that some time back, in the early 1990s, people had come to Hamburg from West Africa to find that there is an abundance of things that are thrown away here, but were wanted in West Africa, or – as they prefer to put it – things are moving, are moving in Lagos, in Gambia, in Ghana. Fridges, TVs, hairdryers, hoovers, water heaters, remote controls – basically everything used in a household and everything with a plug. And that if they could find a way to collect these things and ship them from Hamburg to West Africa that would make a big difference in the lives of their families. Ever since, most people coming from West Africa were trying to do that one way or the other.

geheimagentur conducted extensive interviews with some of them. Everyone who had recently come from West Africa had the same answer to our question, whether they knew someone related to this business or not: 'All the people I know.' All our interview partners introduced themselves as businessmen. Some of them had studied logistics back in West Africa. During the interviews the impression of talking to refugees faded and, though most of them had in fact had horrific reasons for fleeing their country, we realized that we were at the same time talking to a first or

second wave of aspiring African businessmen, of lower middle and working class people from Africa, who were trying to turn things around and
were looking at Europe from the perspective of what to extract from it,
what to set in motion, for the only reason that it is moving in Lagos. All
of them stressed that they were able to do this now because the internet
allowed them to build informal logistical networks between Hamburg and
Lagos with their phones, including ways to regulate money flow.

We learned that another crucial element of these paralogistics are cars.
However, cars are not only cars in this informal supply chain, they are
containers. The car makes use of a hole in the system, as customs will
charge you for the car, not for what is inside the car. Therefore, to send
stuff to West Africa, you first buy a car, a scrap car will do, and then fill
every cubic inch of the car with stuff.

Hidden in the industrial zone in the east of Hamburg – in close proximity to that centre where the anti-piracy forces are trained – there is a
place that is organized by this trade. In Billstraße you find everything that
is moving in Lagos. The place does not look much like Hamburg, it looks
more like Tin Can Island in Nigeria. Whereas logistics makes every port
look the same, a paralogistic zone is more like a passage to a completely
different place. Unfortunately, this is not the kind of trade Hamburg Port
Authority has in mind when it comes to what they call 'development
towards the future' (Hamburg Port Authority).

Most of the West African movers and traders from our neighbourhood
recently came to Hamburg via the Mediterranean Sea in little boats and
ships from Libya, headed towards the tiny Italian island of Lampedusa as
an access point into Europe. Larry Macauley, an activist for refugees'
rights, born in Lagos and now living in Hamburg,[15] has also come via that
route. He told me that the little ship packed with hundreds of people in a
way that reminded him of Hollywood movies he had watched about the
slave trade. The ship was balanced with human bodies and was in danger
of tipping over whenever someone moved. The chance of survival, Larry
said, was equal to the ability of the people to stay motionless for 21 hours,
to keep the balance, to function together as weight. I told Larry about my
plan to do a project about the shippings of the shipped, about the informal
trade between Hamburg port and West Africa, and he connected me
online to his friend, George Adetayo Adewoye from Valuehandlers
International Limited, and sent me to Lagos to see the other side.[16]

Hamburg Port Hydrarchy and the African Terminal

Within the program of the Alternative Cruise Ship Terminal project in summer 2015, people from different initiatives and backgrounds took each other on local cruises to share their practices of reusing the port. A network of people emerged who are active in Hamburg port while trying to stay under the radar of Hamburg Port Authority – a network of port-(non)-citizens one might say. In the end, they built a raft together, the Hydra, and sailed with it from the terminal situated in an old shipyard to the centre of the city. There, next to the town hall, a demonstration on the water took place reclaiming the right to the port for all citizens.[17]

To follow up on this collective effort, Hamburg Port Hydrarchy was founded in January 2016. Mirroring or mocking Hamburg Port Authority, Hamburg Port Hydrarchy is on a mission 'to develop Hamburg port towards a hydrarchical future'.

First, eight members of Hamburg Port Hydrarchy received small grants to travel to different port cities all over the world. They visited 'radical seafarers' and the so-called 'offshore art' scene in Brooklyn, New York. They took part in the uprising of Venetian citizens against the cruise ship industry. They explored the history of the boat people, as well as the current situation of seafarers trapped on board of bankrupt ships in the South China Sea. From each trip, teams brought back to Hamburg port an array of connections, insights and sometimes proposals for a different future. These were presented on board the MS Stubnitz, an old ship for industrial fishing turned into a cultural venue, in a performance consisting of lectures, installations and assemblies. On the MS Stubnitz, Hamburg Port Hydrarchy was collectively performed for the first time, as an experimental claim to a citizenship by the seas that does not yet exist. Transmitting from the old radio room, the Department of Paralogistics argues for a paralogistic approach to hydrarchy by accessing logistical systems through the backdoor, through waste and ruins, through passages that open up in the frictions that logistics is allegedly trying to overcome.

Finishing my own research trip to Lagos Nigeria I came home to a flood. A leakage had turned my basement into a hot tub. The janitor showed up and we smoked a cigarette together, contemplating the damage. It turned out that he had sailed West African waters for years as a member of the former GDR fishing fleet. He had once worked on the MS Stubnitz that had served as a swimming factory, to which other vessels brought their catch to be frozen and stored. Tin Can Island, the port of

Lagos, he remembered, was largely pirate territory back then; they had to keep watch all through the night. However, he also said that the GDR had good and fair business relations with African states. With the Stubnitz, and other ships like it, the GDR provided technical equipment for industrial fishing and therefore got a share of those states' fishing contingents. When the currency of the GDR went down, the industrial fishing fleet of the GDR went down with it. Overnight, it became unaffordable to be fair. The MS Stubnitz was rescued by sound artist Urs Blaser and a bunch of boat punks and is still afloat today. It is now moored at Baakenhöft in Hamburg port and serves as a venue for experimental music and performance. During German colonialism, the ships coming from Namibia were moored not far from here. The huge Afrika Terminal, build in the 1960s and now out of use, is still located next to the MS Stubnitz. In spring 2017, during the theatre festival – Theater der Welt – the warehouse will be open to the public for the first time and will temporarily become a venue for theatre and dance. Nobody knows yet what is going to happen to it next.

After presenting on board of MS Stubnitz, Hamburg Port Hydrarchy will develop an experimental assembly of hydrarchical setups, all to be tried out at Baakenhöft / Baakenhafen, the last remaining part of the old Hamburg port that is in close proximity to the city and not yet sold to investors for 'development'. One element of that assembly will be the re-opening of the Afrika Terminal as an African Terminal in becoming. How might a paralogistic African Terminal operate? What might it sound like, look like, move like? And could it be a place for us to learn more about this new kind of 'citizenship by the seas' that we have to invent?

LOOSE ENDS

On our first day of research in Lagos, our guide refused to take us to the harbour. First, we would have to do this one thing for him and accompany him to a business conference hosted by the government. When I put my name on the list of participants, he stood right next to me and whispered in my ear: 'Put *German Embassy*.' Given my confusion, it seemed about right so, strangely, I obeyed. Then, our guide introduced me to people he wanted to impress. Pictures were taken, me shaking hands, smiling, receiving a promotional plastic bag, and showing the bag to the camera.

At the end of our visit, our guides posed for our camera, too, holding the flag of Hamburg Port Hydrarchy in front of the chart with the business plan we had made together: Back in Hamburg port we were to open a temporary business school, where people who had recently arrived in Hamburg, as well as long-term citizens, could learn about the informal trade between Hamburg and Africa and how to do it. In the end, we would send at least five cars full of stuff that is moving in Lagos from Hamburg Baakenhöft to Tin Can Island.

This is how to get to Tin Can Island: right before you leave Lagos mainland and take the bridge that brings you to the terminal, you have to park the car and take a motorbike taxi. Only the motorbike can pass between those hundreds of oil trucks, which are blocking the highway. The trucks are rocking to the left and to the right, almost bumping into each other each time one of their wheels gets caught in one of the holes in the road. The names of the companies are written on the trucks with paint, one of them reads: *God's Will Limited*. The motorbikes pass through the dust as quickly as possible, calculating the moment when trucks are leaning outwards and not inwards against each other. 'There's no new way to die in Lagos', people say.

When we arrived at the terminal, a man pretending to be an 'authority' took our camera. One hour and 12,000 naira later, we got our camera back. When adrenalin stopped pumping we found ourselves in a yard where people unpacked containers and cars with signs on them saying 'Hamburg to Lagos'. A bunch of kids' bikes and hoovers spilled out. All moving in Lagos. One of the traders wore a shirt saying 'There's less here than meets the eye'. The place looked just like Billstraße in Hamburg.

The business conference we were taken to was about agriculture. During lectures, electricity went on and off. Nobody seemed to care; speakers just went on speaking in the dark, in the pitch-black room. Listening to them, I learned that the state of Nigeria wants the country to change, wants it to become more independent from import, more independent from the oil price. Or maybe does not exactly want, but has to, as the oil price is down and so is the Nigerian currency – the Naira – that lost half its value in 2016. It did not help that the government had tried to fight corruption by limiting the exchange of naira to dollar or euro. We understood that the informal trade we were about to throw ourselves into was in serious trouble, and what it means that the agency of everyone working in worldwide logistics is tied to the oil price, now including our own.

Later on, we met Aderemi Adegbite, an artist who makes a living as a line producer for film crews from abroad. His main service is to pay the authorities 12,000 naira before white people show up with their cameras. He lives in Makoko. Makoko is where migrants from Benin first enter Lagos. They do not actually step on Nigerian soil but build their houses on wooden stilts in the waters of the Lagoon. Makoko looks amazing. No wonder that everyone in the art world loved that project shown at the Venice Biennale in 2013 – *Makoko Floating School* by the Nigerian architecture practice NLÉ. Only Aderemi Adegbite did not. It turns out that Makoko community never wanted a floating school: why would we send our children to a school that can be taken away by the currents or by towing it with a motorboat?

Larry, activist for refugees' rights in Hamburg, is a proud Lagosian. He is no fan of the people of Makoko. They are no Lagosians, they live no Lagosian life; they belong somewhere else he thinks. What would I think, Larry asks me, if people from Africa were living an African life right here in Hamburg?

Wikipedia defines paralogistic as a term for a circular argument, a failing proof.

Epilogue: Searching for Alternative Supply Chains

Epilogue

When this text went to print, the core group of the African Terminal consisted of nine members from Gambia, Nigeria and Ghana and three members from Germany. The first transaction – in which the African Terminal group claimed the space of the old Afrika Terminal to collect goods and send them to Gambia – had just been successfully finished. However, in terms of common logistics, the transaction didn't turn out to be profitable. Even though – due to its partly cultural character – the transaction was partly funded, it didn't pay out for the African members of the group in terms of money. Clearly, the German members of the group were more frustrated by this fact than their African colleagues. The latter were still on board with the project and keen on developing the African Terminal further. Asked for their reasons, they referred to the things we learned during the process but also made it clear that it is simply important not only to be shipped, but to ship something yourself. Important to collectively take the subject position of traders and of citizens that is denied to these group members by the German state. And they convinced us; indeed it seems crucial to go on trying to find alternative supply chains, to chase that dream and to turn logistics around. And it is fruitful to use cultural production as a place to do that. Here, apart from breaking it down to numbers, we can enjoy whatever surplus – or even *jouissance* – the search for the alternative supply chain may produce. In this sense, paralogistics overturn – and at the same time reclaim – logistics as what often appears to be its opposite: a planetary form of conviviality including shared conflicts, shared resources, shared learning, shared memories and shared mourning.

NOTES

1. *geheimagentur* is an open collective working in performance art, cultural studies and activism, www.geheimagentur.net, date accessed 1 March 2018.
2. www.theatreofresearch.org, date accessed 1 March 2018.
3. In May 2013, a delegation from Colombia turned up at the Labour Day demonstration in the Wilhelmsburg quarter of Hamburg and demanded the microphone. They had come to let people know that the charcoal needed for the newly built power station in Hamburg port is imported from Columbia, and that mining it had destroyed their villages and their livelihoods. An alliance of protesters was formed and people managed to block the port with 30 boats and ships for one hour in protest.
4. See Alberto Toscano (2011) 'Logistics and Opposition'.
5. Marcus Rediker and Peter Linebaugh (2013) *The Many-Headed Hydra: Sailors, Slaves, Commoners, and the Hidden History of the Revolutionary Atlantic*.
6. http://www.geheimagentur.net/projekte/ein-kreuzfahrtterminal-3/, date accessed 1 March 2018.
7. Results and insights from this process can be found in the book: *geheimagentur*, Martin Schäfer and Vassilis Tsianos (2016) *The Art of Being Many. Towards a new Theory and Practice of Gathering*.
8. Deborah Cowen (2014) *The Deadly Life of Logistics. Mapping Violence in Global Trade*.
9. Keller Easterling (2014) *Extrastatecraft. The Power of Infrastructure Space*.
10. Sandro Mezzadra and Brett Neilson (2013) 'Extraction, Logistics and Finance'.
11. Fred Moten and Stefano Harney (2013) *The Undercommons. Fugitive Planning & Black Study*.
12. United Parcel Services.
13. Cited after Cowen, p. 204.

14. Rose George (2013) *Ninety Percent of Everything: Inside Shipping, the Invisible Industry That Puts Clothes on Your Back, Gas in Your Car, and Food on Your Plate.*
15. http://www.refugeeradionetwork.net/, date accessed 1 March 2018.
16. http://www.valuehandlers.com/, date accessed 1 March 2018.
17. http://www.geheimagentur.net/statement-der-besatzung-des-alternativen-kreuzfahrtterminals/, date accessed 1 March 2018.

References

Cowen, Deborah. 2014. *The Deadly Life of Logistics. Mapping Violence in Global Trade.* Minneapolis: University of Minnesota Press.
Easterling, Keller. 2014. *Extrastatecraft. The Power of Infrastructure Space.* London/New York: Verso.
geheimagentur. 2016. In *The Art of Being Many. Towards a New Theory and Practice of Gathering,* ed. Martin Schäfer and Vassilis Tsianos. Bielefeld: Transcript.
George, Rose. 2013. *Ninety Percent of Everything: Inside Shipping, the Invisible Industry That Puts Clothes on Your Back, Gas in Your Car, and Food on Your Plate.* New York: Metropolitan Books.
Mezzadra, Sandro, and Brett Neilson. 2013. Extraction, Logistics and Finance. *Radical Philosophy* 178 (March/April): 8–18.
Moten, Fred, and Stefano Harney. 2013. *The Undercommons. Fugitive Planning & Black Study.* Wivenhoe/New York/Port Watson: Minor Compositions.
Rediker, Marcus, and Peter Linebaugh. 2013. *The Many-Headed Hydra: Sailors, Slaves, Commoners, and the Hidden History of the Revolutionary Atlantic.* Boston: Beacon Press.
Toscano, Alberto. 2011. Logistics and Opposition. *Mute,* 3/2.
http://www.geheimagentur.net/. Accessed 1 Mar 2018.
http://www.refugeeradionetwork.net/. Accessed 1 Mar 2018.
http://www.theatreofresearch.org. Accessed 1 Mar 2018.
http://www.valuehandlers.com/. Accessed 1 Mar 2018.

Phyto-Performance and the Lost Gardens of Riga

Alan Read

The 'English Garden Effect'—a phrase borrowed from the poetry of John Ashbery, first written by the novelist Walter Abish in his short story of that name—describes a process by which a landscape might be rearranged to conceal its historical determinants by those who might gain from such scenic concealing. In his story Abish writes, 'Remnants of the old atrocity persist, but they are converted into ingenious shifts of scenery, a sort of "English Garden" effect to give the required air of naturalness, pathos and hope'.[1] I am interested in what such an 'English Garden Effect' might mean for us as artists, outsiders, visitors, to my proposed *phyto-place* of performance—looking for a way to work that eschews the opportunistic occupational mode of the site specific, and thinks itself into site in a more responsive and responsible fashion.

Phyto-Performance, that is, not just theatres representing vegetal matters—of which *The Little Shop of Horrors* (1960) might be taken as an early baroque example—but practices of co-presentation alongside and within plant processes, could be expected to offer affective insights to the deep ecology of these rearrangements. Such performances (in the spirit of the

A. Read (✉)
King's College London, London, UK
e-mail: alan.read@kcl.ac.uk

© The Author(s) 2019
P. Hildebrandt et al. (eds.), *Performing Citizenship*, Performance Philosophy, https://doi.org/10.1007/978-3-319-97502-3_15

plant philosopher Michael Marder) would undermine casual correlations between the vegetal, the whimsical, and the romantic, and might reacquaint us with the robust materiality of flora, the dark side of roots, the infra-thin movement of leaves. The repertoire of such practices, however, has been drastically limited within contemporary performance by a humanist theatre that places *homo sapiens* and their limb-heavy exertions centre stage.

Phyto interests, from the Greek word for 'things that grow', have most recently been championed in all their unpredictability by the philosopher Michael Marder, in his ground-breaking book *Plant-Thinking*.[2] Phyto-thought, you could call it, has been common to the literary and philosophical imagination, vigorously spreading its tendrils since Plato. It is now relevant to the philosophy of a number of thinkers whose broad interest is in *vegetal life*, a decentralizing of the human from plant perspectives, among whom the French philosophers Gilles Deleuze and Felix Guattari's work on the rhizome would be the most obvious example.[3] But that casually metaphoric use, and some might say philosophical and interpretive abuse of plants, is not where I intend to take us in this short essay.

First, by way of a brief biographical sketch to establish the somewhat fanciful link between the vegetal and citizenship here, I would like to recover something more material from Guattari's work—to remind us of the relationship between the questions I am posing on performance and 'troubled citizenship' that I think the vegetal invites. These ideas began to germinate for me in 1992, and were prompted in person by Guattari, who had come to London (just before he prematurely died of a heart attack in 1994), to discuss his newly published essay *The Three Ecologies*.

On finally shoe-horning a considerable audience into the modest Institute of Contemporary Arts theatre space on The Mall (*A Thousand Plateaus*, in the translation by Brian Massumi, had been doing great business at the ICA bookshop for years), I recall him insisting, before he could possibly speak to the assembled expectant group, that this kind of arrangement just would not suffice for the democratic purposes of his work. When the co-author of *Mille Plateaux* says he does not like the seating set up, you take note.

I am committed to the idea that one's ends and means should be linked formally (whether that be the way we conduct ourselves academically or otherwise, in *all* settings, whether they be conference arrangements or the street protests these intellectual assemblies often articulate), and so I readily agreed that we should remove the tiered bench seating, designed to ensure everyone could see, and seat everyone on the floor in a circle around Félix, who promptly positioned himself sitting at their centre, therefore, by definition, with his back to a proportion of the audience who had come to listen to him. Félix had a rather soft voice and started with this passage from the work he was with us to discuss, *The Three Ecologies*:

> Now more than ever, nature cannot be separated from culture; in order to comprehend the interactions between eco systems, the mechanosphere and the social and individual universes of reference, we must learn to think 'transversally'. Just as monstrous and mutant algae invade the lagoon of Venice, so our television screens are populated, saturated by 'degenerate' images and statements. In the field of social ecology, men like Donald Trump are permitted to proliferate freely, like another species of algae, taking over entire district of New York and Atlantic City; he 'redevelops' by raising rents, thereby driving out tens of thousands of poor families, most of whom are condemned to homelessness, becoming the equivalent of the dead fish of environmental ecology. (Guattari 2000, p. 43)

Well, that was Félix Guattari at the ICA in 1992, prescient at least. Few who were present appeared either to know what he was talking about— never really having heard of Donald Trump—nor could they readily get the analogy to algae, as they could not hear what he was saying and his pronunciation of algae was quite baroque. It took a brave heart to suggest at this stage that, given we were all there to listen to Félix, we might want to return to a seating arrangement in which he could be heard—a less formally democratic proposal maybe, but a functional one at least. So we, or I should say, the stage managers and I, set about putting the theatre back into the shape it had been especially put into an hour before, pulling the retractable seating out again, much to the exasperation of the ICA technicians who muttered something about their labour clearly being the one absolutely *infinite* resource available to intellectuals who require optimum circumstances for their *own* labour, with little respect for the call these demands place on others tasked with putting out chairs, taking them away, then putting them out again, in pursuit of the ideal democratic arrangement.

Within this disturbance to the shape of a gathering, Guattari's idea of 'transversality' was already underway within that room. There and then, as much in the *form* of the discussion and disagreement about the seating and ways of resolving that local dispute as it was in his startling theoretical diagnosis, his forensic analysis of the newly empowered rentiers of the

Reagan and Thatcher years, those beyond any constraint of something once called society—Donald Trump's instinct for gated communities, camps of the *über* elite that, like algae, would proliferate across the fetid lagoon of the cosmopolitan class. Beyond the remarkable vegetal allegories that I will return to in the balance of this essay, I was aware—as early as the mid-1990s—that another elite, an educated elite circulating through the theoretical groves that I was responsible for organizing there, at the ICA, had little sense of the question posed to them by those who were responsible for moving those chairs around at their will. A question of the disaffection of labour and also a question that Donald Trump himself would notice provided him with an opportunity and an electoral mandate of 52% some years later. That at that time a certain 'will to power' was manifest within a liberal elite who were beginning to deploy intersectional theory to constitute themselves as polymorphously free of—or at least playful with—multitudinous identity formations, at the same time as forgetting to re-inscribe their analysis with any due regard for that other multitude with *less than one* identity, long left behind by successive government attacks on education and the welfare state. I think these reflections could be inscribed within frames of citizen and non-citizenship.

I returned to Guattari's material thinking about algae and the politics of oppression when Michael Marder[4] visited us at King's College London, where I moved a few years after that time at the ICA. There, Marder offered an audacious, panoramic survey of philosophy's entanglements with vegetal thinking. For instance, selecting one hidden herbalist among many, Friedrich Nietzsche—as Marder drew to our attention—dwelt very precisely upon the vegetal in the form of the 'jungle'—or as it has been more recently translated by Kevin Hill in Nietzsche's newly translated notebooks, 'primeval forest'—in his notes on *The Will to Power* (2017) which were, without his permission and indeed against his expressed view, collected together and published after his death by his sister, Elisabeth Forster-Nietzsche in 1901. But Nietzsche did so only after a detour through the 'arrant misrepresentations' and 'counterfeits' of psychology. In fragment 704 in 'The Will to Power in Nature' (written between November 1887 and March 1888), Nietzsche questioned 'Man's' striving after happiness. To understand anything about life Nietzsche, unusually perhaps for the philosophical tradition, insisted on an expanded sense of life, a 'formula that must apply to trees, and plants and animals'. Nietzsche even takes the trouble to notice the structural problem when asking what a plant might strive after, a false unity which does not exist, given the 'fact of million-fold growth'.

Michael Marder has, since that event, where we first heard these ideas, discussed this passage in Nietzsche's work,[5] fleshing it out, or more appropriately, inter-leafing it with some fascinating material insights borne of his fascination with plant practices. Unbeknownst to themselves, who appear to know little of Nietzsche's view perhaps, Michael Marder suggests that scientists confirm Nietzsche's hypothesis in examining kin recognition of plants. Specimens of the plant *Cakile edentula*, for instance, produce more roots when they share a pot with *strangers* (that is, plants of the same species, grown from seeds that derived from a different mother plant) than when they germinated in the same pot as their kin (defined as plants grown from seeds collected from the same mother plant). So, Marder is drawn to suggest that Nietzsche's interpretation of the 'fight' amongst trees in a jungle is also a 'theoretical fiction', which in turn naturalizes the struggle for survival in human societies, rather as the work of Konrad Lorenz had done with supposedly red of tooth and claw animalities of the mid-twentieth century, against the conclusive research of Ashley Montagu that reframed atavistic nature as altruistic nature.

Such striving, such 'will', will always occur in the face of something that Nietzsche says 'resists', as he posits: 'For what do the trees in a jungle fight each other? For happiness? – *For power! –*'. But amongst these *competitive* columbines there are other million-fold symbiotic forms of species co-existence which with some plant thinking, Marder suggests, some properly environmental thinking of the kind I will offer in this essay, might operate in more sympathetically entangled ways. It is not that 'the jungle' offers another metaphor with which to squeeze the pips of the vegetal, but rather, a material/historical site where kinship relations between plants have been observed; where to *strive* to 'be in the sun' could be conceived as more than an ontological imperative against entropy, where to *persevere* in being is itself the genesis of the performative comportment that will always trouble presumptions of citizenship.

In thinking about some of our *performance* concerns, namely, movement, our awareness of the surrounding world and life itself, Marder reminds us, we do not tend to associate *thinking* with plants. If we consider them at all, we think of plants 'shrouded in obscurity'—as Marder cites Thomas Aquinas in his introduction to *Plant-Thinking*. We maybe fail to recognize ourselves *in plants*. And thus, plants provide us, Marder would suggest possibly unwittingly, with a welcome short-circuit in the anthropocentric machinery. That is, the machinery that ceaselessly compares us with other animals and, having found comparisons wanting, co-opts other animals in *our* interests for our instrumental ends. It is, Marder proposes, a good thing that we do not recognize ourselves in plants. It is their foreignness that might trouble us, but it is this 'otherness' that protects us from too easy assimilation of what they intrinsically are—'Not us'.[6] I would stress here that this writing will have failed if you think what I am promoting is an appetite to cast, to draft in, plants into performance; to squeeze them for their pips, to mimic their movement or to transplant their roots.

But, I would suggest here that a fresh approach to *movement*, to *surroundings* and to *life itself*—in the spirit of Marder's vegetal thinking— might be recognized in plants if we look and listen carefully enough. Just so we can leave some of our zoological bias at the door, movement itself immediately throws up some problems for thinking phyto-centrically. Our ideal movement, we might have to admit at the outset, *is* an animal movement; by which I mean we have the capacity for locomotion. The whole rhetoric of human disability with regard to movement is based upon just such a spurious norm. Just think of words like crawling and striding for their comparative place within an unwritten hierarchy of power to measure something of this loco-normativity. In saying this, and celebrating human locomotion over other movements, we forget, that plants move at their edges, their leaves, at their centre, their stem, and indeed, most voraciously, underground.[7] Growth itself—though in its own time and always patient compared with our pre-emptive leaps and impatient spasms—*is* a kind of movement.

So, while we might not be able to recognize ourselves in plants, we perhaps should be able to recognize—Marder ingeniously suggests—the *vegetal inside us*. The 'otherness' of vegetal life within us is a good antidote to anthropomorphism; we should begin here to recognize something of the plant in *us*, not us in them. And this perhaps is where the affective response to performance might begin to make sense vegetally. Phytocentrism thus halts the anthropocentric urge of humans—for us to situate ourselves as central to a biosphere—which, irrespective of the cultivations of indigenous peoples and the mass-farming of their successors, got on quite well before us. The decentralized nature of plants themselves then, poses some interesting questions for us in performance. By putting plants in the centre, Marder insists—probably in light of a familiar questioning of his project—do we not just repeat anthropocentrism and its humanist ills?

Well, not exactly, as they—plants, that is—are not unified organisms. It is difficult to tell where a part of the plant begins and ends, it is difficult to pinpoint identity in vegetal life. The truth of the matter, for Marder at least, is that to place the plant at the centre of our life is to 'decenter the center'—the centre implodes along with the penumbra.[8] And that might not be such a bad thing when we seek ways of performance that can draw upon the abandonment of plants as a means by which such abandonment *itself* can become the spur to the recovery of lost techniques, disciplines and practices for plants' better protection. The performance *Lost Gardens* is an exemplary act in just one such homeopathic register (Fig. 1).

Lost Gardens, in which I was a participant in the 2013 Riga Homo Novus Festival, was directed by Christine Umpfenbach from Munich, who explores social realities in her performance pieces, focusing on migration,

Fig. 1 *Lost Gardens,* Riga, 2013, Dir. Christine Umpfenbach. (Photo Copyright Homo Novus Festival)

labour, and the realm of the city. The performers one meets in *Lost Gardens*, as in other Umpfenbach projects, are mostly non-actors—people engaged in other professions, older people, children. They could be your neighbours. Umpfenbach collaborates on this occasion with Latvian video artist Katrīna Neiburga and Austrian artist and scenographer Rudolf Bekic—who had been living in Latvia for a number of years, working with hand-made objects and mechanisms. Zane Zajančkausk, a Latvian editor, curator, producer and a researcher of communities, worked as director's assistant on the *Lost Gardens* project, researching 'small garden culture' and helping in the project's admirable and complex commitment to extended communication with the local groups and individuals who wished to be involved in the event.

The programme for the event sets out the context like this:

> In May 2013, a lane was cut through the allotment gardens in Bolderāja to free up the space for railway tracks as a part of the Riga Free Port development plan. Gardeners lost their gardens, fences were knocked down, trees were cut, garden houses were burned down or were demolished by bulldozers. The traumatic event had a big impact on the lives of these gardeners, who after spending every summer there, now have no place to go. Many of them started 40 years ago as young families to cultivate this area from being a swamp into the place in which trees, fruits and vegetables could grow and flowers would bloom.[9]

The 'English Garden Effect' comes to mind as we group here amidst a landscape of 'rearranged' structures, gardens and fences. It is clear that there has been some 'rebuilding' for the purpose of this event, but not so much as to conceal the shattering experience these carers for the soil have experienced. We gather hesitantly, in loose assemblages of between 10 and 14 folk—a community of those who have nothing in common, while looking on at a community who most definitely do. Loss (Fig. 2).

We are split into separate witnessing alliances rather than anything approaching an 'audience', and gently we are asked to follow one of six leaders. We are given a piece of cut fruit or vegetable—something with a distinctive colour—to mark us out from the other groups, as though we might not remember to whom we belong. And indeed, as we walk together slowly through the gathering twilight gloom of a late summer evening in Riga, there is something to be said for this small token of identity. For as one engages with each 'station' in the landscape—a small shed here, a

Fig. 2 *Lost Gardens* conversation station. (Photo Homo Novus Festival)

makeshift stand there, a soup being cooked here, a television playing an episode of some injustice there—the sense of one's own self begins to dissipate and mix with the horticulture that this land was once given over to, before the bulldozers came and made way for the Free Port Authority development that would pour asphalt over 40 years of shared nurturing of this land.

The protagonists in this performance are the displaced gardeners and, peculiarly democratically, a representative from Riga Free Port (who lectures us on the bus *en route* to the location), who explain their perspectives on what had happened and recall the event through their points of view. This is how two of these participants are described:

Asja bought her garden 30 years ago for her father in order to help keep him busy and give him a purpose in life. After his death, she continued to maintain the garden to help her relax. One day, she returned to the garden to find it had been burned to the ground. She wrote to the Free Port authority asking for explanations as to why she was not given notice of the demolition.

Anatolijs and his wife grew fruits and vegetables in their garden so they never had the need to go to the market to buy fresh products. He and his wife stood there watching his fruit trees being cut down. Together with his granddaughter Liza, he explains how his garden house was relocated by a crane to an area 30 meters away from the original location.[10]

Each of the stations one visits as part of the two-hour event is a small bricolage edifice within the landscape, hewn from the materials at hand. Each station is attended to by one of the residents, who in several cases prepare food from the ground nearby and serve a hot bowl of broth or salad and fruits as we perambulate. The pace of each of these hosting gestures—that become the time of the theatre event—is closer to the patience of the slow-grown plants that, in this instance, appear more as co-actors in a network of distributed performances across this threatened landscape.

The evening ends, in as much as it can end, in a tent situated in the landscape, with a glowing fire outside and a supper laid out within, served by those who have been telling their stories of displacement. They stand in simple tableaux in the opening of the tent as we watch on from inside, looking beyond them to the long sunset across the landscape that is now not theirs.

The coaches wait for us in the discrete distance, as though to remind us that this country, this *contra*, is only what it is because of the other it is not: the city to which we are about to be returned, passing through the advertising lights of the petro-chemical companies and banks that edge Riga's fringe.

If plants remind us of anything, it is of the power to wait—both the ability to wait, and the capacity to let others wait. Peter Sloterdijk suggested that democracy could be said to be based on a proto architectonic ability to build waiting rooms, and perhaps glasshouses are just the antithesis of such things.[11] Yes, they allow humans to wait for plants, but their controlled environments represent a strategic quickening of natural growth. If *Lost Gardens*, in its lugubrious pace, wandering dramaturgy and peripatetic pauses showed us anything or invited us to feel something, it was that the time of the landscape and the time of those carers for that landscape—different as they were—contrasted with the time of development. The Riga Port Authority operated to rhythmic imperatives that were just wholly at odds with those who not only had waited four decades for trees to grow amongst them, but were now willing to wait for four hours in the twilight as we made circuits around their makeshift stalls, insisting on trying just about everything that was on offer from their addled ground. There were structures in this landscape, yes, but glasshouses and their urgencies were nowhere to be seen, before or after the heavy-duty lifting gear arrived in this *miserable-en-scene*.

Lost Gardens allows us to consider what Phyto-Performance might look and feel like. There is a commitment here to the cycles of plant growth and retreat. On the one hand, the horticulture of the Rigan allotments sets the pace for the event we wish to enter into, as an audience with its own festival chronotopes to maintain. The programme of the Homo Novus Festival offers so many delights that we *could* move onto, but the entangled, pedestrian pace of this event seems to demand our attention beyond such accelerated departures elsewhere to see 'yet more culture'.

How much longer might we be free to stay here amongst the infinite smells and senses of the landscape should we have nowhere special to go? Festival time, and its topsy-turvy characteristic that Bakhtin made so much play of in his idea of the Carnivalesque, is here substituted by something altogether more alluring for me: plant time. Here there is no topsy-turvy, no day out from the remorseless ministration of power; indeed, the entire event is conducted under an umbrella of ever-present melancholy, of subjection, of the cruel optimism that comes from being down there with plants and knowing one's place when it comes to capital investment. But, critically, finding the words and recipes of the earth and at that very moment expressing that relationship, might be of some significance to the future of the land. Vegetal matter is setting the pace in this environment as Asja is unable, or unwilling, to turn the flame up under those root vegetables and expect them to hurry along for the sake of theatre. They will take their own time to simmer, and that, for me at least, feels for the better.

Lost Gardens digs a vegetal environment and, in so doing, constructs a site of uncertainty, if it is anything, and therein lies its eloquence. The people doing the speaking here—namely, Asja, Zeta, Kosta, and Nina— are, in their doing, marking their own *infidelity* to what lies in those propagation beds, doing what they so beautifully but fantastically suggested the plant-ish humans might be doing in such warm-damp places. Here, that labour of oratory *on behalf* of plants and humans is a properly performative process; it is a Phyto-Performance that, in the playing out, recognizes and measures the degree to which it falls short of its subjects.

Phyto-Performance has no need to translate its matters of concern into matters of fact. That is the stuff of science. It is the 'English Garden Effect' that rearranges these 'old atrocities' into 'ingenious shifts of scenery [...] to give the required air of naturalness, pathos and hope'.[12] Phyto-Performance has always, already, been the ground of the English theatre, as well as its canopy in the plant-adorned proscenium arch. When actors take their leave from responsibility to their character-lives on stage, they do so to a place called the Green Room. Adjacent to the stage, to the side of the wings, in all English theatres from the late eighteenth century on, the Green Room has this designation for ecologically informed reasons. It was the home of the 'green thread' of the stage and provided shelter to the theatre's environmental credentials and vegetal potential. The Green Room was so called because it housed the Greensward, the carpet that would be rolled out from the wings, across the width of the stage, to mark the forthcoming scene as one set outdoors, external, a grassy one; one that was inclusive to the possibility of plant—as distinct to drawing room—matters. The Green Room has long since lost its grass, occupied as it is by those actors who do not know why 'the old atrocities still persist', while audiences look on, in the dark, in serried arrangements of naturalness, pathos and hope.

NOTES

1. Abish, Walter (1980) 'The English Garden Effect' in *In The Future Perfect*, p. 1.
2. Marder, Michael (2013) *Plant-Thinking: A Philosophy of Vegetal Life*.
3. See Gilles Deleuze and Felix Guattari (2004) *A Thousand Plateaus: Capitalism and Schizophrenia*.
4. Michael Marder, author of *Plant-Thinking*, and *Through Vegetal Being* (with Luce Irigaray).
5. *The Philosopher's Plant* (2014).
6. See Marder, *Plant-Thinking*, pp. 3–4, where he describes plants as 'wholly other and foreign to us'.
7. *Plant-Thinking*, p. 12, where Marder discusses the 'spatio-temporal' nature of plants.
8. Marder, *Plant-Thinking*, pp. 1–13. See especially the opening pages of this introduction, in which this manifesto is laid out with incisive flair.
9. See Homo Novus web site archive: http://www.homonovus.lv/eng/performances.php?s=lost-gardens, date accessed 10 March 2015.
10. See Homo Novus web site archive.

11. Peter Sloterdijk (2005) 'Atmospheric Politics' in *Making Things Public: Atmospheres of Democracy*, pp. 944–51.
12. Abish, 'The English Garden Effect', p. 1.

REFERENCES

Abandoned Practices. http://abandonedpractices.org. Date accessed 1 June 2015.

Abish, Walter. 1980. The English Garden Effect. In *In the Future Perfect*, 1–21. London: Faber.

Deleuze, Gilles, and Guattari, Felix. 2004. *A Thousand Plateaus: Capitalism and Schizophrenia*. Trans. Brian Massumi. London: Continuum.

Guattari, Félix. 2000. *The Three Ecologies*. Trans. Ian Pindar, and Paul Sutton. London/New Brunswick: Athlone.

Krauss, Rosalind. 1979. Sculpture in the Expanded Field. *October* 8: 30–44.

Marder, Michael. 2013. *Plant-Thinking: A Philosophy of Vegetal Life*. New York: Columbia University Press.

———. 2014. *The Philosopher's Plant*. New York: Columbia University Press.

Nietzsche, Friedrich. 2017. *The Will to Power*. Trans. Michael A. Scarpitti, and R. Kevin Hill. London: Penguin.

Ophir, Adi. 2000. *The Order of Evils*. New York: Zone Books.

Read, Alan. 2008. *Theatre, Intimacy & Engagement: The Last Human Venue*. New York: Palgrave.

Shiva, Vandana. 1988. *Staying Alive: Women, Ecology and Survival in India*. New Delhi: Kali for Women. http://gyanpedia.in/Portals/0/Toys%20from%20Trash/Resources/books/stayingalive.pdf. Date accessed 10 Apr 2015.

———. 1997. *Biopiracy: The Plunder of Nature and Knowledge*. Boston: Southern End Press.

Sloterdijk, Peter. 2005. Atmospheric Politics. In *Making Things Public: Atmospheres of Democracy*, ed. Bruno Latour and Peter Weibel, 944–951. Cambridge: MIT Press.

Stengers, Isabelle. 2007. Diderot's Egg. In *Radical Philosophy, 144*, July/August. http://roundtable.kein.org/sites/newtable.kein.org/files/Materialism-Diderot.pdf. Date accessed 10 Apr 2015.

Thoreau, Henry David. 1916. *The Maine Woods*. Boston: Houghton Mifflin.

Weiss, Allen. 1999. *Unnatural Horizons: Paradox and Contradiction in Landscape Architecture*. Princeton: Princeton Architectural Press.

Of Mice and Masks: How Performing Citizenship Worked for a Thousand Years in the Venetian Republic and Why the Age of Enlightenment Brought it to an Abrupt End

Mirjam Schaub

INTRODUCTION

While the plague raged in 14th century Venice—eradicating countless patrician families, who were what kept the Maritime Republic alive with its unique system of office rotation and power distribution—the Venetians reinvented their endangered community and polity, with the help of a uniform white mask *(larva* or *volto)*, a black hood and a three-pointed hat.

Presumably, it was in protest against the Black Death—that killed rich and poor without exception—that this so-called *maschera nobile* or *bautà*[1]

Translated from German by Alice Lagaay

M. Schaub (✉)
University of Art and Design Burg Giebichenstein, Halle a.d. Saale, Germany

© The Author(s) 2019
P. Hildebrandt et al. (eds.), *Performing Citizenship*, Performance
Philosophy, https://doi.org/10.1007/978-3-319-97502-3_16

243

was first borne. But it soon developed into a powerful social equalizer, for it permitted the Venetian Republic to regard its own police and spy state as necessary interventions in the fight against corruption and, at the same time, allowed its citizens to lead a relatively untroubled life beyond convention and constraints. As a social mask, the *bautà* grew in popularity between the 14th and 18th centuries, and it played a role at almost every public occasion, as can be seen in countless Canaletto, Longhi and Guardi paintings. Above all, it revolutionized social life by allowing a simple form of anonymization, thus guaranteeing Venetian citizens of both sexes libertine, even voluptuous, practices while respecting etiquette.

The mask reflects the richness of Venetian social and political inventions. The Venetians did not believe in the good of man, which is one of the reasons why the republic survived a thousand years of crusades and slaughter but not the century of enlightenment. Instead, the Venetians believed in institutions, in imposing restrictions to control unwelcome human behaviour. They racked their brains over procedures that would prevent human beings from choosing the easy way. Acknowledging the fact that destroying and doing harm was simple in comparison to the difficulties of re-installing trust and credibility, they invented sophisticated practices and countless precautions from which they expected more benefits and practical wisdom. They had little expectations of weak—but only too corruptible—human beings.

The success of the Venetian Republic depended on its profound pessimism, its distrust in human goodness. Instead of wanting to change the nature of man, say, by affirmative self-declaration, it created a system of procedural interventions and institutional coups whose purpose was to counteract abuse and corruption, like a corset used to fight formlessness.

In the context of a book on 'Performing Citizenship' that focuses rather on contemporary problematizations, the horizon of this essay suggests a new perspective from which contemporary citizens and civil rights movements might perhaps reconsider their usual form of general institutional critique by drawing inspiration from the inventiveness with which historical Venice sought to limit abuses of power, using institutional means and procedures.

Admittedly, the richness of their inventiveness was triggered by a negative image of humanity that Napoleon was not alone in considering premodern and hostile to reason. But in this regard, one might ponder whether our 'enlightened' and idealized image of mankind might not actually be its own comeuppance when accusations of misconduct are directed at a few 'black sheep', instead of the tendency for misconduct being recognized as a *conditio humana*. The Venetian Republic—which subsisted for a thousand years (from around 797 to 1797) without any means of providing for itself except through clever trade—relied heavily on the quick undermining of any suggestion of corruption.

This constellation allowed the citizens of Venice to consider control and freedom of movement, spying, libertinage, and veneration not as opposites, but rather, as reciprocal fires in the expression of their unique concept of performing citizenship. That their political inventions be considered pre-modern or anti-enlightened would appear, as shall be shown, to be based on historical prejudice and is therefore in urgent need of revision.

OFFICE ROTATION AND THE DISTRIBUTION OF POWER

After the deliberate closing *(serrata)* of the politically powerful 'caste' and its limitation[2] to old, established, aristocratic families in 1297, the ideal of ruling among equals was faced with the problem of balancing power and control by the same permanent staff.

The republic could not tolerate being steered (from political responsibility) by the idle. Not even impoverishment was considered an acceptable excuse for the non-fulfilment of aristocratic duties. Little more than two hundred families, who had inhabited the lagoon for generations, were involved in creating the cautious laws of the republic. According to these laws, only male aristocrats over 25 years of age, who had gone to university in Padua[3] or become bowmen to the galleys, were entitled to take over the legislature and the judiciary of the Republic of Venice. The republic kept a turnstile of official jobs that rotated between a fixed number of noble families. No official position was to be occupied for more than 12 or 18 months.

Interestingly, it was their deep and constantly evolving knowledge of real, banal and all-too-human weaknesses that explains why political self-determination, trafficking, cunning, scrutiny and libertinage were so closely intertwined in Venice as to become indistinguishable. Seen in this light, Giacomo Casanova's escape from the lead chambers of the Doge's Palace succeeded not only thanks to the intervention of senator Matteo Giovanni Bragadin, but also due to the *impersonal program*, which emerged from the unique political self-understanding of the Venetian Republic.[4] What if the republic had imprisoned Casanova in 1756, only to let him flee after 15 months, in order to make him return later as a gifted and devoted spy for the flourishing Venetian commonwealth?

How to Avoid Corruption When Everyone Is Corruptible?

Instead of identifying inequality as a disadvantage, Venetian politics were purposefully set out to overcome a scandalous form of *equality* that was considered a threat to society. For it was the long-anticipated *equality* of all members of the Venetian society, regarding their *common corruptibility*, which led to a unique political alliance. This alliance concerned the precautions necessary to undermine or disarm any pseudo-reasons for bribery, such as general distrust in the public order, people's likelihood to choose the paths of least resistance, or clandestine compensation for inadequacies and injustices, and so on.

The chosen method was to organize all social classes—patricians, commoners, craftsmen, soldiers—from the point of view of their *similarities*, in order to secure a lasting base for social peace. This was achieved by introducing independent organizations such as the guilds (from the retailer to the card-maker, from the soap-maker to the mascot maker or goldsmith), from which strong, secular fraternities *(scuole)* derived. Their leading members henceforth wore the costume of the patricians *(toga veneta)*. The chairman of the fishermen's guild even took his seat as 'Doge of the pescatori' next to the noble Doge during the annual procession— *Festa della Sensa* or *Festa dell'Ascensione*—to celebrate the symbolic marriage between the city and the sea.

Thus, even those who had no political decision-making power were still able to participate in the symbolic chain of power transmission. Venetian society worked much like a Märklin railroad according to the principle of miniaturization, whereby train compartments with varying levels of comfort ran and rattled without disturbing each other's circuits. While the noble patricians constantly changed their offices, the *cittadini*—commoners or civics—ensured continuity by dealing with the administrative offices of the executive.

The bourgeois Grand Chancellor of the republic, appointed as the chief executive for life, was the only Venetian not to bow before the noble Doge. He was privy to all the secrets of the state but had no right to vote or speak in any council. The coats of arms of the 45 bourgeois Grand Chancellors that ruled Venice between 1297 and 1797 were placed prominently on the walls of the Doge's Palace, as were the Doges' portraits in the marble section—albeit locked away in a wooden cabinet, hidden to the eyes of ordinary visitors. If, since 1315, the hand-painted coats of arms of the noble families and their names were collected in the Golden Book of the City, then the citizens' names were to be found in the Book of Silver. Each social class mimicked the rituals and privileges of the class above them in the *stato misto* of Venice, reflecting them while introducing slight differences. This ensured the satisfaction of all and established a degree of distance built on familiarity.

Given the small number of staff members that had known each other for generations, abuse of authority in Venice was never considered to be the unfortunate affair of a few 'black sheep'. Quite the contrary, corruption was exactly what was expected of everyone all the time.

Venetians were such pessimists that, by 1275, they had invented an elaborate system of precautionary measures. It consisted of a well-organized mixture of personal votes and impersonal lotteries, alternating between random, intuitive and strategic decisions and supplemented by prescribed interruptions of office that sometimes lasted as long as the office itself. Thus, for a thousand years, all urgent or controversial political tasks rotated successfully among the male, adult members of only 204 different patrician families *(case vecchie)*, without a single family ever gaining too much power.[5]

Thus, corruption was prosecuted forcefully, and the misuse of power often resulted in expropriation and exile. In order not to be suspected of corruption, local traders in Venice were not allowed to put foreign merchants up in their houses, nor allowed—under any circumstance—to accept any gifts.[6] Those operating outside the republic, if suspected of mischief, would immediately be brought back to Venice, imprisoned in the Doge's Palace's wet *pozzi* and, later, publicly executed. Thus, an example was set between two bloodthirsty pillars of the Loggia of the Doge's Palace, installing a strong and close-knit network of mutual control, fear and retaliation.

PARTICIPATION AND EXCLUSION WITHIN THE DOGE'S PALACE

Thus, in the Doge's Palace of Venice in the 14th century, ideas of *political participation and exclusion* became both effectively and architecturally visible, that remain to this day uniquely radical in the history of Europe: the political inclusion of many (within the patrician republic), and the simultaneous exclusion of almost all (by the police and spy state), coexist as *equally welcomed powers*, in peaceful harmony and great spatial proximity.

After two devastating fires (1574 and 1577), and on the ruins of a 12th-century citadel built without a defence system, the bells of the Trotteria of the campanile of St. Mark's Cathedral would ring out on Sundays and the electoral patricians would gather in the *Sala* of the Great Council (*Maggior Consiglio*) within the renovated Doge's Palace. The whole palace itself can in fact be considered as no more than a pretext to have built a space of this magnitude (55 by 25 metres) with the capacity for so much participatory impetus. The ceiling seems to float, unsupported by columns. Venetian carpenters simply erected an inverted ship's hull over the gigantic ceiling to absorb the weight of the sides. If you look closely, you can still see how many rusty nails penetrate the ceiling—and its bombastic paintings—in order to make the construction safe.[7]

Thanks to the repeated reduction of the electorate by means of a lottery and the steady reconstitution of numbers through numerous rounds of deliberation, the system—which was especially designed to install the Doge for life as the highest representative of the republic—was indeed hellishly complicated but, ultimately, exceptionally fair. Five times the lottery would decide, five times the electors would debate the pros and cons of the remaining candidates. Since it was impossible to predict whether or not one would still be a member of the electoral college at the end of ten rounds, pre-arrangements were simply hopeless.

In this bombastically magnificent room—modestly called the room of the 900—not only the Doge, but also the sixty senators, the nine treasurers (*procuratores*) and all the important offices were elected. It was also the venue for special ceremonies, such as the occasion of Morosina Grimani's inauguration to the office of the Dogaressa (1597), and the place where the Venetian ambassadors would present their reports on the world beyond the lagoon. These reports, the so-called *relazioni*, were famous for their considerable accuracy, since only an exact study of the gestures and states of mind of driving forces could be used to predict the future plans of action by foreign peoples with some certainty. These portrayals by Venetian diplomats had to be written and stored in the archives where, still today, they remain a fruitful source of information. Clandestinely, Venetians celebrated themselves as clever traders and as equally clever informers, which guaranteed the lasting mastery of *la serenissima*, the most illustrious republic. By refraining from judgement for the sake of precise descriptions, the reports were so insightful, that they even became much admired—and envied—by foreign powers.

Fig. 1 Giovanni Bellini, *Doge Leonardo Loredan* (after 1501), oil on tempera on poplar wood, 61.6 × 45.1 cm, National Gallery, London

The art of reading minds through studying the characteristics of facial features, and the knowledge of how to index and interpret the slightest show of emotion, belonged, as it were, to early childhood education in the Venetian Republic. It was in Venice, not Florence, that the art of portraiture was born, with the Bellini brothers, Giorgione, and later Titian and Tintoretto. Precisely because the exhibition of Venetians was strictly forbidden in public places, patricians and wealthy citizens first began to commission portraits for themselves for private display only. Even the Doge was only allowed to have his portrait painted for his own private collection, like Leonardo Loredan—painted by Giovanni Bellini after 1501 (Fig. 1).

In the narrow streets of Venice, it was essential to always know exactly whom one might encounter by chance, and to be able to greet them by name and actual status—no easy task given the annual office rotation. To solve this problem, the Venetians invented an unconventional and effective solution: the mask.

THE VENETIAN *BAUTÀ*: A SOCIAL MASK AND ITS MULTIPLE FUNCTIONS

Of course, the masks in question differed from the ones people are most familiar with now. Not the traditional, colourful carnival masks of harlequin, lawyer, *dottore* or *capitano* (since the late Middle Ages), nor the grotesque half masks of the actors of the *commedia dell'arte* (since the 16th century); these were used to emphasize character, or exaggerate certain features, they did not primarily serve to anonymize. The austere white mask that is meant here is often depicted in the paintings of Canaletto (1697–1768), Pietro Longhi (1702–1785) and Francesco Guardi (1712–1793).[8] In allowing a person to look dignified and yet unrecognizable as a particular person in the middle of the public sphere, the so called *bautà* enabled its bearer to mind his or her own business. Visible but opaque, singular but anonymous, the mask would allow the person to disappear in the crowd, like a black dot with a white stipple.

In terms of external appearance, this type of mask complemented the traditionally black, ankle length coat *(tabarro)* of the Venetian merchants. The whole outfit consisted of five garments and accessories: a black hood *(bautà)*, a silk chest cape, a short gown of black gauze, a three-pointed hat and a white *larva* for the face. The *larva* was placed over the chin but pointing sharply upwards so that the person could eat and drink whilst remaining unrecognizable under the mask. For brevity, this mask was commonly referred to as *bautà* in its entirety and compiled with the *tabarro*. It became appropriate for both men and women. In fact, it soon became impossible to tell whether a woman or a man was wearing it, because the clothes hidden under the long cloak became yet another opportunity to dress up in disguise.

This mask was invented by the nobles but was soon no longer restricted to them. Although it started as a *maschera nobile,* its overwhelming popularity gradually made it into a social mask.[9] It was worn outside the carnival season for every conceivable social occasion—in the streets, at weddings, banquets, processions, during elections, theatrical and theatre shows, indeed, even in honour of the Indian rhinoceros Clara (Fig. 2).[10]

In the simplest way, the *bautà* made it possible for people—who otherwise knew each other perhaps all too well—to become inconspicuous, unidentifiable and equal. What a relief it must have been to have been able to pass unidentified in the small republic, whose entire social realm otherwise depended on one presenting the appropriate *attitudine* and

Fig. 2 Pietro Longhi, *Exhibition of a Rhinoceros at Venice* (1751), oil on canvas, 60.4 × 47 cm, National Gallery, London

contegno—the right facial expressions and dignified physical postures. The purpose of this mask was not to facilitate role-finding or roleplay, but to allow for distance and anonymity. Even one's voice would sound strange and hard to place, darkly sonorous, when resonating from under the leather mask. Whoever encountered such a masked person on the street would certainly have had to bow to them and say, 'Hail, honorable mask' ('*Sióra, Maschera*').

Exclusive to Venice, the precise origins of this social mask still lie in the dark. In the context of the gruesomely raging pestilence of 1348, one might plausibly imagine that it came about as an alliance between forces of nature and the morbid pleasure people got from blurring differences of rank. The chronicler Lorenzo de Monacis notes a few years after the events,

> Right at the beginning of this plague, within a few days, [it] removed leading figures, judges, and civil servants who had been elected to the Grand Council, and then those who had taken their place. In the month of May it increased so much, and the contagion became so strong that the squares, courtyards, tombs, and cemeteries filled with corpses.[11]

Tens of thousands died within a few months; Dorsoduro, Santa Croce and Cannaregio were basically depopulated. In June 1348, the Grand Council was unable to grant resolutions, due to the loss of most of its members. However, what remained of the Senate continued to rule: ordering quarantine, forbidding alcohol, and even banning the wearing of mourning clothes in an attempt to raise the general mood. Meanwhile,

> ...the moderates, the restrained, the chaste, the sober, died as the drunks and the sluggishers died, the frugal and extravagant, the bold and timid, those who fled, as well as those who remained behind, all without confession and the sacraments of the Church. Even the pious clerics and priests were seized with horror, and the plague also killed them. The whole city was a grave.[12]

The uniformity of death stifled one particular ritual of the nobles, dating back to the Roman Republic, which was the ritual of taking death masks from the deceased. They would normally wear the masks of their ancestors—who otherwise were on display in the atrium—at each funeral. It is thus conceivable that the uniform *larvae* of the white *bautà* arose out of the nobles' growing protest against these restrictions during the first plague. Indeed, to this day, the mask still looks like the unfinished, raw prototype of a mask. Such a presumed origin, in line with the gloomy veneration of the whole appearance, would also explain why the *bautà* was traditionally worn *outside* the carnival season. The first plague broke out in Venice at the end of March 1348, and only receded in the late summer of that year.

Ignazio Toscani—who in the 20th century dedicated a monograph to the *bautà*—argues that its success, its uncanny popularity, was due to the versatility of its use and the ambiguity of its functions. He suggested that the *bautà* compensated for the experience of social constriction by providing anonymity as protection. It transcended the finesse of the envoys, in the same ways as Venetian portraiture did, by promising relief from reciprocal facial examination. At the same time, it allowed for secret scrutiny of others under the protection of one's own mask. It thus respected the Venetian code of modesty, in that it appeared as a sign of pure honourable value. It equalized what was different (people and their class), and thereby neutralized what might otherwise be considered a cause for enmity (the mask as a uniform). It protected one against blackmail (as in the case of the election to be held publicly in St. Mark's Square) and when facing one's creditors; indeed, it helped one not lose face in any circumstance. A good example can be seen in the case of public begging, which was in fact not a rare occurrence, for there were many impoverished patricians who were obliged to fulfil their political duties nevertheless. The Venetian social mask was, in short, *an institution of far-reaching socially equalizing potential*, reconciling the particular with the general, or anonymous and the general, or anonymous with the particular.

The Venetians discovered the virtue of anonymity; that it need not be considered as a threat, but as protection, a promise. They understood that from under the appearance of equality, diversity and a variety of desires could in fact blossom and flourish. It can thus be seen as a kind of logical counterpart to the territorial and social constraints, which, combined with the limitations brought about by the presence of the sea and the closed nature of the different social classes, but at the same time guaranteed the extraordinary liberties that characterized Venice (both inwardly and outwardly). The freedom to wear the *bautà* became the subject of countless restrictions and conditions, which had to be renewed at ever shorter intervals because no one seemed seriously concerned in adhering to them. A special magistrate for dress codes, the *Magistrato all Pompe*, was founded in 1514. The mask also presented a particular challenge for the secret police because it facilitated the clandestine transportation of weapons, as well as surreptitious changes of gender identity.[13]

It is no surprise, therefore, that the Venetians understood well that, in addition to their exotic goods from all over the world, their knowledge of human beings was a valuable means of power—with its own particular sell-by-date. Consequently, they developed techniques to collect, examine, stretch, mix, weigh, exchange, sell, or buy that knowledge profitably. No individual piece of information would ever be taken at face value, but would become the subject of an intricate procedure of examination. Thus, in analogy to the commodity business, businesses dealing with knowledge began to flourish—services especially designed to counteract the easily perishable nature of knowledge and the fragility of cunning, using secrecy and person profiling. Participation of the many was not desired here.

WHY THE PATRICIAN REPUBLIC AND THE POLICE STATE WERE MUTUALLY DEPENDENT IN VENICE

Just one floor above the *Maggior Consiglio* was an elaborate architecture of secret passages, false wall panelling, torture and denunciation. The archives of the Doge's Palace were no less meticulous than those of the Vatican, despite the complete lack of religious zeal. They gathered not only folkloristic, but concise, applicable knowledge regarding foreign peoples. Simultaneously, they worked to acquire more knowledge about the predilections of their own noble families than a present-day *Facebook* 'friend' could even imagine.

Management of the Doge's Palace functioned, as Ursula Krechel's award-winning novel *Landgericht* (2012) describes, as

[...] a cave, a beehive, chamber to chamber, [where] from wall to wall people would be punished, and prosecuted [...], witnesses would be channelled into chambers, interrogated, defended.

The non-public part of the Doge Palace,

vibrated, [...] lived, [...] crushed, and in the end spat out judgments. It was a large, oiled machine. You would put your hand in the mouth of truth, and it would come out, bitten, scratched, bloodied. Or it would have remained, miraculously, just as uninjured as before. You had been released for lack of evidence.[14]

In fact, there was a 'mouth of truth' in all public places in Venice but, in 1797, when Napoleon and his troops invaded the city during their Italian campaign, they could not distinguish it from denunciation. The *bocce di leone* were publicly displayed letter boxes for complaints, especially designed to prompt the citizens of Venice to remain vigilant over misuse and corruption. The inscription was always the same. It called for the written denunciations of anyone found suspicious of granting privileges, or of speaking cryptically in order to obscure the 'true interest' of their intentions.

However, the rules stated that any anonymous such letters were to be destroyed and left unread. A denunciator was required to sign with their name. It was only after an in-depth investigation, and if several complaints were collected around a given suspect, that a possible prosecution was made. The denouncer would also be prosecuted if what he claimed proved to be false; if his suspicion was confirmed, on the other hand, then his name would remain undisclosed to the public.

When, in 1797, the French attacked the Venetian Republic and its institutions—forcing the 120th Doge to abdicate—one of the first things they destroyed, in order to break the power distribution amongst noble families, was not only the only copy of the handwritten Golden Book, but they also demolished and mutilated the lions' mouths. Most importantly, however, was their forbidding of the wearing of masks in public under any circumstance. Their intention was to crush the symbols of an autocratic police and spy state, which no longer belonged in the century of enlightenment. Yet, without knowing it, in so doing, they hit the logistic heart of the Venetian power distribution, which did not organize participation and exclusion by reference to different groups of people or different classes, but rather, *assigned* both to the same people as equals among equals. Corruptible nobles, merchants and citizens were treated equally, and only tamed by institutional wisdom and clever procedures, not by reason, insight or deliberation.

The patrician republic and its police state were inseparable in Venice, just as the black *bautà* was to the white *larva (volto)*, and just as inclusion and exclusion, strict secrecy and the greatest possible participation applied, not to different people and different things, but to everyone and everything equally. In the republic's self-conception, the Grand Council *(Maggior Consiglio)*, the Council of Ministers *(Minor Consiglio)*, and the feared secret police—the Council of Ten—pursued similar tasks such as seeking to undermine corruption, but with different means. The primary task of the resulting police and spy state was to investigate high treason amongst patricians, like activities involving gunpowder and plotting (often made possible thanks to the use of the mask). Greatest possible participation, paired with a strategic use of the lottery system, had a similarly preventive effect on corruption as strict secrecy had among a constantly rotating staff.

Their understanding of the fallibility of each individual led the Venetians to limit the power even of the unique jurisdiction of the Council of Ten. Measures were put in place to undermine corruption: limited terms were implemented with yearly elections, the participation of the Doge and his six independent consultants *(consiglieri)* was required, the presence of '*avogadori de comùn*' (attorney general) was necessary to testify to the legality of the secret ballot. The Council of Ten also elected three chairmen *(capi)*, who were compelled to rotate every month on their own terms and whose names were kept strictly secret. No patrician family was allowed to send forth more than a single member to this council at any given time. And, as a precautionary measure in especially politically charged cases, the investigating *capi* were even locked up in the Doge's Palace to prevent any influence from outside.

THE SYSTEM OF OVERLAPPING COMPETENCES

The republic had its doctrines, which historians of the enlightenment mistook for paranoia. In the course of the trial against the Doge Marino Faliero for treason in 1355, the Council of Ten was flanked by a further council, the *zonta* (the Council of Twenty). This was twice as strong and equipped with similar competences so that, for instance, controversial death sentences would be shouldered by thirty, rather than just ten people. Consequently, both magistrates began to keep each other in check, developing a curious system of balances between rivalling councils. Thus, the Council of Ten and the Council of Twenty gradually developed into double committees, which, over time, claimed all sorts of overlapping competences for themselves: state acquisition, secret police, chancellery of the Doge, war ministry, morality police; thus, controlling the alms of the cloisters, the health of the prostitutes, the ban on public duels, masks and masking habits, fun in the street theatres, and so on.

It took centuries for the Great Council and the Senate to undo these double structures. Indeed, it was not until 1644 that the *zonta* was disbanded, for the Venetian patricians soon got the hang of it, with their mandates limited in time and the obligatory breaks before entering into a new office; if dysfunctional dynamics could not be resolved (such as dubious power struggles between certain noblemen), then certain offices and institutions would simply be doubled up. The Venetian rules of conduct, to which the *serenissima* owed its proverbial serenity, was thus as follows: Political conflicts can be defused by means of targeted, institutionally anchored competence overlaps. This is achieved by temporarily doubling up a particular office with rotating staff. The gist is to create mirror councils that are mutually interrelated and keep each other in check; in other words, by undermining and ridiculing each other, say, by arriving at opposite conclusions to the same simple question as, for instance, with regard to the question of whether or not to allow the Venetian society mask (*bautà*) to be worn in public on a particular day.

And so, it is no wonder that Casanova was once condemned, once helped to escape, and then declared honorary citizen of Venice, before being sent to France and Bohemia as an informer. In the end, he left his birthplace, full of contempt forever. To the Venetian *nobili*, to which he never fully belonged, he devoted a pamphlet in 1782: *Né Amori, né Donne* ('Neither Love, nor Women').

In the twenty-fifth chapter of his posthumous recollections (*Histoire de ma Vie*, in the French original)—after having become acquainted with forms of government in Austria-Hungary, Prussia and France—Casanova, with a sideways kick to his home town, declared:

> Like all worm-bitten institutions, it continues to exist. Most of today's governments resemble those old dams whose foundations are completely decayed, and which remain in their place only by virtue of their own weight.[15]

NOTES

1. The term *bautà* literally meant the black hood, but soon became an umbrella term for all the components of the costume.
2. This limitation doesn't simply mean that the 3500 members of noble families rule over 136,500 others. We will soon see why.
3. The historian Renan therefore sees at work an 'Averroean rationalism of Paduan scholars'. [Author's translation]—Ignatio Toscani: *Die venezianische Gesellschaftsmaske. Ein Versuch zur Deutung ihrer Ausformung, ihrer Entstehungsgründe und ihrer Funktion*. Inaugural-Dissertation der Universität des Saarlandes, Saarbrücken 1972, p. 108.
4. Casanova's *nom de guerre* as spy is Antonio Pratolino.—Giacomo Casanova: *The Story of my Escape from the Prison of the Republic of Venice*, otherwise known as *'The Leads'*, written in Dux in Bohemia in 1787. Translated from the French edition by Andrew L. Lawston, Kindle Edition 2014.
5. After the first plague in 1348 had extinguished whole families, and the Genoese had given up the siege of Chioggia in 1381 (with the help of

all Venetian citizen), the total figure of noble families was increased at once by 30 bourgeois families, the *case nuove*. Later, after significant losses against the Turks in the 17th century, the *case novissime* gained access to peerage by paying large amounts of money to the Venetian state. Over the centuries, the number of male nobles over 30 years of age and with families with at least two children—in other words, those qualified to elect the Doge and all other offices—varied between 1000 and 2746.

6. Cf. Insa Holst (2007) *Handel im 15. Jahrhundert: Der Kaufmann von Venedig*, in: *Venedig (810–1900): Macht und Mythos der Serenissima*, GEOepoche Nr. 28, (Hamburg), 48–63.

7. Wolfgang Wolters (2010) *Der Dogenpalast in Venedig. Ein Rundgang durch Kunst und Geschichte*, (München).

8. Unfortunately, in the National Gallery of London, the *bautà* is still falsely labelled as a 'typical Venetian carnival mask'. Nothing could be more wrong.

9. 'The social role is not an "arbitrary corset of behavior" but a distinct social element [...]. It thus stars at every "seam", where the individual meets his social milieu, that is, where man and the impersonal system of relationships merge into a role which man has to play in society' [Author's translation]—Toscani (1972) (typo-script in German), p. 99.

10. The rhinoceros was exhibited as a fierce beast, as her keeper carries a whip and shows a horn of a bull instead. But alongside the disguised Venetian nobles, it quickly becomes apparent that with her ears flattened at her head, Clara is really just a badly dressed, harmless ruminant.

11. Lorenzo de Monacis, as quoted by Eva-Maria Schnurr, in: 'Venedig: Die ganze Stadt ein Grab', in: *Der Spiegel*, May 30, 2012. See, http://www.spiegel.de/spiegel/spiegelgeschichte/d-85776628.html.   [Author's translation]

12. Ibid.

13. Originally reserved for the patricians, it was soon also worn by members of other classes, as well as by educational travellers (such as Goethe in 1786). Through the semi-transparent black gauze, anyone could tell a person's status by 'reading' the clothes that they were wearing underneath. However, it soon became fashionable to dress up under the *bautà* as well, like as a clergyman, for example, in order to enter into a convent of women without causing suspicion.

14. U. Krechel (2012) *Landgericht*, (Jung und Jung, Salzburg/Vienna), p. 58.

15. Author's translation. For further reading, cf. Jörg-Uwe Albig (2007) 'Der Verführer, 1725–1798: Casanova', GEO Epoche—*Venedig (810–1900): Macht und Mythos der Serenissima*, 28, 142–156.

REFERENCES

Ackroyd, Peter. 2009. *Venice. Pure City*. London: Chatto & Windus.

Agamben, Giorgio. 1998. *Homo Sacer. Sovereign Power and Bare Life*. Trans. Daniel Heller-Roazen. Stanford: Stanford University Press.

Albig, Jörg-Uwe. 2007. 'Der Verführer, 1725–1798: Casanova' ('The Seducer, 1725–1798: Casanova'*). *GEO Epoche – Venedig (810–1900): Macht und Mythos der Serenissima* 28: 142–156.

Casanova, Giacomo. 2014. *The Story of My Escape: From the Prisons of the Republic of Venice Otherwise Known as the 'Leads'*. Trans. Andrew Lawston, Kindle edition. North Charleston: CreateSpace Independent Publishing Platform.

Crowley, Roger. 2011. *City of Fortune. How Venice Ruled the Seas*. New York: Random House.

Directorate of the Doge's Palace. (ed.) 1959. *Der Dogenpalast. Kunsthistorischer Führer*. Venice: Officine Grafiche Ferrari.

Ferrari, Simone. 2010. *The Doge's Palace in Venice*. Milan: Skira.

Gualdoni, Flaminio. 2010. *[Pietro] Longhi*. Milan: Skira.

Holst, Insa. 2007. Handel im 15. Jahrhundert: Der Kaufmann von Venedig.' ('Trade in the 15th Century: The Merchant of Venice'*). *GEO Epoche – Venedig (810–1900): Macht und Mythos der Serenissima* 28: 48–63.

Krechel, Ursula. 2012. *Landgericht. Roman*, 58. Jung und Jung: Salzburg and Vienna.

Norwich, John Julius. 1977/2012. *A History of Venice*. London: Penguin.

Rademacher, Cay. 2007. "Spanische Verschwörung" (1618): Tod in der Lagune. ('Spanish Conspiracy' (1618) Death in the Lagoon*). *GEO Epoche – Venedig (810–1900): Macht und Mythos der Serenissima* 28: 110–122.

Rancière, Jacques. 1999. *Disagreement: Politics and Philosophy*. Trans. Julie Rose, Minneapolis: University of Minnesota Press.

———. 2004. *The Politics of Aesthetics*. Trans. Gabriel Rockhill, London: Bloomsbury. (*Le partage du sensible. Esthétique et politique*, Paris 2000).

Strempel, Johannes. 2007. Flottenbau, um 1570. *GEO Epoche – Venedig (810–1900): Macht und Mythos der Serenissima* 28: 94–104.

Toscani, Ignazio. 1972. Die venezianische Gesellschaftsmaske. Ein Versuch zur Deutung ihrer Ausformung, ihrer Entstehungsgründe und ihrer Funktion ('The Venetian Society Mask. An Attempt to Interpret Its Formation, Origins and Function'*). Inaugural Dissertation for a Doctorate in Philosophy, Saarbrücken. (Typoscript).

von Hadeln, Detlev Freiherrn. 1911. 'Beiträge zur Geschichte des Dogenpalastes' ('Contributions to the History of the Doge's Palace'*). *Jahrbuch der Königlich Preussischen Kunstsammlung* 32: 1–33.

Wolters, Wolfgang. 2010. *Der Dogenpalast in Venedig. Ein Rundgang durch Kunst und Geschichte ('The Doge's Palace in Venice. A Tour of Art and History'*)*. Munich: Deutscher Kunstverlag.

*Translation by author

PART IV

Emerging Agencies

Perform, Citizen! On the Resource of Visibility in Performative Practice Between Invitation and Imperative

Maike Gunsilius

'I did not choose this theatre course. I do not want to go on stage'. Leyla, a 13-year-old student with whom I was working in my artistic research project *School of Girls I*, said this when we were preparing a public presentation of our research about what it means to be a female citizen—in the sense of being an active member—of our postmigrant[1] society. I was disappointed, irritated, disempowered. Actually, my project was *about* inviting the 12 co-researching girls to take the stage, so becoming *visible* and *audible* as citizens in public. I noticed that I presupposed performing on stage would be a desirable moment of agency and would form an emancipatory approach to my research setup. However, Leyla' s statement made me rethink the relation between visibility, performance, agency and citizenship.

Consequently, this chapter asks: what exactly do we offer by inviting young citizens to become part of a performative research project? Who and what exactly has to become visible on stage, and in what way, to provide an experience of self-efficacy and to create agency, or maybe even

M. Gunsilius (✉)
Graduate Program Performing Citizenship, HafenCity University Hamburg, Hamburg, Germany

© The Author(s) 2019
P. Hildebrandt et al. (eds.), *Performing Citizenship*, Performance Philosophy, https://doi.org/10.1007/978-3-319-97502-3_17

produce citizenship? The essay looks first at the theoretical relation between visibility,[2] performance, agency and citizenship in general and then goes on to question the promise of visibility in the context of cultural education projects. The text finally relates these two areas of investigation and asks how the *resource of visibility* can be used in performative practice to generate agency—for both children and adults.

CITIZENS BECOME APPARENT AND PERFORM

Whenever we talk about citizenship being more than just a national status connected with civil rights and duties, we talk about it as a question of social rights and participation (Marshall 1950). Following Allman and Beaty, citizenship describes the idea of a subject position that articulates itself by 'a set of learned and constantly reproduced practices and conducts, as well as expectations and claims' (see Allman and Beaty 2002; Peters 2016). Agency as a condition of such an articulation can be defined here as the capacity to choose how to act within a social structure. Articulations and 'acts' (Isin 2008) of citizenship—including claims and fights for it—are constitutively connected to the public sphere (Arendt 1998; Butler 2004, 2011; Mackert 2006; Isin 2008; Schaffer 2008; Holston 2009; Spivak and Butler 2011; Hess and Lebuhn 2014). However, the relation between citizenship and public visibility/audibility is seen ambivalently within the citizenship debate. In Hannah Arendt's notion, human acting—strongly connected to speaking—is generally performed in front of the eyes of others, of a public. More than that, identity, for her, is constitutively performative: the self 'appears' visible in the world, speaking and acting.

> With word and deed we insert ourselves into the human world, and this insertion is like a second birth, in which we confirm and take upon ourselves the naked fact of our original physical appearance. (Arendt 1998, p. 176)

Intersubjective acting as the moment of becoming visible and audible in front of each other creates a 'space of appearance' (Arendt 1998, p. 199), it constitutes the citizens' stage—*the public*. Power and freedom for Arendt emerge when people act and create something together. The efficacy of this acting lies in its execution, in its performance itself (see Arendt 1998, pp. 198–9). The hesitant reception of Arendt, and her concept of *acting in public* within feminist and postcolonial theory, results from the critique of her distinction between public and private that traces back to the model of the Greek polis, without questioning the exclusion of women and others from this public (Benhabib 1998; Spivak and Butler 2011). Focussing on this exclusion from *appearing* and *performing* on the world's stage, Judith Butler brings in the term 'intelligibility', explaining that norms provide a structure in which an emerging subject position is recognized and recognizable. But, if a human way of living is foreclosed by repressive social norms, this life is excluded from visibility, from intelligibility, from agency as the possibility to 'matter' (Butler 2004, 2011). Postcolonial theory has identified the lack of access of marginalized groups—especially women to rights and to means of social, cultural and political participation—as a missing possibility to be seen and heard in public. Gayatri Chakravorty Spivak, as well as (her readers) Nikita Dhawan and María do Mar Castro Varela, insistently point out that her notion of 'the subaltern' (Spivak 2011) is not to be understood as an identity, but rather, it is asking to move focus from the capacity of the marginalized subject (or group) to the mechanisms of and the power structures behind his or her marginalization—to make active exclusion *visible*.

The discussion about visibility, regimes of visibility and representation shifted from affirmative claims for visibility, raised by antiracist and feminist contexts in the 1980s and 1990s, to the critique of different forms of representing 'the other' as the moment of creating 'the other' (Steyerl 2002; Rogoff 2005; Spivak 2011; Schaffer 2008; Varela and Dhawan 2015), and to the claim for the 'right for opacity' (Glissant and Wing 1997). The concept of 'becoming imperceptible' (Deleuze and Guattari 2002), has been developed further on to the 'imperceptible politics' by Vassilis Tsianos, Dimitris Papadopoulos and Niamh Stephenson (Papadopoulos et al. 2008). In answer to increasing debates about migration movements and illegal migration, here, the authors radically question the concept of the political subject. Visibility, as a resource of recognition, undergoes change within the neoliberal logic of today's urban and national life; a society that values the acting of people in all areas of life in terms of efficiency and productiveness. The right, or the chance, to become visible, to be recognized and to perform citizenship, has turned into an imperative: *Be* citizen! Citizens often see themselves called upon to become *visible*, to perform as active and responsible members of society, as Nikolas Rose has pointed out:

> This transformation from citizenship as possession to citizenship as capacity is embodied in the image of the active entrepreneurial citizen who seeks to maximize his or her lifestyle through acts of choice, links not so much into a homogeneous social field as into overlapping but incommensurate communities of allegiance and moral obligation. (Rose 2000, p. 99)

Migrants, especially, find themselves under obligation to show their efforts; for example, to fulfil integration agreements and other conducts, to 'earn' citizenship—as a legal status as well as a possibility of social and cultural participation (see Rose 2000, p. 98). If the *visibility* of a citizen is considered as her or his social inclusion and participation, claims for imperceptibility can be better understood 'as "not being included like this, in that way and under these conditions"' (Schaffer cited after Lorenz et al. 2012, p. 286); as a pushback of a hegemonic power relation. Claims and fights for visibility, as well as its rejection, question and negotiate spaces, ways and conditions of participation and power relations. Agency has to include a possibility to choose a position towards *visibility* and *performance,* either to use this resource for public articulation and appearance, or else to reject a performative imperative through strategies of invisibility, disappearance and resistance.

If we look at artistic practice, the ambivalence of *visibility* and *audibility* as a resource of agency on the one hand, and as a regime of representation on the other hand, remains widely discussed in different artistic fields. Artistic strategies, like 'giving a face' and 'lending a voice' to marginalized positions from an artist's privileged perspective, are questioned (Schaffer 2008; Steyerl 2008; Lorenz et al. 2012). With regard to performative and theatrical works with children in the context of cultural education, this discussion is in its early stages. *Visibility,* most of the time, is created affirmatively in these projects.

THE PROMISE OF CULTURAL EDUCATION: BECOME VISIBLE AND PARTICIPATE!

Cultural education holds a promise, a promise for agency and, following this, even for citizenship. In the German context, *cultural education* is strongly connected to eighteenth-century concepts around aesthetic experiences shaping the human character (The term *aesthetic education* is used further on.). Since Friedrich Schiller's *Letters Upon the Aesthetic Education of Man* (Schiller 2000), art and aesthetic processes are seen as means to empower, or maybe even generate, the free civic subject. On the basis of this promise, many performative projects in the context of aesthetic education—especially projects in which art and educational institutions, like theatres and schools, cooperate—are about creating 'cultural, social and political participation by enabling children to speak and to be seen in public by their brought in or newly developed artistic forms of expression'[3] (Sting 2014, p. 44). Curricula and funding guidelines are built on the promise: performance = public visibility = participation, for young citizens of our postmigrant society.[4] Particularly in times of bigger social change—like the increase of migration, diversity, and social segregation—in times when citizenship is transforming radically, aesthetic education seems a promising tool for solving complex questions of citizenship such as 'how can living together work? How can we organize it justly?'

Principally, aesthetic education projects focussing on disadvantaged or migrant (or both) children and teenagers, often reproduce the dubious construction of deficient young citizens that have to be motivated by the arts to work hard, to make the 'bodily experience of music, dancing or acting' that finally leads to the fulfilling 'success of the collective performance' in a (maybe even hegemonically structured) public space—for example, in a theatre (see Mörsch 2011, p. 12, translation by author). The participants quite often are *made visible*, are represented (on purpose or not) as formerly deficient, but now happily empowered subjects who finally learned some soft skills on their way to becoming active, participating, performing citizens. To appear, to speak and to act on stage means to be seen and heard in public, to receive attention and potentially appreciation. But '[…] is someone already self-effective only because he or she succeeds in drawing the attention of the others on him or herself? Or does the wish for attention have to stand in for other participatory needs and desires?' Sibylle Peters asks (Peters 2012, p. 9; translation by author). In other words, if *visibility* within a compulsory school project is to provide participation, it has to be used for first creating the experience of self-efficacy within a social or cultural question, or a process in which one wants to involve oneself—this applies to children as well as to adults. Of course, *acting* on a theatre stage does not have the same social efficacy as *acting* in the frame of 'reality'; it will not change the world's structures immediately, or on its own. However, art has the possibility to build up temporary 'zones' of 'acting on trial' (Peters 2012; Plischke 2016, translation by author) in which children and adults are able to claim agency, to build up and enact alternative social orders—and to make this *visible* in public. Sometimes, this 'acting on trial' even goes beyond the frame of art and extends into the social arena.

Childhood, as a protected space, constructs children as citizens in becoming—with temporarily limited rights and duties—who at the same time are affected by social decisions quite directly. Their demands for social or cultural participation bring up questions of power and power relations (Deck 2014). How are these articulated in theatrical and performative projects with children and teenagers? In what way is *visibility* used here so far, and how else could we use it, knowing about the ambivalence of this resource?

BIOGRAPHIC THEATRE AND THE VISIBILITY OF THE INDIVIDUAL

The concept of biographic theatre has become a common strategy used in order to connect to complex, and perhaps abstract, topics and questions, in theatrical works with non-professionals and children. What is made visible here, the young individual and their biographical experiences and stories—from past, present and future associated with certain social, cultural or political questions—are told on stage to give a narrative quality to their knowledge, perspective or appropriation of the world. Ingrid Hentschel has pointed out that biographic theatre has to transform authentic material into a play between self and world without becoming a theatre of illusion, but also without reproducing the publishing of privacy as found in social media. The theatre stage and the assembly of the presentation enables this play with difference by playing with the contrast of showing and not showing[5] (see Hentschel 2016, pp. 258–62). Regardless, in a setup like this, typically, children perform and speak on stage and parents and teachers are sitting in the dark watching, while the initiating artist is proudly standing behind the lighting desk. An intergenerational public dialogue about questions of power and participation within this constellation is limited, inevitably a children's public in which adults *make* and children *become* visible implies a pedagogic framing and reproduces a distinct power relation.

VISIBILITY, POWER RELATIONS AND POSTMIGRANT SOCIETY

Researching on children's agency as citizens within the structure of state schools in Germany today means to collaborate with the generation in which the majority situation between people with and those without a migrant background is tipping within German society. Today, nearly 50 per cent of the students have a so-called migrant background,[6] whereas 90 per cent of their teachers,[7] and 75 per cent of theatre-makers working with them, do not (Ahrens 2009, p. 25). Educational and cultural institutions have been identified as powerful spaces that create difference and exclusion (Sharifi 2011, 2014; Mecheril 2014; Castro Varela and Mecheril 2016). Given this situation, art projects within these structures inevitably are part of, and reproduce, their exclusive logic. Questions of participation and power arising within these projects are crucial issues to be negotiated in a postmigrant society. For example, who allows whom to speak about what, and to become visible in what way here? What happens if somebody does not want to be seen? What if he or she does not want to take part? Is it possible for students not to be made visible, or necessarily be empowered the way I—as the initiating artist—advocate or facilitate?

VISIBILITY AS A DRAMATURGIC JUNCTION

Using the resource of *visibility* for creating agency for children *and* for adults within performative practice means to look at it as a dramaturgic junction for negotiating relations, structures and conditions of *acting* and participating as citizens. Instead of adults solely administrating this resource, children should also be in control and fully able to decide if and how to use the resource. In effect, this addresses not only the chances and limits of *becoming visible* as individuals on stage, but also the strategies of *making* something or someone *visible*. For example, to make the structures and relations that frame encounters between children *and* adults visible, including power relations like teacher-student, parent-child, artist-participant. Or to make other social mechanisms and conditions of participation and exclusion visible. Or to make the co-acting of children and adults visible.[8] Further, we should think about strategies of using *visibility* for 'playing by the rules of the game' (Sternfeld 2013). What if we used the theatre stage—the space of showing and making things public—to play with the difference of showing and not showing? If we used it as a space for hiding, for not appearing, or for disappearing? What would that ask of the audience and of other participants in aesthetic education processes—like teachers, artists, parents? And how would that change our concept of (aesthetic) education?

A play like this could offer possibilities for collaborative *acting* in a self-effective way—not despite, but precisely because, it is irritating previously accepted common orders.

To look at three examples:

Example I: Public Incantation (Turbo Pascal) – Hiding and Looking Back

The first example is a work produced by the performance collective Turbo Pascal. The two artists, Plischke and Oberhäusser, were working with students of the Hector-Peterson-Gesamtschule[9] (most of whom have migrant backgrounds), on the project *Public Incantation* ('*Publikumsbeschwörung*').[10] On stage, there is a white box. Students are inside the box, not visible to the audience. They glimpse out through a venetian blind, watching and commenting on the audience (Fig. 1).

Later on, they step outside the box and invoke the audience by mirroring the assumed projections of the audience regarding them. The students call the audience 'the poor, the deficient, the victims, the lost, the being rescued persons, the anti-socials'. The artists also take stage and reveal their own projections before the students in front of them and are subsequently interrogated by them. Children and adults are questioning one another's positions.

Fig. 1 *Public Incantation*, Turbo Pascal 2011, © Alexei Fittgen

Example II: The Godfathers (Turbo Pascal) – Showing Relations in Constructing and Deconstructing Difference and Similarity

In another school project, the artists met 17-year-old Alper. Following comments quoting Francis Ford Coppola's *The Godfather* in relation to each other's bossy behaviour that arose in certain working situations, Alper and the male artist Frank agreed to work together on a project focussed around that film. The two male actors—17 and 37 years old—share and confront their different views of, and associations to, different figures within the film and thereby present biographically inspired stories about manhood and power. Both of them build up (fictional) self-images; but in the next moment, the other one is challenging this image, by proposing his own view and ascriptions (Fig. 2).

Surprisingly, in their face-to-face-encounter on stage, these two men—both in their appearance as well as in some of their intentions—seem quite similar, sometimes even indistinguishable from each other. Different images of each other, alternative perspectives on their relationship, are constructed and deconstructed—teacher-student, father-son, German-Turk, competitor-friend. They continuously interchange the roles they represent for one another. All these constellations become visible and negotiable.

Fig. 2 *The Godfathers,* Turbo Pascal 2015, © Milan Benak

Example III: School of Girls I (Maike Gunsilius) – Resisting Performance
With this final example, I return to Leyla, the girl who did not want to perform on stage during my artistic research project about female citizenship, with students from Hamburg Veddel. Having observed that women and girls in the neighbourhood of Hamburg Veddel are underrepresented in public forms of civic or political practice, I started an art-based research project with 13 year-old girls from this neighbourhood (students of the local school). We started looking into how their everyday practices influence their surroundings, their social life and whether and how these practices produce citizenship. We developed tutorials about these practices to make the girls'—maybe implicit—knowledge explicit: to make it *visible*. I had thought about the possibility that the girls' practices of citizenship might be not recognized, and perhaps might not be presentable as such. However, I was sure that their visibility on stage in public would let them experience attention and appreciation as active citizens who would show us—the adults—what to learn from them. Leyla, and her friend Sietara from Veddel, resisted this setup when they said about the project: 'It is our school!' 'I just want to do *nothing* here, just chill' (Sietara). 'I do not want to perform on stage' (Leyla).

What can be learned from this opposition to performing within an art-based research framework?

- The opposition against a pedagogically framed power relation within an intergenerational encounter like this should be read as a claim for agency.
- A setup that offers enough space for agency to the participating children first of all includes the choice of whether to take part or not. It also provides different possibilities for *performing* and *appearing* in public. If it fails to do so, a well-meant invitation quickly turns into an imperative to 'perform' in a double sense: to show one's effort and achievement.
- Convinced that it is the responsibility of the initiating artist to build a clear and strong art-based research setup, this should still stay flexible enough to allow for unexpected results, or even opposition, and view this as a chance to rethink and adjust the framework.

Leyla's statement, expressing her wish not to perform on stage, changed the presentation of the project quite radically from the one I had planned. After welcoming our audience, the girls walked off the stage, whereby I

Fig. 3 *School of Girls I*, Maike Gunsilius 2016, © Margaux Weiss

was left there alone. I was the one to present our research about citizenship, while the girls watched off-stage and commented on it with short remarks and videos. I put on my mother's old Norwegian pullover and displayed some posters bearing slogans from protest movements in the 1980s. The girl's opposition, their 'wanna-do-nothing', was mirrored by biographical images of my childhood and stories about my own socialization as an active, or even activist, citizen in which opposition and resistance were central strategies for me to appropriate spaces of action. In a monologue, I started a speech towards the girls about rights and duties of the performing citizen that became more and more paradoxical; this finally revealed my invitation to perform as active citizens within the *School of Girls I* as being an imperative (Fig. 3).

What became visible:

- The clash of interests, motivations and socializations of the different co-researchers, concerning questions of everyday practices, regarding acting in public and citizenship.

- The power structures within our encounter: a well-meaning white, middle-class theatre-maker doing research *with* students of a socially disadvantaged neighbourhood, 95 per cent of whom have a so-called migrant background—and at the same time doing research *on* them.
- The unfulfilled promise of *visibility as agency* being rejected and turned around; the girls were in return researching on *me* in a way that made my agency as a theatre-maker implode.

On the topic of agency for children and adults, achieved through collaboration and negotiation, we tried to 'do nothing', to 'destroy something', we tried to appear on and to disappear from stage. We confronted our different expectations and approaches concerning the *School of Girls I*, concerning ambivalent wishes and fears of becoming visible, of *performing* in public as citizens. We made our positions visible in a way that was irritating.

Who Is Performing? How to Play with the Visibility of a Social Constellation on Stage

In these examples, *visibility* is used for constructing and deconstructing relations between adults and children *on* stage, as well as between on- and off-stage. Visibility is used to negotiate structures, mechanisms and conditions of our ideas and possibilities to participate, to act as citizens.

I tried to demonstrate ways of using the resource of *visibility* within performative practice that go beyond the imperative of having to perform oneself, and thereby to fulfil the paradoxical order for self-empowerment. Returning to the initial question: What do we offer when we invite children and young people to take part in a performative research project? I would suggest thinking of this collaborative research process and its public presentation as a possibility of *co-acting*—for children *and* for adults. Agency, as the capacity to choose how to act (on stage), means to use the resource of visibility not only for *becoming*, but also for *making* visible. This has to encompass letting *all* participants of cultural education processes, including children, define what is seen as worthy to be made visible and how. It might also include bringing *all* participants, also adults, with their different or similar perspectives, on to the stage to create collective forms of agency. It might also incorporate claims to refusal, to denial; a resistance of citizens against a performative imperative by using the stage for hiding, for looking back, for disappearing, for irritating each other.

NOTES

1. The term 'postmigrant', originally deriving from American cultural and literature studies, was brought into the German discussion by Smhermin Langhoff, director of the *Maxim Gorki Theater* in Berlin. The prefix 'post' does not name an end of migration, but marks cultural and social transformation and negotiation processes that occur after migration has become characteristic for (German) society as a whole (Foroutan et al. 2014; Widmann 2014).

2. Talking about *visibility* in this text usually means audibility as well. The visual is connected to the audible appearance of citizens here.

3. For example, Wolfgang Sting describes a cooperation between schools and artists by TUSCH-projects in Hamburg, See also http://www.tusch-hamburg.de/TUSCH/index.php

4. Compare funding guidelines of German programmes like, for example, 'Kultur Macht Stark': https://www.bmbf.de/de/kultur-macht-stark-buendnisse-fuer-bildung-958.html; 'Kultur Bewegt': http://www.hamburg.de/kulturbehoerde/kultur-bewegt/; and so on.

5. Although Norma Köhler points out that 'biographying' in theatre is nothing that happens in just one direction, that the audience members also involve themselves in what is shown and told on stage with their own biographical perspectives—*on* stage it is the biographies of children that are told and performed *on* stage (Köhler 2015)—that become visible and audible in public.

6. 44.9 per cent of the pupils in Hamburg overall have a so-called migrant background; in the Hamburg neighbourhood of Veddel, it is 95 per cent (Behörde für Schule und Berufsbildung Hamburg 2016).

7. See, Hamburger Netzwerk Lehrkräfte mit Migrationshintergrund: http://www.wegweiser-kommune.de/projekte/kommunal/hamburg/, date accessed 13 December 2017.

8. Compare examples such as the works: *Haircuts by Children, Eat the Street,* and so on, by Mammalian Diving Reflex, http://mammalian.ca/projects/, or projects of the Forschungstheater / Theatre of Research, like *Die Kinderbank* or *Playing Up* http://www.fundus-theater.de/forschungstheater/

9. A high school in Berlin Kreuzberg.

10. The title refers to Peter Handtke's play *Publikumsbeschimpfung* ('Offending the Audience') (1966), in which the idea of theatrical representation is rejected: the audience's expectations and thoughts are analysed, the audience is watched back from stage.

REFERENCES

Ahrens, P.A. 2009. Bestandsaufnahme: Theaterarbeit mit Kindern und Jugendlichen mit Migrationshintergrund. In *Theater interkulturell: Theaterarbeit mit Kindern und Jugendlichen*, ed. K. Hoffmann, 16–76. Uckerland: Schibri

Allman, D.D., and M.D. Beaty. 2002. *Cultivating Citizens: Soulcraft and Citizenship in Contemporary America*. Lanham: Lexington Books.

Arendt, H. 1998. *The Human Condition*. Chicago: University of Chicago Press.

Behörde für Schule und Berufsbildung Hamburg. 2016. *Hamburger Schulstatistik Schuljahr 2015/2016*. http://www.hamburg.de/contentblob/5323720/97e5 b9e0c5f28c7767347b5947f04ce5/data/2015-16-hamburger-schulstatistik. pdf. Accessed 22 Sep 2016.

Benhabib, S. 1998. *Hannah Arendt – die melancholische Denkerin der Moderne*. Hamburg: Rotbuch.

Butler, J. 2004. *Undoing Gender*. New York/London: Routledge.

———. 2011. *Bodies that Matter: On the Discursive Limits of 'Sex'*. Abingdon, Oxon/New York: Routledge.

Castro Varela, M. do M., and P. Mecheril, eds. 2016. *Die Dämonisierung der Anderen: Rassismuskritik der Gegenwart*. Bielefeld: Transcript.

Deck, J. 2014. Paradoxe Verhältnisse. Zum biopolitischen Kontext der Theaterarbeit mit Kindern und Jugendlichen. In *Stop Teaching! Neue Theaterformen mit Kindern und Jugendlichen*, ed. P. Primavesi and J. Deck, 47–67. Bielefeld: Transcript.

Deleuze, G., and F. Guattari. 2002. Intensiv-Werden, Tier-Werden, Unwahrnehmbar-Werden…. In *Tausend Plateaus*, 317–422. Berlin: Merve.

Foroutan, N., C. Canan, S. Arnold, B. Schwarze, S. Beigang, and D. Kalkum, eds. 2014. *Deutschland postmigrantisch. 1: Gesellschaft, Religion, Identität: Erste Ergebnisse*. Berlin: BIM.

Glissant, É., and B. Wing. 1997. *Poetics of Relation*. Ann Arbor: University of Michigan Press.

Hentschel, I. 2016. Zwischen Ich und Welt. Zeigen und Verbergen im Theater mit Jugendlichen. In *Theater zwischen Ich und Welt: Beiträge zur Ästhetik des Kinder- und Jugendtheaters: Theorien – Praxis – Geschichte*, 253–267. Bielefeld: Transcript.

Hess, S., and Lebuhn, H. 2014. Politiken der Bürgerschaft. Zur Forschungsdebatte um Migration, Stadt und citizenship. *sub\urban. zeitschrift für kritische stadtforschung*, 2(3/2014): Stadt und Migration: Neue Forschungsansätze zu Citizenship, Macht und Agency, 11–34. http://zeitschriftsuburban.de/sys/ index.php/suburban/article/view/153. Accessed 20 Dec 2017.

Holston, J. 2009. Insurgent Citizenship in an Era of Global Urban Peripheries. *City & Society* 21 (2): 245–267.

Isin, E.F. 2008. Theorizing Acts of Citizenship. In *Acts of Citizenship*, ed. E.F. Isin and G.M. Nielsen, 15–43. London/New York: Zed Books.

Köhler, N. 2015. Biografieren auf der Bühne – Theater als Soziale Kunst an der FH Dortmund. Tagungsrück- und Ausblick. *Zeitschrift für Theaterpädagogik* 31 (66): 68–69.

Lorenz, R., J. Schaffer, and A. Thal. 2012. Sichtbarkeitsregime und Künstlerische Praxis. *Feministische Studien* 30 (2): 285–295. https://doi.org/10.1515/fs-2012-0212.

Mackert, J. 2006. *Staatsbürgerschaft: eine Einführung.* Wiesbaden: VS Verlag.

Marshall, T.H. 1950. *Citizenship and Social Class.* Cambridge: Cambridge University Press.

Mecheril. 2014. Die Illusion der Inklusion: Bildung und die Migrationsgesellschaft. In *Vielfältiges Deutschland: Bausteine für eine zukunftsfähige Gesellschaft*, ed. U. Kober and Bertelsmann-Stiftung, 200–216. Gütersloh: Verlag Bertelsmann Stiftung.

Mörsch, C. 2011. Watch This Space! – Position beziehen in der Kulturvermittlung. In *Theater Vermittlung Schule: ein Dialog*, ed. M. Sack, 8–27. Zurich: Zürcher Hochschule der Künste.

Papadopoulos, D., N. Stephenson, and V. Tsianos. 2008. *Escape Routes: Control and Subversion in the Twenty-First Century.* London/Ann Arbor: Pluto Press.

Peters, S. 2012. Forschung und Teilhabe. Vom ästhetischen Lernen der Gesellschaft. *Kukturelle Bildung* 6 (10): 9–11.

———. 2016. Performing Citizenship: Performance Art and Public Happiness. In *Artistic Citizenship: Artisty, Social Responsibility, and Ethical Praxis*, ed. D.J. Elliott, M. Silverman, and W.D. Bowman, 469–479. New York: Oxford University Press.

Plischke, E. 2016. *Was wäre, wenn Kinder...? Gesammelte Gedanken über Teilhabe an Forschung & das Erforschen von Teilhabe.* Leipzig: Unpublished manuscript.

Rogoff, I. 2005. Looking Away: Participations in Visual Culture. In *After Criticism*, ed. G. Butt, 117–134. Oxford: Blackwell Publishing. https://doi.org/10.1002/9780470774243.ch6. Accessed 13 Dec 2016.

Rose, N. 2000. Governing Cities, Governing Citizens. In *Democracy, Citizenship and the Global City*, ed. E.F. Isin, 95–109. London: Routledge.

Schaffer, J. 2008. *Ambivalenzen der Sichtbarkeit: Über die visuellen Strukturen der Anerkennung.* Bielefeld: Transcript.

Schiller, F. 2000. *Über die ästhetische Erziehung des Menschen in einer Reihe von Briefen.* Stuttgart: Reclam.

Sharifi, A. 2011. *Theater für Alle? Partizipation von Postmigranten am Beispiel der Bühnen der Stadt Köln.* Frankfurt am Main: Peter Lang.

———. 2014. *Bestandsaufnahme zum postmigrantischen Theater für ein junges Publikum in NRW.* http://2014.westwindfestival.de/fileadmin/user_upload/Westwind_Sharifi_Studie.pdf. Accessed 20 Dec 2017.

Spivak, G.C. 2011. *Can the Subaltern Speak: Postkolonialität und subalterne Artikulation.* Vienna: Turia + Kant.

Spivak, G.C., and J. Butler. 2011. *Who Sings the Nation-State: Language, Politics, Belonging.* London/New York: Sea Boating.

Sternfeld, N. 2013. CuMMA Papers # 1: Playing by the Rules of the Game. *CuMMA – Studies in Curating, Managing and Mediating Art.* https://cummastudies.wordpress.com/cumma-papers/. Accessed 6 Feb 2017.

Steyerl, H. 2002. *Can the Subaltern Speak German? Postkoloniale Kritik.* Transversal texts. http://transversal.at/transversal/0902/steyerl/de. Accessed 13 Dec 2016.

———. 2008. *Die Farbe der Wahrheit: Dokumentarismen im Kunstfeld.* Vienna: Turia + Kant.

Sting, W. 2014. Theater und Schule: TUSCH. Ein KulturLernModell. Zentrale Merkmale am Beispiel von TUSCH Hamburg. *Zeitschrift für Theaterpädagogik* 30 (64): 41–44.

Varela, M. do M. C, and N. Dhawan. 2015. *Postkoloniale Theorie: Eine kritische Einführung.* Vol. 1. Bielefeld: Transcript.

Widmann, A. 2014. Was heißt postmigrantisch? Interview with Naika Foroutan. *Berliner Zeitung.* http://www.berliner-zeitung.de/naika-foroutan-was-heisst-postmigrantisch%2D%2D487520. Accessed 19 Dec 2016.

Practices of Politicizing Listening (to Migration)

Nanna Heidenreich

Already, before the 'summer of migration' in 2015—the supposed 'refugee crisis'—strategies such as 'giving a face' and 'lending a voice' have become catch phrases in addressing migration and flight. However, no voice is just nature, reality, truth, or simply 'there'. In particular, what a voice is, can do, is also a question of listening. The famous question posed by Gayatri Chakravorty Spivak is pertinent here: 'Can the subaltern speak?' Pointedly, her response reveals that the answer to this question is based on the subaltern voice getting heard. In this way, listening plays a crucial role: it critically allows a voice to be heard. Such active listening is an act of response rather than a simple act of recording; it does not defer responsibility by placing it on 'the Other's' ability to speak, to find their voice within the frame given to them in the act of 'giving' or 'lending'.

The German term *Aufnahme* speaks volumes here with its threefold translations as recording, admission and inclusion.[1] Replacing the long established German neologism of *Nichteinwanderungsland* (a country of

---

'*The point of language will no longer only be about communication, but also about pleasure and politics*'

N. Heidenreich (✉)
ifs internationale filmschule köln, Berlin, Germany

© The Author(s) 2019
P. Hildebrandt et al. (eds.), *Performing Citizenship*, Performance Philosophy, https://doi.org/10.1007/978-3-319-97502-3_18

non-immigration), the term *Aufnahmegesellschaft* became a keyword in 2015. It means host society, referring to the moment of arrival as well as to civil society's active engagement in providing support and many of the services German bureaucracy actually fails to provide for migrants and refugees.[2] What the term misses is the incorporation of duration—it inherits, after all, the well-established frame of non-immigration. The question therefore continues to be: how to think arrival—*The Enigma of Arrival*, as V. S. Naipaul titled his 1987 novel—or, how to think *Aufnahme*. One way to do so might lie in the semantic layers of the word: let's turn to the sound of *Aufnahme*, let's listen to arrival, let's think migration through the ear.

Philip Scheffner's films testify to the art of listening as a form of (political) activation. In 2012, he and his co-author Merle Kröger[3] made a film about the death of Grigore Velcu and Eudache Calderar, two Romanian Roma who were shot at the German-Polish border in 1992, supposedly a hunting accident. The German hunters responsible for their deaths claimed they thought the men they spotted in the wee hours of the morning in a corn field were wild boar; they were put on trial and acquitted. The families of the men who were killed were never informed about the trial. Not one single representative of the law nor any other involved party considered contacting them, thus depriving them of a chance to participate in negotiating justice and having the possibility to make civil claims. Instead of reading this violent inactivity as individual or group negligence or failure, rather, this configuration needs to be understood as an expression of structural violence (which does not dilute individual responsibility). Through their film, titled *Revision*, Scheffner and Kröger set out to open a space for negotiation withheld by police investigations and court proceedings. The very space which the systematic violence of racism, bureaucracy and diffused responsibility foreclosed. In reopening a legally terminated case for a different agenda, a new 'hearing room', *ein neuer Verhandlungsraum* could emerge. A space was created in which the families of the victims could participate, as well as all the other parties involved; a cinematic revision in which reflection on the very form of the witness testimony gives shape to a listening/recording practice allowing for voices to be heard which were silenced before. The film did not aim to produce a different judgment, but created instead the possibility for different versions of contemporary European history to have meaning and resonance. The violence of the deaths and ensuing silence cannot be undone; thus, *Revision* does not resort to the narrative and institutional form of either the verdict or of revenge, two familiar sites of 'justice'. Instead, it opens up a space for speaking and, more so, for listening. The film documents their 'revision', their reviewing, rather than first encounters—the 'original' interviews. Each protagonist is shown listening to their prior statements. Everybody gets the chance to speak, to listen, and to comment.[4]

One of the participants in this process of revision was Colorado Velcu, the oldest son of Grigore Velcu. His presence in *Revision* is striking. He has a clear command of the position of the camera and of relational configurations in operation in the space that lies between who is behind the camera and who or what is in front of it, and what actually speaking within the camera's frame entails. He clearly has no interest in just 'giving' his face or his voice to the piece. He questioned the filmmakers and actively configured the meeting grounds, as Philip Scheffner and Merle Kröger have described in their encounter.[5] It is their shared love for Bollywood that lays the foundation for mutual openings: cinema as a space of negotiation, also in its colorful grand version of song, dance, and endless passion.

A few years after the completion of *Revision*, Colorado Velcu, (temporarily) single father of seven,[6] moved to Germany with parts of his extended family—first to Essen, then to Berlin. The relationship between Philip Scheffner and Colorado Velcu has always been via the camera. They set out to film their arrival; it is a form of communication (also in the absence of a shared language 'proper'). This begins to shift very quickly: the camera becomes several cameras, and Colorado Velcu—with the support of his family—begins to collaborate on what will become the film *And-Ek Ghes...* (2016). Fittingly, the film begins in a recording booth. We see Colorado Velcu wearing headphones, listening to a recording of his voice. He hears, we hear

> I started a few times to write a personal diary. But that was all. I never managed to keep at it, even for a few weeks. Today, I've decided to write. As one sees, I've picked up my pen here in my apartment in Berlin. I begin with my arrival in Germany, in Essen. As I have to begin there.

He pauses and then begins to speak on camera, addressing Philip Scheffner, whose reflection we see in the soundproof glass of the recording booth:

I think it wasn't so good. We should do it again. We can do it still better. Let's do it again.

And from the off, Philip Scheffner:

Ok.

And-Ek Ghes... means: 'One fine day...' A song, a promise to the beloved, to the children, to oneself. Members of the Velcu family—from Fața Luncii, Romania—move to Berlin and perform themselves into a possible future. It is the refrain of the title song that was written by Colorado Velcu. It is this song that adds yet another layer to the many cinematic formats and languages deployed and worked through by Velcu and Scheffner in their film; they transform the piece into a Bollywood style music video that lays claim to a city and its venues: this is our story, our scenery, our stage.

Feminist theorist and musician Christina Thürmer-Rohr published an article in 1994 called '*Achtlose Ohren. Zur Politisieren des Zuhörens*', translated as: 'Careless Ears. On the Politicization of Listening',[7] in which she establishes a connection between *Aufnahme* and *Aufnahme*: inclusion and recording, starting and absorbing, receiving and accommodating, taping and adopting. *Aufnahme* is the verb used to describe the current arrival of refugees and migrants. *Aufnahme* outlines the bureaucratic processes migrants have to pass through as imposed by the supposed 'host' society, that is Germany. As *Aufnahme*, the sites of their registration are called *Aufnahmezentren*, or 'reception centers'. These euphemisms should indeed be held by their word. Thürmer-Rohr writes:

> Listening shows that the Other concerns me. It signals interest in the world, interest in the Other(s). Listening to is a metaphor for openness, a person's being open, hospitality on the inside. S/he who listens makes herself accessible and vulnerable, wants to know about the Other, is concerned by the Other, wants to answer to the Other. Listening to contradicts the monological consciousness, is not only reception but attention and irritation.[8]

> Listening to is not about recognizing what one already knows,...it leads to something missing and not to something already known.[9]

It doesn't confirm or indeed reaffirm; it means slackening the realm of certainty and stepping into an arena of uncertainty.

Thinking about listening is not so much about advocating sound instead of images, as if the recording of sound would be less imbued with 'perspective' than recording with a camera. Listening as a political act is more about a shift in focus, a shift in the attunement of one sense by using another. Listening might actually teach us to see (otherwise).

Philologist and communication scholar Lisbeth Lipari, in a short article called 'Listening Others',[10] addresses the practice of listening to the others as 'Other'. If we fail to do so, she argues, we 'deny their alterity and limit our own horizons of meaning. But when we listen to the other as other, we pave the way for an ethic that can listen others to speech, and in doing so, put our self-conceptions and dearly held certainties at risk.'[11] Lipari continues by looking at the transitive and intransitive uses of speaking, listening and hearing. She wants to convey a sense of listening as constitutive of, and prior to, speaking: 'listening is an invocation, a calling forth of speech'.[12]

In this sense, Judith Butler and Gayatri Chakravorty Spivak were listening together to the 2006 protests of illegalized immigrants in the US, who were collectively singing the US national anthem in Spanish. In their dialogue, 'Who sings the Nation-State. Language, Politics, Belonging',[13] they hear it not simply as an expression of a new—a pluralist, more inclusive—nationalism, but rather, they hear it as the longing for enfranchisement.[14] In German, this is translated as '*Verlangen nach Stimmrecht*',[15] that is, the desire to enter the law, the desire for having the right to vote, and the longing for the right to have a voice: *Stimme*—voice, and *Stimme*—vote.

The doubling of the meaning of voice as *Stimme* und *Stimmrecht*, between voice and vote, gains another angle in the context of the films I chose as examples—it needs to be *revisioned*. If we discuss arrival under the premise of citizenship, that is, as a question of arrival in the sense of becoming part of the political community (which always also pertains to the question of rights, even if one considers citizenship as constituted from below), we need to ask again what this entails, as it is obviously not simply a question of legal status or passport. In the case of the Romanian Roma people, they—like all other EU citizens—have the right to establishment (in other words, residence). Yet Romanian Roma are clearly not treated as equal citizens, and even have been deported from countries such as France and Germany in blatant violation of the law—acts of unlawful violence enacted by the state. So, what if the entitlement to participate is not defined by one's passport (as in the case of Romanian Roma who are citizens with EU membership, but are still not counted in)?

One of the expressions of everyday racism in Germany has become the demand to speak German ('Here we speak German (only)!'). Monolingualism (as attitude) feeds into the use of the German language as a tool of exclusion and discipline. And yet, the critique of this form of violent refusal to speak, and thus to listen otherwise, does not mean that being able to relate to Otherness is based solely on knowledge. Understanding—or actually, the willingness to understand and to relate—does not reside in subtitles, and most certainly not in the dubbing, to use another cinematic term. Eva-Ruth Wemme worked as one of the translators on the making of *And-Ek Ghes*.... Wemme is the author of the book *Meine 7000 Nachbarn*[16] ('My 7000 Neighbors'), a publication based on the blog under the same name, in which she chronicles her work as translator—and facilitator—with Romanians and, in particular, Romanian Roma in Berlin. When she was asked to work as a translator for the film, she expected a familiar situation:

> When I interpret between Roma and Gajikané [non-Roma people, ed.], fear usually rises up against me – in the worst case, from both sides – and I need good standing. Two meet who can't understand one another, not just linguistically, and who also don't even believe understanding is fundamentally possible.

But:

> Working with Philip and Colorado, nothing rose up against me. Unaccustomed to that, I started to totter. I almost felt superfluous; nothing hurt when we spoke. There were no cultural presuppositions or dreams that also needed to be interpreted. Philip and Colorado encountered one another in a world whose points of reference they had created themselves. They understood each other; it was only one another's words that were unfamiliar. A matter of the tools of my trade. And when, beyond the question of language, they didn't understand each other, they considered it as something to be expected. People can't see through one another like shards of glass.[17]

The ability to understand might thus be found elsewhere, in a different form of relation (to language, to speaking, and of course to listening). As

Daniel Hendrickson—musician, author, translator and member of the artist collective CHEAP—writes in his 'The Rhizome of Babel',[18]

> Each of us will speak whichever language he or she chooses, as the situation arises. The choice of language will be left to the speakers, to be negotiated according to ability, context, or simply personal whim. We will be free to switch from one to the other as we see fit. We will not be required to speak only one, and we will not even be required to announce which one it is that we are speaking. I will not require you to understand me, nor will I blame myself if I don't understand you. The point of language will no longer only be about communication, but also about pleasure and politics. After all, what is the point of 'nations and tribes' if it's not that we should get 'to know one another'? I may very well try to learn your language(s), but if I do, it probably means that I'm flirting with you.[19]

*   *   *

The film *And-Ek Ghes...* ends as it begins, with Colorado Velcu in the recording booth, a trace of Philip Scheffner visible in the reflection of the glass. Velcu reads from his diary. Then he looks up and addresses Philip, the camera, and us: 'Let's listen to it again. Let's see how it turned out.'

NOTES

1. See Julia Tieke's working through the meanings of *Aufnahme* in her audio play *'Achtung, Aufnahme!'*, *Recording in Progress!* which she wrote and realized for the series *Tonspuren/Soundtracks*—I curated this work for the Haus der Kulturen der Welt in Berlin in 2015. http://hkw.de/en/programm/projekte/veranstaltung/p_128515.php, date accessed 31 January 2017.
2. See the two 'EFA' studies 'Strukturen und Motive der ehrenamtlichen Flüchtlingsarbeit (EFA) in Deutschland' conducted by BIM—Berliner Institut für empirische Integrations- und Migrationsforschung. https://www.bim.hu-berlin.de/en/about/, date accessed 31 January 2017.
3. Together they formed the production platform 'pong' in 2001, http://pong-berlin.de/, date accessed 31 January 2017.
4. See also the director's statement on the film's website: http://revision-film.eu/en/2/film-texts-revision/directors-statement, date accessed 31 January 2017.
5. For example, at the conference *Wessen Wissen?* in July 2016 at the University of the Arts in Berlin, https://www.udk-berlin.de/forschung/dfg-gradui-

ertenkolleg-das-wissen-der-kuenste/veranstaltungsarchiv-des-dfg-gradui-ertenkollegs/wessen-wissen-kuenste-situiertheit-materialitaet/,   date accessed 31 January 2017.

6. At the time of the making of the film, his wife—the mother of his children—was in prison in Romania.

7. Published first in Christina Thürmer-Rohr (1994) *Verlorene Narrenfreiheit. Essays* (Berlin: Orlanda), pp. 111–29.

8. Christina Thürmer-Rohr (1994) *Verlorene Narrenfreiheit. Essays*, (Berlin: Orlanda), p. 111 [author's translation].

9. Christina Thürmer-Rohr (1994) *Verlorene Narrenfreiheit. Essays* (Berlin: Orlanda), p. 115 [author's translation].

10. Published in Angus Carlyle & Cathy Lane (2013) (eds) *On Listening* (Axminster/Devon: Uniformbooks), pp. 156–9.

11. Angus Carlyle & Cathy Lane (2013) (eds) *On Listening* (Axminster/Devon: Uniformbooks), p. 156.

12. Angus Carlyle & Cathy Lane (2013) (eds) *On Listening* (Axminster/Devon: Uniform books), p. 157.

13. Judith Butler & Gayatri Chakravorty Spivak (2011) *Who sings the Nation-State. Language, Politics, Belonging* (London/New York/Calcutta: Seagull).

14. Judith Butler & Gayatri Chakravorty Spivak (2011) *Who sings the Nation-State. Language, Politics, Belonging* (London/New York/Calcutta: Seagull), p. 63.

15. Judith Butler & Gayatri Chakravorty Spivak (2007) *Sprache, Politik, Zugehörigkeit*, translated by Michael Heitz & Sabine Schulz (Berlin: diaphanes), p. 44.

16. Eva-Ruth Wemme (2015) *Meine 7000 Nachbarn* (Berlin: Verbrecherverlag).

17. Eva-Ruth Wemme (2016) *Everything Merely Language* (Berlin), http://andekghes.pong-berlin.de/en/10/eva-ruth-wemme, date accessed 26 March 2017. The text was written in German and, in that language, has a particular beauty, as has all of Wemme's writings.

18. Daniel Hendrickson (2011) 'The Rhizome of Babel' in Sebastian Cichoki & Galit Eilat (eds) *A Cookbook for Political Imagination* (Berlin: Sternberg Press), pp. 232–5.

    A Cookbook for Political Imagination was a publication for Yael Bartana's art/political enterprise 'The Jewish Renaissance Movement in Poland', a critical investigation of Zionism and of notions of origins and dreams of return, together with its mix into historical and present anti-semitism, as well as Schengen/Dublin Europe's anti-immigration politics.

19. Daniel Hendrickson (2011) 'The Rhizome of Babel' in Sebastian Cichoki & Galit Eilat (eds) *A Cookbook for Political Imagination* (Berlin: Sternberg Press), p. 235.

Childish Citizenship

Darren O'Donnell

The left's pivot over the last thirty years towards a politics of identity has been blamed by some commentators for driving people apart and contributing to the recent rise of an extremist, racist, sexist, homophobic far right. But, whether that's true or not, the politics of identity has not provided the tools to create a movement with enough mass to provide alternatives to the current economic order. Judith Butler, a leading figure in challenging the gender binary in both academic and popular contexts, also has doubts about the efficacy of identity politics. She believes it 'fails to furnish a broader conception of what it means, politically, to live together across differences' (Butler 2015), and she turns to the idea of precarity, or precariousness—living with no stable, reliable and consistent employment—as a concept to rally around, a site of alliance.

If we're looking for a population with nearly infinite identities expressed by the individuals within it, all of whom share the condition of precarity, we don't have to look much further than children, even the richest of whom are denied many basic rights, including the right to work for money. Children are everywhere, all identity groups have them, and all of us, no matter our identity or our politics, have been a child and experienced the acute powerlessness that is the child's condition. Can the child—and

D. O'Donnell (✉)
Mammalian Diving Reflex, Toronto, ON, Canada
e-mail: darren@mammalian.ca

© The Author(s) 2019
P. Hildebrandt et al. (eds.), *Performing Citizenship*, Performance Philosophy, https://doi.org/10.1007/978-3-319-97502-3_19

efforts to infiltrate much of the world with the presence of children—provide a strategy for destabilizing the status quo? And if so, can this strategy attract the critical mass currently missing from the many fractured movements that wrestle with the question of fairness? Our understanding of what it means to be a child and what children are capable of contributing is rapidly evolving. I believe we do have the possibility of both subverting business as usual and finding a common cause to organize around, a stealthy little cause that, at first, seems naive and innocuous—sure, let the kids in—but that might radically revolutionize the world.

But it is adults—not children—who are the universal legal subject. As full citizens, adults can legitimately stake their claim as members of civil society, with the possibility of political citizenship being central to the contemporary understanding of citizenship. Children are denied this in law, they are not full citizens.

What defines children and what constitutes the place and domain of childhood is not static across time or space. There is huge variation in what it means to be a child, what their capacities are understood to be, and how they are expected to behave. Currently, our society largely views children as *becoming* and not as being. Children are on their way towards a destination: adulthood. They are constituted as children in opposition to adulthood and considered to be in a state of preparation for taking on life's 'real' responsibilities once they are old enough—an age that is locked in law. They are *on-their-way-towards* being finished.

Or,

Is it possible to conceive of young people as not headed towards this more perfected state, but considered for who they are now? This approach prioritizes the young person's being over their eventual becoming. This is the recognition that their being is as legitimate as anyone else's and that, ultimately, they not only have a stake in all discussions affecting them, but that most issues affect them.

This shift away from the psychology of development recognizes that adults themselves hardly resemble the complete and fully formed entities that are popularly understood as adults. There is vague definition, let alone consensus, on what it means to be adult. To be an adult is to be many things that are regarded as being childlike: vulnerable, mistaken, confused, petulant, afraid, irrational, despairing (Pedraza-Gomez 2007). Making mistakes, learning and growing up never stop—so how can we ever mark where adulthood begins? Incorporating vulnerability does not preclude competence.

Adulthood produces the subcategory of childhood; the idea of the autonomy of adults makes absolutely no sense without the lack of autonomy implied in the idea of children. As we have witnessed the disintegration of the gender binary, so too can we anticipate, if not actively work towards, the dissolution of the binary that is adult and child. An obvious first step—as in the approach to gender or race—is to stop associating essential and unchanging qualities to either of the binaries, adult or child. When we think of children, we tend to think they are vulnerable and in need of care, while adults are understood to be able to take care of themselves. But, in reality, each adult and each child have innate capacities and abilities: Some adults are more childlike than others, some require the same care that a baby requires for their entire lives, and some children are, at quite a young age, completely resilient, rational and independent—qualities more often associated with adults. Again, like gender and race, any generalizations or assumptions we make about the 'typical' behaviours of children and adults inevitably fall into question in the face of a multitude of exceptions.

In order to re-evaluate and define entitlement to full citizenship, it requires that the notion of adults—as commonly understood—simply does not exist. We all can be viewed as remaining as children, we are all vulnerable and continue to figure out how to cope with complex situations. Ultimately, the existing notions of childhood and adulthood are stereotypes, with all the coercion that being a stereotype entails (Watson 2009). But beyond a stereotype, childhood is a way to relegate a big chunk of the population into being an 'eternal other.' Political economist Alison M. Watson claims that:

> the implications of children's 'otherness' have not been tackled in a sustained way within the social sciences generally or geography in particular, because of the genuine difficulty of doing so. The otherness of childhood is profound, as many of the symbolic orders which routinely but deeply structure adult life, such as time, money, property, sex, mortality, and Euclidean space melt away as one tries to see the smoother, or perhaps differently striated spaces of childhood. (p. 33)

As a way to address this otherness, feminist legal scholar Martha Albertson Fineman argues that we need to look at a vulnerability, which is 'universal and constant, inherent in the human condition' and that the vulnerable subject should be 'at the centre of our political and theoretical endeavours' (Fineman 2008, p. 1). Fineman contrasts this idea of vulnerability with the liberal theory of the autonomous and independent subject, the 'competent social actor capable of playing multiple and concurrent societal roles: the employee, the employer, the spouse, the parent, the consumer, the manufacturer, the citizen, the taxpayer, and so on' (p. 10).

This idea of the liberal, autonomous, subject is 'indispensable to the prevailing ideologies of autonomy, self-sufficiency, and personal responsibility, through which society is conceived as constituted by self-interested individuals with the capacity to manipulate and manage their independently acquired and overlapping resources' (p. 10). As Fineman points out, this liberal subject does not account for everybody, and it certainly does not account for the trajectory of a life which has constant variation in degrees of autonomy, self-sufficiency and personal responsibility, with the ever-present threat that that autonomy, self-sufficiency and personal responsibility will be wiped out entirely. It is just an accident away, after all.

And, of course for our purposes here, another problem with the liberal subject is that 's/he can only be presented as an adult' (p. 11). Instead, Fineman points to the idea of the vulnerable subject as a 'more accurate and complete universal figure to place at the heart of social policy' (p. 11). In addition to social policy, the very idea of citizenship itself needs to be retooled to include the vulnerable subject as an active political subject, even as their actions may be quite circumscribed or need the help of others to be fully expressed. As such, the vulnerable citizen should be the citizen around which political participation is conceived, designed and implemented.

Vulnerability, being the idea around which state and other institutions intervene into the social sphere, opens things up to consider children in the same moment that we consider adults. Within this framework, children and adults are exactly the same, in that that which is understood to be universal is now tweaked to include aspects central to the experience of children—which are also increasingly certain to be aspects of the adult experience towards the end of life. The liberal universal of autonomous, self-sufficient and personally responsible individuals means that children are excluded and become just another 'Other' but, within a vulnerability framework, children are *included* and, as such, have a right to participate in the world like any one of us.

Article 12 of the *UN Convention on the Rights of the Child* (The United Nations 1989), which provides the basis for a way to consider the participation of young people, states:

States Parties shall assure to the child who is capable of forming his or her own views the right to express those views freely in all matters affecting the child, the views of the child being given due weight in accordance with the age and maturity of the child.

While 'expressing views' is a narrow way to describe participation, Article 12 has been taken up and commonly understood as protecting children's participation rights (Pare 2015). The realm of these rights is extensive, outlined therein as: 'all matters affecting the child.' It is hard to think of any important social or political institution, process or system that does not, to some degree, affect young people: the market, the education system, the judicial system, the electoral system, the entertainment industry, the medical industry, almost all technology, and so on. The list is endless and, perhaps, is best summed up with one word: everything. *Everything* affects children.

Increased participation rights for children are essential—as reasoned extensively by scholars—for young people to develop a sense of control, increased ability to handle stressful situations, enhanced trust in others, self-esteem, the sense of being respected, contribution to education and development, to learn how to respect the views of others, and so forth. All admirable reasons, most of which are at the level of the individual child. But more importantly, the participation of children has the potential to completely renovate the way in which we think of citizenship, as the inclusion of young people within the political process is very likely to decisively alter that process.

Advantages emerge for all of us when children are amongst us, ways of being with each other that are oriented towards efforts at a calm civility. Adult behaviour is often modified around children, for example, as seen in the common endeavour to shield young children from aggressive conflict. In addition to guiding us towards better behaviours, children are also experts at small joys and masters of play; attributes we can all enjoy and learn from. So, in these senses, the participation of children as citizens not only benefits the young, but all of society.

References

Butler, J. 2015. *Notes Toward a Performative Theory of Assembly.* Cambridge, MA: Harvard University Press.

Fineman, M. 2008. The Vulnerable Subject: Anchoring Equality in the Human Condition. *Yale Journal of Law and Feminism* 20 (1): 1–23.

Pare, M. 2015. Inclusion and Participation in Special Education Processes in Ontario, Canada. In *International Perspectives and Empirical Findings on Child Participation*, ed. T. Gal and B.F. Duramy, 51–73. Oxford: Oxford University Press.

Pedraza-Gomez, Z. 2007. Working Children and the Cultural Perception of Childhood. In *Working to Be Someone*, ed. B. Hungerland, M. Liebel, B. Milne, and A. Wihstutz, 23–30. London: Jessica Kingsley Publishers.

The United Nations. 1989. *The United Nations Convention on the Rights of the Child*. Geneva. www.ohchr.org/EN/ProfessionalInterest/Pages/CRC.aspx

Watson, A. 2009. *The Child in International Political Economy*. New York: Routledge.

I Do. From Instruction to Agency: Designing of Vocational Orientation Through Artistic Practice

Constanze Schmidt

Henry, a 16-year-old boy, is standing in the entrance hall of a large Chinese logistics company in the HafenCity in Hamburg. He is playing the recorder. It is lunchtime; employees are pouring out of the elevators to go out for lunch. A few of them turn to glance at Henry. Normally, Henry plays the recorder at small concerts, with his family, or alone, just for relaxation. He even plays it during the breaks of rehearsals when he is stressed. He always carries his recorder with him. At the moment, he is doing a mandatory internship at China Shipping, and had the idea that maybe some of the employees might enjoy hearing him play his instrument. Shortly afterwards, he said, 'Of course, it was embarrassing. But it was a lot of fun too'.

In this particular context, Henry's playing becomes a micro practice, by which he triggers something within a micro framework. Such a sense of

---

I am here.
And as a result, something happens.

C. Schmidt (✉)
Graduate Program Performing Citizenship, HafenCity University Hamburg, Hamburg, Germany

© The Author(s) 2019
P. Hildebrandt et al. (eds.), *Performing Citizenship*, Performance Philosophy, https://doi.org/10.1007/978-3-319-97502-3_20

agency, the capacity to act and to prompt an effect, is probably not experienced so often by young people during their internship. In general, interns will focus primarily on adapting to given structures at the workplace and in trying not to attract too much attention. Together with Henry and other ninth-grade teenagers, I have been researching a new form of vocational orientation with artistic practice. In this context, I initiated internships where teenagers performatively explore different places of work. The following questions were decisive for our project:

- How can vocational orientation be combined with an education of agency?
- Ideally, could this take place by introducing an artistic, performative form of agency?

To answer these questions, I will first refer to given theories and research around the notions of work, performance, citizenship and agency, and then describe our specific research setup of a vocational orientation that was informed by artistic practices.

Working Citizen. The Longing for Agency in Current Vocational Orientation

Concerning professions, the German Basic Law states:

Article 12

(1) *All Germans shall have the right freely to choose their occupation or profession, their place of work and their place of training.* (Basic Law, p. 3)

Vocational orientation has so far been understood as a life-long process in which an individual can tailor his skills and align his own aspirations with the professional requirements of the outside world. In school-based vocational orientation, the parents, employment agency and school support the young individual's career choice by providing counselling and informing him or her about different vocational fields and corresponding requirements.

Working as a teacher in the German school system at a Hamburg academic high school, I have noticed that many teenagers—in view of the given freedom and an ever-changing world of work—feel overwhelmed when it comes to choosing their professional education.[1] They tend to make short-term decisions, without much reflection, which often have far-reaching consequences—such as later breaking off from their studies or education. Students are confronted with two key challenges in the context of their vocational orientation: firstly, their efforts to obtain good grades, in the sense of fulfilling external requirements, do not prepare them for their working life. According to Paul Collard, more than half of the professions that will be socially relevant in the future do not even exist yet. Young people will thus also need to be capable of one thing in the future: to invent careers for themselves (cf. Collard 2013, p. 2).

Additionally, many students have neither been taught nor encouraged how to develop a critical attitude towards our neoliberal working society, and to develop this attitude within their career choices and life planning.

I understand a vocational orientation in which both of these challenges are taken into account as being designed around the idea of a *working citizen*.

Performing Work

In post-Fordism, labour is no longer defined as a self-explanatory concept. The same occupation can be perceived by those executing it as either labour or non-labour. For Paolo Virno, the distinction between labour and non-labour has become obsolete, and has been replaced by a politically motivated differentiation between remunerated and non-remunerated life (cf. Virno 2004, p. 117). Thus, it is not solely the occupation itself, but other factors that will determine what is considered as labour.

Companies nowadays expect their employees to optimally organize their work themselves; to not only execute a work-related task, but also to perform it. According to Kai van Eikels, social and communicative skills (negotiating, communicating, presenting), one's personal standing and the corresponding recognition from colleagues, all play a vital role in the assessment of a person's proficiency. What is being assessed is 'their self-enactment – in the double sense of their behaviour and self-presentation as a performing subject in an inter-subjective network of collaboration' (van Eikels 2013b, p. 8, translation by author). A person's occupations are possibly perceived less as work when fulfilled independently within the environment of a company based on teamwork. This also involves the assumption that workers who dedicate themselves to their tasks with their entire personality are less able to distance themselves from their work.

For work performance in a company, particularly the 'performative sovereignty' (van Eikels 2013b, p. 4, translation by author) is attractive. A person can attain performative sovereignty by exposing themselves to situations which they are able to cope with, not through an existing position of power, but only by virtue of their own behaviour in the given situation. Acting, in such a situation, affords the performing person the freedom to shape reality in concrete terms (cf. van Eikels 2013a, p. 32); it never implies merely executing what has been predetermined. Performative sovereignty thus develops only with the actual performance of actions. According to van Eikels, the sovereign here disengages from the political—understood here as institutional authority—and appears as a performative sovereignty in processes of work and collaboration.

Labour—in the context of post-Fordism—in the eyes of Paolo Virno takes on traditional characteristics of political action in the sense of Hannah Arendt, because 'it is in the world of contemporary labour that we find the "being in the presence of others", the "relationship with the presence of others", the beginning of new processes, and the constitutive familiarity with contingency, the unforeseen and the possible' (Virno 2004, p. 51).

Following van Eikels' and Virno's thoughts, citizens thus have the possibility to understand work as a form of political action and to perform it according to their own needs and desires.

The Concept of a Working Citizen

The concept of a working citizen has been proposed by Ulf Schrader (2013). He suggests that, in view of an exponential economic growth that implies the exploitation of ecological and social resources, work—besides earning a living—should follow the principle of achieving social, ecological and economical fairness. According to Schrader, a working citizen follows a professional self-concept in the course of his working life, in which he 'preferably contributes his labour and time for the benefit of societal objectives relevant to him as a citizen' (Schrader 2013, p. 1, translation by author).[2] However, Schrader's approach neglects both a broadening of the definition of work and the possibility of a fundamental reorganization of work in our society.

Therefore, concerning vocational orientation and how to design it, I would like to expand the notion of the *working citizen* through the following ideas[3]:

Colin C. Williams criticizes the fact that, in most US top-down models for the promotion of security, esteem and identity, a *working citizen* is always understood as someone who participates in formal, paid employment. 'In this view, everything is linked to a paid job, including citizenship itself as manifested by the lack of distinction drawn between citizens' rights and workers' rights' (Williams 2007, p. 235). Williams promotes the redefinition and expansion of both grassroots and top-down models of the *working citizen* to encompass informal work. By extending the 'voluntary and community sectors', integration could be enhanced through informal work and *active citizenship*. In this context, Williams assesses the programme ACC (Active Citizen Credits) as being inclusive and sensible. The intention of this active citizens' service is to document, present and reward endeavours—such as caring and other work, conducted anyway—for the benefit of their community, for example, by granting tax credits. Individuals would thus voluntarily engage in a self-designed portfolio of work of their choice. 'The result would be the creation of a society founded upon the principle of multi-activity without a radical policy overhaul' (Williams 2007, p. 237).

Impulses towards a fundamental redistribution and reassessment of work in our society are found in the more holistic concepts of 'time prosperity' from the post-growth debate. The proposals made by Friederike Habermann (cf. Habermann 2013, pp. 14–24), and Frigga Haug (cf. Haug 2013, pp. 26–38) and others open up temporal spaces (cf. Konzeptwerk Neue Ökonomie 2013). Their ideas are of interest for the conception of a *working citizen,* even if they do not explicitly use the term. Here, the citizen takes responsibility for the sustainable organization of paid and unpaid work in our society. Internalized logics of growth are broken up and gainful employment is reduced to one quarter of the former allotted time. The individual will engage in activities, which she/he perceives as meaningful, based on the assumption that people are less interested in optimizing their personal economic situation but instead will use their own, and other, human resources with great care in all areas of life.

The German artist Juliane Stiegele extends post-growth concepts of work organization through the dimension of creativity. The question 'what is humane work?' is examined from different perspectives; for example, with regard to ecological responsibility, economic considerations, social aspects or the need for creativity and culture. In view of ongoing crises and negative impacts on human existence, Stiegele suggests the redefinition of all fields of work, involving rethinking and actively shaping them in the sense of creating a *social sculpture*, similar to the way Joseph Beuys described it in his 'expanded concept of art'. The concept includes the kind of human action aimed at shaping society for the benefit of all (cf. Beuys 1985). Stiegele finds an answer to the question of what humane work could be in artistic practice:

> If a person shapes things, works beyond his own interest toward a relation with others and does not lose sight of the overall picture, then he is an artist. [...] This would also serve as a plausible definition of humane work. (Stiegele 2014, p. 6, translation by author)

In the light of the concepts outlined above, I understand the working citizen to be an individual who principally acts in a socially, ecologically and economically fair manner and, within these activities, finds and invents their own profession.

The Longing for Agency in Current Vocational Orientation

For vocational orientation in adolescence, this concept of a *working citizen* provides various ideas that can be structured according to two interpretations of the term 'orientation': orientating oneself in the sense of determining one's personal standpoint or as an alignment towards a profession. A holistic vocational orientation comprises the development of a differentiated perception of one's own needs, desires and skills—including a form of aesthetic intelligence, and the readiness to allow new perspectives, and to think and act empathically and socially (cf. Collard 2013). The idea of developing and orientating oneself on both personal and social values is based on a comprehensive concept of work, equally including non-paid endeavours like house-work, individual work or civic work (cf. Famulla, Butz 2005). Moreover, Ulf Schrader emphasizes the importance of the principle of sustainability. He notes that this topic has, until now, merely played a minor role in the academic study and implementation of vocational orientation in schools (cf. Schrader 2013).

In the light of continual changes in the realm of work, orientation in the sense of 'alignment' refers mainly to aspects like flexibility and adaptation; they have been the subject of controversial discussions in the field of vocational orientation for some time. While Karin Schober considers them to be essential (cf. Schober 2001), Marisa Kaufhold suggests that one should indeed develop an inner flexibility, but only acquire such new professional competencies that one personally perceives as meaningful. One should not submit oneself to the pressure of constant adaptation to changes on the job market (cf. Kaufhold, pp. 223–4). Both positions underline self-reliance as a necessary feature.

Within the specific discussion on suitable vocational orientation, a paradigm shift—from professional guidance towards the promotion and support of an individual planning ability and capacity to act—has already taken place. Currently, for practical implementation, this implies that young people are only offered impulses that will motivate them to shape their own educational, professional and life planning (cf. Butz 2008).

In my view, the very experience of difference gained through artistic processes, as Ulrike Hentschel describes (cf. Eckert, Hentschel 2015), offers a chance to break with habitual modes of perception in the working world. Following Martin Seel (1993), for Hentschel, the peculiarity of art is 'to point to "the world". The art can only do this by distinguishing itself from "the world", thereby enabling the experience of difference or distance' (cf. Eckert, Hentschel 2015, p. 3, translation by author). Thus, artistic performative strategies may evade exploitation on the economic level.

From this, I conclude that what is called for to achieve a vocational orientation towards a *working citizen* is a performative, artistic form of agency.

Agency

Based on Cornelia Helfferich's compilation of various social-scientific concepts of agency (cf. Helfferich 2012, pp. 9–39), agency can be understood like this: agency describes a person's conscious capacity to act and be effective, which they themselves perceive as meaningful and creative. A possibility to act depends on social factors. It determines the preconditions for and/or a consequence of agency. A subjective experience of agency does not necessarily coincide with factual circumstances.

Michel De Certeau sees routine practices as presenting an opportunity for creative practices of appropriation—individuals decisively integrate predefined structures into their everyday life in a joyful process of resignification. To him, 'walking in the city' exemplifies the process of active consumption of a place—a city has a system of streets; its inhabitants, however, take shortcuts that best suit their purposes. Thereby, they create new paths, and thus impact the prevailing system. De Certeau ascribes an element of creative resistance to such tactical practices, whereby an individual would not be aiming at revolution, but rather, simply evading the control efforts deployed by the 'disciplining forces' (cf. de Certeau 1988).

With de Certeau, the term 'agency' thus becomes a description of creative processes of appropriation. Agency signifies the capacity to consciously individualize, influence and re-signify prevailing structures.

How Artistic Instructions May Lead to Agency: The Project *Internship Report*

The project 'Internship Report'[4] was conceived as follows: in January 2016, ninth-grade students at the Europaschule Gymnasium Hamm in Hamburg undertook the usual three-week internships in different companies in order to gain their first work experience—for example, at a bank, a dental practice or a Chinese shipping company. During the preparation of our vocational orientation project, 22 teenagers and I worked with various artistic practices. In this context, we discovered that an artistic, performative form of agency could be developed and supported by means of particular art-based instructions. Usually, the tasks related to an internship are aimed at helping teenagers find out for themselves whether they are suited for a particular job and the given structures at that workplace—or not. The instructions of the 'internship through artistic practice' served as a research tool, aimed at testing the work environment and designing one's own internship. A series of questions were formulated to guide the process:

- What does the working environment need?
- In carrying out their work, what kind of experiences do the teenagers see as also pleasing their colleagues?
- How would they like to design their *own* work?
- What kind of new professions do they invent for themselves?

Based on these questions, the students developed specific artistic interventions within the workplace—using sounds, images, actions or movements—and then documented the reactions of their colleagues.

In the weeks before their internship, the young people had tried out different artistic tasks in businesses throughout the neighbourhood. The special form of instructions had emerged because these teenagers seemed to enjoy carrying out tasks in general. The students also seemed accustomed to receiving clear instructions, as they were used to transparent rules and their rigorous implementation from school ('the strictest school in Germany' cf. Gall 2012). In my role as artist, and by working with art-based instructions, I could give them 'license to do things differently'. The project was aimed at providing the students with small spaces, where they, for once, would be allowed to bypass the rules set by their environment. This also enabled them to withdraw from the neoliberal logics of adaptability, usability and achievement orientation, which are found in economy as in common educational contexts. Instruction-based education is turned inside out by instruction-based art.

Instruction-Based Art: Permission and Scope for Action

On August 29, 1952, the pianist David Tudor sits down at the grand piano, starts the stopwatch and closes the piano. In the four minutes and thirty-three seconds that follow one cannot hear any piano music, only an occasional coughing from the audience, the shuffling of feet and someone sneezing. The repeated opening and closing of the piano lid marks all three movements of this premiere of the composition, whose score was defined as follows:

I

Tacet

II

Tacet

III

Tacet

By measuring the time, and the opening and closing of the piano lid, John Cage's composition *4'33"* (Cage 1960) creates a framework that directs the audience's attention to incidental sounds occurring in the music hall. The recipient is thus referred to his own expectations of a concert. By reinterpreting the sounds all around them as music, the audience may become aware of their own participation in the concert. Cage upgrades such ordinary sounds as essential elements of our world. He reflects the function and the material of art through art itself (cf. LaBelle 2002, p. 48).

Cage's conceptual compositions had a decisive influence on the Fluxus movement of the 1960s. In Fluxus, I found the same features and effects of instructions manifested that became relevant for our project *Internship*

Report. With the introduction of scores, according to Ken Friedmann, a 'core principle of musicality' was transferred to Fluxus art (cf. Friedmann 2002). Whilst in the field of music, the 'musical score' represents a script for music notation, the 'event score' in Fluxus describes already performed or yet to be realized actions. Like in Cage's composition *4′33″*, such actions develop on the basis of everyday activities, which anyone could perform. As the event score used in Fluxus addresses, in linguistic form, the original artist themselves, the performer and/or the audience, it becomes an instruction understandable for all.

The 'core principle of musicality' of instruction-based art is not focused on an original work, but rather, on the specific realization of an event score by different individuals with the participation of varying audiences in different contexts and at different times. In Yoko Ono's work *Cut Piece* (1964), performed on various occasions by herself and other artists, people in the audience were instructed to cut off pieces of the performer's clothing with an available pair of scissors.

Yoko Ono, Cut Piece

First version for single performer:

> Performer sits on stage with pair of scissors placed in front of him.
> It is announced that members of the audience may come on stage – one at a time – to cut a small piece of the performer's clothing to take with them.
> Performer remains motionless throughout the piece.
> Piece ends at the performer's option.[5]

By conceiving her work as a score, Yoko Ono enabled the transformation of one idea into multiple different experiences. Ono herself once characterized her performance of 1964 as a spiritual act, as a genuine contribution, an experience of giving the audience what it wishes to take. The male performer Jon Hendricks, who performed the score in front of and with his new students of the Douglas College in New York, experienced a transition in the relationships of authority. During some other performances of *Cut Piece*, the audience displayed particularly sexually aggressive behaviour (cf. Concannon 2008, pp. 83, 85). As the author of the instruction, Yoko Ono becomes a kind of 'facilitator', who provides the active recipient with specific actions and experiences (cf. Umathum 2004). This, and other event scores, departed from the physical space of art venues; Ono made the scores publicly accessible in her book *Grapefruit* (Ono 2000).[6]

Artistic instructions question the conventional concept of the author and recipient. In Cage's *4'33"*, the audience's participation is rendered visible through the given specific framework. In instruction-based art, as in Yoko Ono's *Cut Piece*, control over the work is partially surrendered by the author by delegating the realization of the artistic work explicitly to the recipient. The instruction is completed only through the performance of the recipients; their participation and artistic decision-making become indispensable. For Ken Friedmann, the proposition of participation defined in the scores corresponded with Joseph Beuys' democratic concept of 'Everyone is an artist' (cf. Friedmann 2002, p. 126). In the sense of an extended definition of art, Beuys understood every human being as being capable of creatively shaping society (cf. Beuys 1985).

Through the instruction to act, the recipient receives permission. As Mary Patterson says about *Playing Up, a Live Art Game* by Sibylle Peters, performed at the Tate Modern in 2016: 'The rules of this game are simply to follow the rules, which are less like rules and more like permissions' (Paterson 2016, p. 1). In the instructions of this *Live Art Game* it is stated, 'that to commit to a task can set you free' (Peters 2016, p. 6).

Similar experiences, from a special form of instruction—the self-commitment—were made by contemporary artist Sophie Calle:

> I like being in control and I like losing control. Obedience to a ritual is a way of making rules and then letting yourself go along with them [...] I'm always dreaming of situations where I won't have to decide anything. Where I can really let myself go. (Calle, in an interview with Christine Macel. (Macel 2003 p. 75))

The method of the artistic instruction produces the liberating effect (cf. Umathum and Rentsch 2006, pp. 9–10) that the composer Igor Strawinsky describes as a special essence of an artistic attitude and work:

> My freedom consists in acting within the tight framework that I have set for myself for each of my projects. [...] Whoever deprives me of my restraint, also strips me of my force.
> The more compulsion you impose, the more you are freed from the chains that bind the spirit. (Strawinsky 1949, p. 46)

An artistic instruction gives permission and provides new space for actions and experiences. This new space is designed by the performing person, who creates their own set of rules.

Even by refusing the scope for action, the recipient performs an attitude. I would infer that the appropriation of an instruction may lead to independent, self-reliant action—to agency.

Opening Up Scope for Action Within Institutions

The scope for action—the new space—created with the help of instructions, always develops within an existing space that, according to de Certeau, has in turn constituted itself through activities and agreements.[7] During an internship, these spaces and the supervisory bodies of workplace and of school overlap for three weeks. In this situation, it is not quite clear which rules actually apply. One may have to break one rule in order to follow another. This is where, in the guise of school assignments, our artistic instructions come in. The instructions allow for a new space, which can be designed according to one's own rules. Such scope for action is normally not foreseen within institutions. Neither employers or schools, nor even authors of such instructions, have complete access to this space. The prevailing rules of workplace and school thus become unstable.

This process opens up new perspectives onto institutional rules, creating potential for their appropriation. The scope for action here provides a form of freedom, as defined by de Certeau—by adopting the instructions for themselves, in using their own approach, the students temporarily allow a new space to emerge in the frame of their internship. They perform a new space.

Through the medium of their bodies, boundaries between art and everyday life are dissolved. Action remains action. Through the artistic, daily and political dimension of action, routine activities at school and the workplace are affected. By experiencing new scope for action, an intern has the possibility of attaining a new self-understanding. Thus, there is potential space for agency.

The Licence for 'Doing Things Differently'

Two Different Kinds of Artistic Instructions

For the students' internship, I devised a set of instructions in their research journals, which they then could use as blank permissions. How would the teenagers deal with this new scope? What would they wish for at their working environment that normally was not considered as belonging there? Or—in the sense of Cage's composition—which coughing, which shuffling of the feet would they choose to make heard?

Generally speaking, there were two different kinds of instructions involved:

Testing the Working Environment—Instructions with a Predetermined Micro Practice

The interns carried out a number of activities in order to test reactions in their working environment. In this phase, the content of the instructions was based on concepts for a post-growth society, including concepts of time prosperity. Besides this, they were based on practices that the students had previously used as forms of micro resistance at school against achievement orientation, for example, 'talking to their classmates' or 'snoozing at their desk'. These sensorial physical practices were examined with regard to their reflexive, subversive and experimental potential, and then exaggerated in the form of instructions in the work context. Following Elke Bippus' definition, I refer to them as micro practices (cf. Bippus 2015, pp. 216–21). Initially, a constitutive element for micro practices, according to Bippus, is their pharmacological dimension—as both formative and deformative practice simultaneously (cf. Mikropraktiken). However, regarding this research project, I would expand her concept to include individual practices which, when transferred to a new context, have an interventionist effect. To break the rules was therefore set up as a new rule and the students were empowered to follow it.

For their internship, some students had in their research journal the instruction to:

> Take two additional breaks, during which you sleep at the workplace for three minutes.

Pauline, a student, did her internship at a bank. The manager of the bank took a keen interest in the tasks Pauline found in her research journal. He suggested a solution for following the instruction: not to sleep at the counter or in the customer area, but in the back office of the bank. This would provide the opportunity to 'make everything ok, afterwards'. In this case, the creative enactment of a predetermined micro practice within prevailing structures was at stake, and the straightforward character of the instruction indeed had a productive effect. It gave Pauline permission to break with, or at least question, rules at the workplace by referring to the licence of an 'artistic research task', in the face of—or even together with—her superior, the bank manager. The result of this testing of the working environment was that the bank manager used the newly created intellectual leeway actually as an opportunity for reflection. In an interview with both Pauline and me, he talked about what it meant to take your breaks with self-responsibility or to 'test the limits'.

Shaping the Working Environment: Instructions with Self-Created Activities

The other form of instruction given to the students was more open, and implied self-determination—implementing their own ideas and taking their own decisions. An example of such an instruction might be:

> Perform an activity at the workplace that you enjoy doing and that also pleases your colleagues.

A girl named Bintou had undertaken a boring internship in a dental practice. The atmosphere there was marked by mutual disinterest. She had hardly any tasks to do and she stood around a lot. At this time, many refugees were coming to the dental practice. Bintou is a native English speaker. After just a few days, she had invented the job of interpreter for herself in dental practices.

Perhaps she would have engaged in this activity even without the instruction. By fulfilling her research tasks, however, she consciously experienced her scope for action and could appreciate her activity as meaningful. After this, she gave herself permission to no longer follow any instructions from the research journal.

Another performance of this instruction was enacted by Henry, mentioned earlier, by playing his flute in the entrance hall of the Chinese shipping company. After the internship, we jointly reflected the students' experience, based on an artistic presentation titled *Internship Report* ('*Praktikumsbericht*'). In making the presentation, Henry took advantage of his newly found scope for action by making himself heard on a Wagner tuba (Fig. 1).

Agency became visible in the students' meaningful and creative appropriations of pre-existing structures. The corresponding instructions provided them with a space they could design for themselves by developing their own set of rules within the rules of their chosen workplace. In this sense, 'To commit to a task can set you free' meant empowering them to

Fig. 1 During the presentation, Henry watches footage of himself playing the recorder in the China Shipping company (Hamburg, 2016)

contribute something of their own to the workplace—independent from the requirements of the workplace—and so shape the environment for themselves and others. The instructions required reflection upon oneself and on existing structures—the act of translation and the playing of a recorder counted, amongst the young people, as answering human need that was found in their working environment. They thus performed their self-understanding as interns within an institution and manifested their identity as young *working citizens*.

The instructions, and their performance by the students, can be seen as an experimental embodiment of the above-mentioned Article 12 of the Basic German Law regarding the freedom to choose one's occupation; an article, in this light, that can itself be interpreted not only as a right but as an instruction that might be embodied individually in an ever-changing world of work: Choose your vocation freely. Design your vocation. Invent your vocation. As *working citizen*.

The project *Internship Report* opens up the possibility to experience one's own present or future workplace as being malleable through action; thereby reinterpreting, redefining and appropriating both this space and one's occupation in a positive sense. In his composition *4'33"*, Cage was able to provide a framework capable of directing the audience's attention to incidental sounds during a concert; sounds which usually are considered disturbing. He distinguishes the ordinary noises of the audience—the coughing, the shuffling of feet, the snoozing—by redefining them as independent sounds. Based on its instructions, the project *Internship Report* provides a comparable framework aimed at directing one's focus, within the scope of one's activities, more towards recognizing individual human needs that, in the context of neoliberal working relations, are normally neglected—such as sleeping, language translating and playing the recorder. If this concept were transferred to the level of social responsibility and designing of working practices, which opportunities would it signify for the future of work and the citizens' participation within the process?

By providing space for agency in Article 12 of the Basic Law, responsibility is returned to each individual in two key respects: the responsibility to respect and honour one's own wishes, values and abilities and the responsibility to perform one's own activities as civic action. This raises the question for every subject, according to which values one intends to shape the space:

Through which practices would a person like to become a *working citizen*?

This is the chance for citizenship to be reconsidered and negotiated from the perspective of an active subject being an inclusive phenomenon.

NOTES

1. Also, Heinz Dedering writes about the overwhelming situation for young people (cf. Dedering 2002, pp. 25–6).
2. Schrader's definition of citizenship is oriented on the tradition of the republican understanding of citizenship, by which a good citizen actively contributes to common welfare and voluntarily fulfils duties.
3. In Germany, the concept of the *working citizen* is currently of particular relevance in view of its integrative qualities. Until 2014, it could take several years before persons seeking asylum, or with a 'tolerated' status of residence, was granted a work permit. Considering that, especially since the summer of 2015, an increasing number of people sought refuge in Germany, the policymakers and economists have made an effort to facilitate entry to the job market. Reasons for this are the costs of social benefits that otherwise would be due, a shortage of skilled workers in Germany and, not least,

the prospects successful 'professional integration', as 70% of the refugees are under 30. Here, the law of integration of August 6, 2016 plays a vital role (Cf. Pro Asyl 2017).

4. The project was conducted at the Europaschule Gymnasium Hamm in Hamburg, from November 2015 to May 2016. Concept and research: Constanze Schmidt; artistic assistance: Teresa Rosenkrantz; educational assistance: Ulrike Mack.

5. Yoko Ono's *Cut Piece*, quoted after Concannon, p. 82.

6. From my point of view, an interesting approach to enabling the artistic scores to enter the recipients' everyday life is George Brecht's idea of distributing artistic scores via newspapers and postcards (cf. Dezeuze 2002, p. 79).

7. De Certeau distinguishes between space and place. A place is the structure of relationships between elements. Two items can never be at the same place. A place signifies clarity and stability. The space develops from changeable elements—like direction, speed and time—as a 'polyvalent unity of conflictual programs and contractual proximities' (de Certeau 1988, p. 117).

REFERENCES

Basic Law for the Federal Republic of Germany. 2012. *Article 12 (Occupational Freedom)*. https://www.gesetze-im-internet.de/englisch_gg/englisch_gg.pdf. Accessed 9 Mar 2018.

Beuys, J. 1985. Sprechen über Deutschland: Rede vom 20. November 1985 in den Münchner Kammerspielen. In *Reden über das eigene Land: Deutschland*, ed. H. Mayer, J. Beuys, M. Mitscherlich-Nielsen, and A. Schönherr. Bertelsmann: Munich.

Bippus, E. 2015. Adrian Pipers Funk Lessons. Eine Mikropraxis transformierender Affirmation. In *Kunst und Wirklichkeit heute: Affirmation – Kritik – Transformation*, ed. L. Everts et al. Bielefeld: transcript.

bridge – Das Berliner Netzwerk zur Unterstützung von Bleibeberechtigten und Flüchtlingen auf dem Weg ins Unternehmen. www.aub-berlin.de/fuer-erwachsene/bridge/. Accessed 9 Mar 2017.

Butz, B. 2008. Grundlegende Qualitätsmerkmale einer ganzheitlichen Berufsorientierung. In *Berufsorientierung als Prozess – Persönlichkeit fördern, Schule entwickeln, Übergänge sichern. Ergebnisse aus dem Programm 'Schule -.Wirtschaft/Arbeitsleben'*, ed. G.-E. Famulla. Baltmannsweiler: Schneider Hohengehren.

Cage, J. 1960. *4'33: For Any Instrument or Combination of Instruments*. New York: Peters.

Collard, P. 2013. Vortrag auf der Tagung der Kultusministerkonferenz und der Stiftung Mercator im März 2013 quoted after *Grundsatzpapier zur Kulturellen Bildung in den Kulturräumen des Freistaates Sachsen Vogtland-Zwickau,*

Leipziger Raum, Erzgebirge-Mittelsachsen, Niederschlesien-Oberlausitz, Chemnitz, Leipzig und Dresden, p. 2. www.dresden.de/media/pdf/kulturamt/ Grundatzpapier_KuBi_Kulturraeume_Sachsen.pdf. Accessed 3 Mar 2018.

Concannon, Kevin. 2008. Yoko Ono's Cut Piece: From Text to Performance and Back Again. *PAJ: A Journal of Performance and Art* 30 (3 (MIT Press)): 81–93.

de Certeau, M. 1988. *The Practice of Everyday Life*. Berkeley/Los Angeles/ London: University of California Press.

Dedering, H. 2002. Entwicklung der schulischen Berufsorientierung in der Bundesrepublik. Deutschland. In *Berufsorientierung in der Schule. Grundlagen und Praxisbeispiele*, ed. J. Schudy. Bad Heilbrunn/Obb.: Klinkhardt.

Dezeuze, A. 2002. Origins of the Fluxus Score. *On Fluxus. Performance Research* 7 (3): 78–94.

Eckert, C., and Hentschel, U. 2015. 'Constanze Eckert im Gespräch mit Ulrike Hentschel. Über mögliche Zusammenhänge von Kunst (Theater) und Bildung' in Mission Kulturagenten – Onlinepublikation des Modellprogramms "Kulturagenten für kreative Schulen 2011–2015. http://publikation.kultura-genten-programm.de/detailansicht.html?document=160. Accessed 3 Mar 2018.

Famulla, G.-F., and Butz, B. 2005. *Schule – Wirtschaft/Arbeitsleben -Glossar:Berufsorientierung*. http://www.swa-programm.de/texte_material/ glossar/index_html_stichwort=Berufsorientierung.html. Accessed 9 Mar 2017.

Friedman, K. 2002. Working with Event Scores: A Personal History. *On Fluxus. Performance Research* 7 (3): 124–128.

Gall, I. 2012. *Hamburgs strengste Schule setzt glasklare Regeln*. https://www.welt. de/regionales/hamburg/article112176008/Hamburgs-strengste-Schule-setzt-glasklare-Regeln.html. Accessed 6 Jan 2017.

GGUA Flüchtlingshilfe e. V. *Arbeitserlaubnis mit Duldung*. http://www.einwan-derer.net/uebersichten-und-arbeitshilfen/. Accessed 9 Mar 2017.

Habermann, F. 2013. Die Freiheit, so zu leben, wie wir es wollen. In *Zeitwohlstand. Wie wir anders arbeiten, nachhaltig wirtschaften und besser leben*, ed. Konzeptwerk Neue Ökonomie. Munich: oekom Verlag.

Haug, F. 2013. Zeit, Wohlstand und Arbeit neu definieren. In *Zeitwohlstand. Wie wir anders arbeiten, nachhaltig wirtschaften und besser leben*, ed. Konzeptwerk Neue Ökonomie. Munich: oekom Verlag.

Hellferich, C. 2012. Einleitung. Von roten Heringen, Gräben und Brücken. Versuche einer Kartierung von Agency-Konzepten. In *Agency. Die Analyse von Handlungsfähigkeit und Handlungsmacht in qualitativer Sozialforschung und Gesellschaftstheorie*, ed. S. Bethmann et al. Weinheim/Basel: Beltz Juventa Verlag.

Kaufhold, M. 2009. Berufsbiografische Gestaltungskompetenz. In *Eigen-Sinn und Widerstand. Bildung und Arbeit*, ed. A. Bolder and R. Dobischat. Wiesbaden: VS Verlag für Sozialwissenschaften.

Konzeptwerk Neue Ökonomie. 2013. *Zeitwohlstand. Wie wir anders arbeiten, nachhaltig wirtschaften und besser leben*, ed. Konzeptwerk Neue Ökonomie. Munich: oekom Verlag.

LaBelle, B. 2002. Reading Between the Lines: Word as Conceptual Project. *On Fluxus. Performance Research* 7 (3): 47–53.

Macel, Christine, ed. 2003 *Sophie Calle, M'as-tu vue*. Exhibition catalogue. Munich/Berlin/London: Prestel.

Mikropraktiken: Formen des Widerstandes und Engagements. https://mediaand-participation.com/ueber/teilprojekt-5/. Accessed 12 Mar 2017.

Ono, Y. 2000. *Grapefruit: A Book of Instructions and Drawings*. New York: Simon & Schuster.

Paterson, M. 2016. *Playing Up* London: Live Art Development Agency. http://playingup.thisisliveart.co.uk/playing-up-by-mary-paterson/. Accessed 9 Mar 2017.

Peters, S. 2016. Instructions. In *Playing Up! A Live Art Game for Kids and Adults*, ed. S. Peters. London: Live Art Development Agency.

Pro Asyl. 2017. *Integrationsgesetz in Kraft: Die Neuerungen im Überblick*. https://www.proasyl.de/news/integrationsgesetz-in-kraft-die-neuerungen-im-ueberblick/. Accessed 9 Mar 2017.

Schober, K. 2001. *Berufsorientierung im Wandel – Vorbereitung auf eine veränderte Arbeitswelt*. http://www.swa-programm.de/tagungen/bielefeld.html. Accessed 9 Mar 2017.

Schrader, U. 2013. *Nur noch kurz die Welt retten? Konsequenzen der Diskussion um eine nachhaltige Entwicklung für die Berufsorientierung*. http://www.bwpat. de/ht2013/ft02/schrader_ft02-ht2013.pdf. Accessed 3 Mar 2018.

Seel, M. 1993. Intensivierung und Distanzierung. *Kunst und Unterricht* 176: 48–49.

Stiegele, J. 2014. *UTOPIA TOOLBOX. Eine Anstiftung zur radikalen Kreativität. Kunst als Antrieb einer zukunftstauglichen Ökonomie*. http://www.postwachstumsoekonomie.de/wp-content/uploads/2014-11-12_Stiegle-Utopia-Toolbox.pdf. Accessed 27 Feb 2018.

Strawinsky, I. 1949. *Musikalische Poetik*. Mainz: Schott.

Umathum, S. 2004. Do It Yourself! In *Kunst der Aufführung. Aufführung der Kunst*, ed. E. Fischer-Lichte, C. Risi, and J. Roselt. Berlin: Theater der Zeit, Recherchen 18.

Umathum, S., and Rentsch, S. 2006. 'Vom Gehorchen. Über das Verhältnis von Handlungsanweisungen und ästhetischer Erfahrung' in Sonderforschungsbereich 626 (ed.) *Ästhetische Erfahrung: Gegenstände, Konzepte, Geschichtlichkeit*. http://www.sfb626.de/veroeffentlichungen/online/aesth_erfahrung/aufsaetze/umath_rentsch.pdf. Accessed 3 Mar 2018.

van Eikels, K. 2013a. *Die Kunst des Kollektiven. Performance zwischen Theater, Politik und Sozialökonomie*. Munich: Wilhelm Fink Verlag.

————. 2013b. *Was uns deine Spontaneität wert ist: Improvisieren zwischen Kunst und Ökonomie.* https://kunstdeskollektiven.wordpress.com/2013/06/29/was-uns-deine-spontaneita%CC%88t-wert-ist-improvisieren-zwischen-kunst-und-okonomie. Accessed 9 Mar 2017.

Virno, P. 2004. *A Grammar of the Multitude.* Los Angeles/New York: Semiotext(e).

Williams, C.C. 2007. *Rethinking the Future of Work. Directions and Visions.* Basingstoke/New York: Palgrave Macmillan.

INDEX[1]

[1] Note: Page numbers followed by 'n' refer to notes.

© The Author(s) 2019
P. Hildebrandt et al. (eds.), *Performing Citizenship*, Performance Philosophy, https://doi.org/10.1007/978-3-319-97502-3

Printed by Printforce, United Kingdom